T0274995

"An incredibly well-researched guide to an often understudied magical subject….This must-have book adds a unique body of knowledge that any Witch would do well to have on their bookshelf as it is an all-inclusive guide: from magical mixology to barista-based coffee, tea, water, and all points in between."

—JENNA MATLIN, author of *Will You Give Me a Reading?*

"Troy has thought of all the details to guide you toward practical sippable magic. You'll not only learn what tools and ingredients can help you create your sacred magical space and perfect spellbound libations, but also the vital mindsets and energetics required to make your intentions come to life. Woven with heartwarming stories from her own life and years of witchy knowledge, Troy guides the reader on a fantastic journey."

—ANITA AVALOS, women's embodiment and eating psychology coach

"A delightful manual on the magic we can sip, slurp, and imbibe. Including lots of recipes and wonderful instructions, Runa's work needs to be on every witch's shelf!"

—BRIANA SAUSSY, author of *Making Magic*

"Dive into a world where magic flows freely from your goblet in *Magic in Your Cup*. With each spell and recipe, you'll learn how to concoct potent elixirs and add enchantment to your cocktails, teas, waters, and more. A must-read."

—ETHONY DAWN, author of *Tarot Grimoire*

"Join author Runa Troy around the table or at the bar to shake up cups, mugs, and glasses full of magic."

—RACHEL PATTERSON, bestselling author of thirty books on Witchcraft and Paganism

"A brilliant volume of practical magick!…Loaded with interesting tips and recipes to infuse your life with magick, *Magic in Your Cup* is a must-have for any magickal library."

—LAUREL WOODWARD, author of *Kitchen Witchery* and *Wellness Witchery*

Magic in Your Cup

© g. rothe

About the Author

Runa Troy (Seattle, Washington) is a solitary witch with more than forty years of experience cooking, starting as a child making food for her large family. She has volunteered her cooking skills for homeless shelters in her community and studied food preservation and safety with her local food conservation district. For two years she provided weekly kitchen witchery content on the Country Dwellers podcast. Visit her at RunaTroy.com.

Magic in Your Cup

A Witch's Guide to Sippable Spellcraft

RUNA TROY

LLEWELLYN
WOODBURY, MINNESOTA

FIRST EDITION
First Printing, 2024

Book design by Rebecca Zins
Cover design by Shira Atakpu
Illustrations by Llewellyn Art Department

Llewellyn Publications is a registered trademark of Llewellyn Worldwide Ltd.

Library of Congress Cataloging-In-Publication Data
Names: Troy, Runa, author.
Title: Magic in your cup : a witch's guide to sippable spellcraft / Runa
   Troy.
Description: First edition. | Woodbury, Minnesota : Llewellyn Publications,
   2024. | Includes bibliographical references and index. | Summary:
   "Blending ancient wisdom and modern mixology, this book invites the
   reader to embrace the alchemy of intention one beverage at a time. Tap
   into the power of your coffee, cocktails, cocoa, and other cauldron
   concoctions while pouring more magic into your daily life. Includes
   sixty recipes"—Provided by publisher.
Identifiers: LCCN 2024037539 | ISBN 9780738776163 (paperback) | ISBN
   9780738776200 (ebook)
Subjects: LCSH: Witchcraft. | Magic. | Formulas, recipes, etc. |
   Beverages—Religious aspects. | Cocktails—Religions aspects. | LCGFT:
   Cookbooks.
Classification: LCC BF1572.R4 T76 2024 | DDC 133.4/4—dc23/eng/20240924
LC record available at https://lccn.loc.gov/2024037539

Llewellyn Publications
A Division of Llewellyn Worldwide Ltd.
2143 Wooddale Drive
Woodbury, MN 55125-2989
www.llewellyn.com
Printed in the United States of America

Significant portions of this book contain instructions for herbal medicine. The author is not a doctor but a longtime user and lover of herbal alchemy. Pregnant women and nursing mothers should not use any type of herbal treatment without consulting with their medical care team first. Please be discerning and understand that your mileage may vary when using herbal treatments. The information provided is for educational and entertainment purposes only. Magic is never a substitute for medical care.

Additionally, there is a lot of fire usage in the Craft. Throughout this book there are instructions for using incense and candles. Please practice good fire safety when working with these items. Don't burn incense or candles unattended. Trim the wicks. Snuff the candles. Make sure hair is tied up when working with fire. Ensure incense is in a heatproof container and you're burning it in a well-ventilated area. Be careful.

Do everything the Witches have been telling you to do regarding not setting the world on fire with errant matches. As a Witch who lives in wildfire country, I can tell you this is important. Please follow those guidelines. We don't want to burn down New Orleans again.

My path informs much of this text. Please understand my practice is eclectic, non-Wiccan, and leans heavily on the mythos and traditions of my ancestors, who come chiefly from northern and northwestern European locations. My workings are heavily colored by the lens of animism and my deep and daily energetic connections to everything around me, especially what I put inside my body. Regardless, I'm sure there are many places where your curiosities, beliefs, and spiritual practices intersect.

for Skaði and Njörðr

Contents

PART I
Sippable Spellcraft Basics

PART II
Magical Mixology in Practice

RECIPES

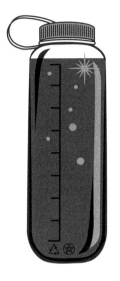

FOREWORD
The Cauldron in a Cup

I've been aware of the power of beverages from the time I could hold my sippy cup on my own. Even as a tot, I knew something good would happen as soon as that tiny plastic mug was in my hands. In that case, it was ice-cold milk to nourish my body and strengthen my bones. Drinking this at every meal ensured I would be healthy. While you may not consider that magical, it is actually pretty potent when you think about it.

After all, every single thing you put in your mouth becomes a part of you. When you eat or drink, your body goes to work on transmuting it into fuel or waste. Because your body is efficient, it happens rather quickly. Some things affect you immediately while others have long-range consequences. Eating and drinking are alchemical processes, and that's magic AF.

I began to see the connection between libations and spirituality when attending church as a young lass. My parents were strict Catholics, so Sunday mornings were always spent in a pew or confession booth. Once they confessed their sins, they joined the other parishioners, hands piously folded as they marched up the aisle for the communion wafer and wine.

I was fascinated with this process. The idea of being forgiven for anything bad I could conceive of doing was appealing, but what drew my attention most was the priest, decked out like Liberace and turning water into wine. How could he do that? I needed to know.

My time came soon enough when I received my first communion. As I walked toward the priest behind a line of other little girls dressed in frilly white outfits like mini brides, I was giddy with excitement. Finally, I would taste the "blood of Christ"! Imagine my disappointment when it tasted like flat grape soda. That didn't matter, though. I was still thrilled that I got to eat that wafer and drink the wine . . . plus, now I could sin and get away with it!

I had an inkling that organized religion wasn't going to be my future. However, I was still intrigued by the spiritual power of drinks.

My mother may have been Catholic, but she was also witchy in her own ways. She had premonitions. An ace in the kitchen, she could transform simple ingredients into a luscious meal and stretch leftovers to feed her small army of unruly children for days, something vital because we didn't have much money. Mom also seemed to know the magical, curative properties of beverages.

A crisp can of soda or a steaming cup of coffee delivered a jolt of caffeine, keeping me buzzing for hours over school projects. When blizzards raged outside—a common occurrence in Wisconsin—a mug of cocoa soothed my belly and warmed my hands. And then there was the medicinal hot toddy spiked with brandy for flu and colds. I never liked the taste, but it did make me feel better.

Every drink had a different effect. My mother may not have been a legit mystic or priest, but she knew how to pour the right thing at the right time.

As I got older, other drinks became my potion. A glass of wine signaled the day was done, while green tea meant it began. The ritual of putting the leaves in the little wire strainer, pouring hot water at just the right temperature, and steeping for a minute before placing the cup to my lips felt like the priest at the altar from so long ago.

When I began to follow the Moon, I became more sensitive to everything I put in my body. Food cooked by someone I didn't like made me unwell. Some drinks brought out the best in me, while others turned me into someone I didn't like. I also noticed how liquids created magical effects in other ways. For example, a glass of water on my table as I read tarot seemed to keep the energy contained, while pouring libations to my ancestors calmed the vibe in this old house.

At some point I began experimenting with writing words on glasses of water like the scientist Masaru Emoto, who believed our thoughts influenced the molecules in H_2O. I also drank water that had sat on the windowsill overnight under a full moon and noticed how my intuition seemed stronger afterward. Once again, I made notes. Whether we approach it from a medicinal or a witchy perspective, there is power in what we consume. Our cups are portable cauldrons.

In *Magic in Your Cup*, Runa Troy turns the act of hydration into something holy and potent. This book's instructions, recipes, and stories will inspire the reader to gather all their glassware and get brewing.

Instructions for every magical purpose, from the first energizing sip of the morning to a nightly dream recall tea, will have you drinking with intention—and probably getting your recommended daily eight glasses of water in a fun way. A coffee ritual turns your cup of joe into something that powers you in a new way, while the cocktails will have you look at "spirits" in a different light. The party-friendly punch recipes are the perfect toast for the bonfire at your next witch's night out, while the cannabis options help you float down to earth like a feather. You can transform your mood, situation, or day with these clever witchy concoctions.

Runa's meticulous attention to detail and history makes this more than a witchy drink book. I'm a fan of learning about the history and story behind everything we eat or drink, and she delivers that here. But the best part is her personal stories that breathe life into her recipes. It's like a conversation with your cool BFF witch bartender—honest, fun, and soulful.

Whether you're a Pagan, witch, magically curious, or a fan of bubbles and brews, you'll want this book on your shelf next to your mugs and bar equipment.

Cheers!

Theresa Reed
author of *The Cards You're Dealt—
How To Deal When Life Gets Real: A Tarot Guidebook*

INTRODUCTION

An Invitation to Magic

This book invites you to take a magical journey through all the drinks in life. From the morning cuppa to that evening nightcap, there are many opportunities for you to turn favorite liquids into ritual, spell, and daily practice within the framework of Witchcraft. However, even if you do not call yourself a Witch but enjoy a life of intention and mindfulness, this book also has a lot for you. Those who have an earth-based spiritual practice but don't consider themselves a Witch will also find lots of good magic inside this book.

Throughout the text, you'll learn about all the things that might affect the magic you're mixing up: the season, the moon, a dash of astrology, and the corresponding energies within the physical ingredients. This book contains dozens of ways to perform a little drinkable potion to start, get through, and end the day. You'll investigate the magic behind all the components, dive deeper into things you likely drink already, and see the path to make them an even more powerful partner in life. You may already know that Witchcraft, the Witch, and brewing have a long history. Some of it is true. Some of it is a myth. This book will cover that as well.

This path has many wells of knowledge to explore, from quality and quantities of ingredients to tips and tricks to make magic with what is at hand, all while being delicious. This book will help you be a drink weaver and employ drink as a foundation within spiritual practice. I hope that from my experience and that of others, you'll find that the Craft and craft drinks go hand-in-hand—whether they are bubbling up through the coven-stead, sipping at the local cafe, or toasting community at a favored pub.

Powerful Magic Every Day

If we are what we eat, we most certainly also reflect what we drink. This fact is good for Witches as drink gives us another path, both close to home and even mobile, to hydrate, heal, nourish, spread love, and do magic. The water bottle you drink from can be some daily magic. Even brewing tea on the go can be magic. You'll also learn a juicier, slower kind of magic from creating something over an afternoon, an entire moon cycle, or from sea-son to season. Magic in our glasses during celebrations, already so full of good energy, levels up to something mystical when the Craft is applied. It's all in your cup. Layer some magic, and now it's a spell. Do it regularly and a ritual is created. Layer in different areas of magic, couple with a spell, and that is a working.

A Life of Drink Magic

Searching for that mystical something for a good portion of my life has led me to be an honored guide through this drink exploration. The spells, rit-uals, and recipes contained within were born from this path. I spent most of my twenties as a bartender while learning everything I could about the Craft. From nightclubs to concert venues to dive bars and even a stint in a historic pub in Germany, I would craft cocktails, conduct dream interpre-tations, or cast runes for the guests who would belly up to the bar.

In the lulls between serving drinks, I read everything I could get my hands on dealing with being a Witch. I was especially drawn to elemental magic, dreams, herbalism, mediumship, runes, and the northern Euro-pean mythos from where my ancestors hailed.

After becoming a mother, my magic was mainly daily rituals at home, especially with food and drink. Planning a menu daily for a growing family forces a Witch to get crafty while compiling lots of practice. With my family topping the ultimate number of seven in total come 2006, that practice was mastermaking. Fortunately, my role allowed me to continually learn more deeply about everything that can bring us to magic every day, and that foundationally includes what we drink.

I learned and then applied this magic from clients who gave me a look behind the curtains of coffee production and roasting, where the magic of bean water deepened to become a tool for every day. I wanted to be illuminated all about tea in the Middle East and the Balkans, where my witchy heart saw everything from healing to connection from some leaves and hot water. And finally, to this present time, living on a small permaculture holding in the wild Pacific Northwest, where my partner and I seasonally brew cider, beer, mead, and wine, which helps bring deeper earth magic into the lives of those who drink these fruits with us. This path is varied and seemingly unending but always magical. It is also easily emulated, followed, and made personal.

Becoming a Witch of Cups

This book will show you how to put the Craft in a glass, mug, or cup. Give yourself that cafe coffee experience right in the kitchen, and make the dining room its own Algonquin Round Table sessions with those who share passions. The after-school snack time with children becomes a ritual of connection so everyone in the house can be safe and loved. Part of the medicine we consume daily can look like a glass of water enhanced by magic. Every classic cocktail out there is transformed into a literal potion when you imbibe it to raise energy and power. We can have magic every day by looking at what we drink. We can turn routine into mindful and intentional rituals. It enriches our lives in a multitude of ways. Moving through all these daily drinks and working with the seasons empowers us to create a life where we can be our truest selves and live our best lives.

When you move to put magic in your cup, whatever is in it, you create a new energy level into the act and the liquid. Magic is personal, but we all need to start somewhere. Again, this is an invitation to explore and adapt everything contained here to make it personal. You may even be reading this while sipping on something—and that's as good a place to start as any other.

Allow my journey to inform your journey. Take from it what speaks to you; leave what doesn't vibe. But given the curvy road that brought me to this type of magic, my intuition tells me that many of you will morph these workings to your personal preference. None of the magic contained in this book works without the reader as a partner. You are the most powerful tool in all modalities mixing magic and drink. You put it all together. Once together, you're ready to drink that magic.

That intention, the energy you put into every action you do in life, whether focused on Craft or mundane tasks, is key. For example, when I started making a Dark and Stormy cocktail to bring serenity and security to an actual dark and stormy night, my ability to be calm in the face of destructive storms and wind increased. Alternatively, I find myself more grounded and centered when I choose my coffee beans or tea blends to complement or combat seasonal energies. Blessing water under the moonlight for drinking can help make that water holy in the eyes of a Witch and is a ritual that brings one closer to the earth and its rhythms. When we're in sync with the land—or water, as the case may be—that sustains us. It can be both powerful and transformative. I can also attest that it heightens the fun in life, too. This element will be necessary in every working within this text. Who doesn't like more fun?

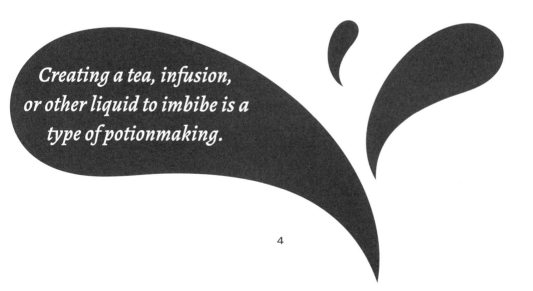

Creating a tea, infusion, or other liquid to imbibe is a type of potionmaking.

Additionally, we will focus on seasonal energies and resources and how they impact the magic we want or choose to do. Whether it's marking a solar celebration, lunar phase, or benchmark in the life of the Witch or her kindred, using the season to add more magic to liquids is the goal. Trying to make something with strawberries in November will be tough and likely change the texture, taste, and magical properties of said brew. In short, different seasons call for different drinks.

Witches have been doing sippable spellcraft in one way or another throughout history. Creating a tea, infusion, or other liquid to imbibe is a type of potionmaking. Whether it's termed potionmaking, teamaking, tinctures, or magical mixology, these crafts all require working with energy. This book aims to show you how your energy and the ingredients' energies work intentionally to invite positive and poignant impacts in our lives—and the lives of our kindred and community—one cup at a time.

Let's dive in and find out.

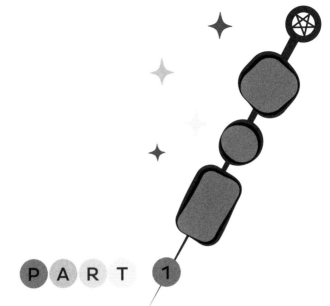

PART 1

SIPPABLE SPELLCRAFT
basics

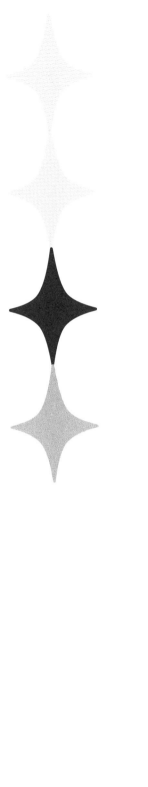

DRINK
like a
WITCH

The image of the Witch, or at least a woman, next to a brewing, bubbling cauldron, chalice, or stein has a long and sordid history. Understanding why that image came to be—what it truly indicated and who the people were who helped bring this knowledge forward to how we use it today— informs so much of how we understand the present. This knowledge is another power source, bringing an extra level of potency into our magical life. When you see the Witch from the past, it helps you understand the Witch in the mirror. It doesn't mean you need to make beer or kombucha, but understanding what makes something magical and why you may be drawn to it is important to note. It wouldn't be a journey or an exploration without a little history. You may even begin to recognize how working with drink in your practice is an act of resistance.

A Sordid Drink History

From the earliest distillers of ancient Mesopotamia to the lychee wine-making concubines of the Tang Dynasty to the beer nuns in the medieval Germanic Alps to the alewives of the later Middle Ages to the Irish brewsters making mead and the women in the Othama and Tohono O'odham tribes in the Sonoran Desert making saguaro wine, brewing drinks for the home and direct community fell to women. It has always been this way. However, for the likes of the brewing women of history, many lost their livelihood, if not their actual lives. They were imprisoned, tortured, and often killed because they dared to be self-sufficient and not beholden to men who wanted a piece of the beer-money pie. Knowledge of that history adds a sacred intention to creating drinks now both as a woman and a Witch. Even if the women distillers and brewers didn't identify as a Witch, they were called one. Ask Sarah Osborne of Salem Witch Trial infamy. She was the owner of the best tavern in town—best because it turned a profit, which the men of her family cheerfully thought was theirs, not hers. She died in jail. Unfortunately, the tale of Sarah Osborne is not singular. Innumerable cases ring similar or horrifyingly worse.

If patriarchal culture fueled by capitalism wasn't stealing the livelihood from women and other nonconforming souls, it was telling them how they could live or what to drink. In the early to mid-1700s, after a long fight to be able to sip some gin with their besties in small female-centric dramshops in

The drinks in this book are not primarily alcohol. You'll be able to dive into everything we sip, from water to juice, tea, and—my favorite—coffee.

London, the temperance movement began, beginning first with reformers in England calling gin "mother's ruin." It didn't take long before such attitudes spread to the United States. At that time, the reformers were more focused on getting women out of the taverns as employees, owners, or customers. Men could still imbibe—well, men of a certain social class could. Regardless, the fight for control of who was allowed to drink took a turn with the passage of the Eighteenth Amendment in the United States. From 1920 until 1933, the United States was dry, meaning alcohol was illegal.

However, as Catherine the Great learned in the eighteenth century, drink can propel an entire country. Her thirty-four-year reign was fueled by her understanding that a nightcap can help quell rebellions. Catherine knew that the people of Russia would not allow the government—or empress as the case was—to step on their liberties. Vodka and Russian Imperial Stout had to flow freely, first and foremost, for the ruling classes to feel liberated. As a former soldier, I can attest to witnessing similar situations in different places around the globe. Maybe I'll tell you sometime over a drink. Suffice it to say, don't stand between people and their drinks.

But the overculture and patriarchy continued to do that, especially where the poor and women were concerned. Today, with dry January, new mocktail commercial production, and sober-only places, an argument could be made that it feels like the corporate machine—again, still fueled by capitalism and patriarchal values—doesn't want people to imbibe so they can be busy workers toiling for their corporate overlords for too many hours and not enjoying the life we have here on planet Earth. You had a mimosa with Sunday brunch? You must be a drunk.

The prohibition comes culturally now.

There are health benefits to abstaining from or limiting alcohol consumption—in other words, moderation—particularly so for those who may have a drink with their dinner (Elagize et al. 2021). According to the National Institute on Alcohol Abuse and Alcoholism, drinking has moderate or low-risk levels (Zhao 2023). For women, they say, this is no more than three drinks per day and seven drinks per week. For men, it is no more than four drinks a day and no more than fourteen drinks per week.

There was a mere 0.5 percent increase in health problems for people who had a daily drink (Harvard 2018). That's like saying there is an increased radiation risk when flying, which there is, but people still do it.

The drinks in this book are not primarily alcohol. You'll be able to dive into everything we sip, from water to juice, tea, and—my favorite—coffee. Whatever the drink, there is a history from which to understand and move forward. Besides, personal choice is one of the greatest aspects of Witch-craft. The aim of this book is that there are lots of choices.

Not Just Gin Makers

From the brief and summarized history you've just read, you can deduce that water and plants were the first things people used to create medicine and drinks.

Again, we can go back to that ancient fertile crescent of Mesopotamia. More than 5,000 years ago, the Sumerians took to clay tablets and doc-umented herbal recipes, which included 250 plant species. Carving into stone wasn't available to the average person, so teas, tinctures, and the like were taught orally from one generation to the next. As written lan-guage developed and became more widely accessible, considerable work was invested to document this knowledge. The Ebers Papyrus, authored in Egypt around 1550 BCE, includes descriptions of ways to turn these herbs and plants into soup or tea to help with everything from digestive ailments to skin diseases and even urinary tract infections. The ancient Greeks then took herbal medicine and combined it with scientific think-ing. Hippocrates, the father of Western medicine, was among the first to separate medicine and religious theory. He is allegedly quoted as saying, "Let food be thy medicine and medicine be thy food." It is easily attributed to Hippocrates because nutrition was one of the big tools for doctors of his time, for which he did write extensively, founding a whole study of nutri-tion (Klesiaris 2014). Without a doubt, giving ourselves the fuel we need to carve out the life we want is foundational. Nutrition includes drinks. And drinks, as you'll discover throughout this book, are essential.

Give a Witch a Plant

We're still turning all parts of the plant and water into drinks and food to nourish and heal. Making tinctures, shrubs, vinegars, teas, and non-alcoholic brews has been something humans have been doing for eons. Like the brewing of alcohol, these activities have long been associated with the occultists, Pagans, and Witchcraft. This association is not surprising because these populations have an ever-present connection to the natural world. This natural world sustains humans. It was natural that people would find treatments for illness and injury in that world. We know that this has been especially true from the Middle Ages when wise women healers "served as herbalists, midwives, surgeons, barber-surgeons, nurses, and empirics, the traditional healers" (Minkowski 1992). Those traditional healers in my lineage were called *wortcunners*, a word with Indo-European etymology combining the words of *root* and *to know*. In short, wortcunners were early botanists. But broadly accessible botany texts didn't exist back in those dark ages. Much of what those healers knew was passed down orally and only recorded initially through "drawing, sculpture, song, and story." Medieval monks learned from these healers and then wrote that knowledge by hand and disseminated these remedies and studies throughout their religious organization's libraries.

Again, like the pub owner Sarah Osborne, many of these healers revered as wortcunners and even called physicians in the thirteenth century were branded witches in the fourteenth and fifteenth centuries. Unfortunately, the knowledge those early physicians curated was burned at the stake with them.

Fortunately, some things have changed since then, and today, creating potions for health and healing is fairly attainable. This book's approach looks at the nourishment, healing properties, and, more uniquely, the magical energies of the ingredients. We'll be leaning heavily on the magic-making part of it. You'll have access to many works that continue this long tradition of plants and Witches and how the two connect. There's something very magical about that.

During the moments I'm within these workings, I can see the land returning the energy I give it. Whether that's my kitchen windowsill herbs or tending to orchards, hops, and other crops, I feel the struggle and the success of all those women, healers, and Witches throughout history. Their spirit, their energy, lives on in what you and I brew and drink. At a minimum, it can be an exercise in gratitude—grateful for all those ancestral brewsters, alewives, beer nuns, midwives, wortcunners, healers, wise women, and Witches. Their work and its energies exist within the concoctions, potions, and brews we create today. The simple act of recognizing this connection between right now and back then may be a path to deepen a spiritual practice. In honor of the Sarah Osbornes of the world, let's take beer, wine, spirits, and all the other homebrew potions away from the overculture and back into the hands of the Witches.

DRINK WEAVER spaces

Doing magical workings in a sacred space with magical tools is a part of many witchy paths. Sippable spellcraft, as well, requires a few tools of the trade. It ranges from what to put in drinks to the stirrers, knives, strainers, and other mixology equipment and where you create liquid libations. As Kate West says in her book *The Real Witches Kitchen*, "Witches do not have special buildings where we gather" (West 2009, 8). Instead, we create spaces—often temporarily—that become sacred. Additionally, every item we use in these workings can represent a particular energy, a magical tool, or a sacred space. Let's start with where you create the drinks and then work through all the likely tools.

Spots of Energy

The place where the Witch creates drinks can be approached as a general sacred space, an altar, or both; you decide. It could be a counter in the kitchen, a table in the bedroom, or some other space you decide on. Anywhere you prepare drinks can be designated as a sacred space. There is a true sense of magic in a sacred space. These spaces often allow practitioners to move between the physical and spiritual worlds. It is a place where you feel protected and empowered.

Most importantly, it is where the Witch shows up authentically as their truest self. It is where you will do the energetic exchange that is the Craft. Comparative mythologist Joseph Campbell said, "Your sacred space is where you can find yourself again and again" (Campbell 1991, 180). I have found this to be true.

Where you choose this space is purely subjective and not necessarily permanent. If you're a solitary eclectic practitioner like me, how you set it up, consecrate it, and work in it is all up to personal preference. Witches that work together in covens or more prescribed Craft traditions may have different and more ritualistic methods to create a sacred space. As the years turn into decades, most dedicated occult practitioners maintain a ritual to create sacred space at any given moment in any given place. It can be as immediate as taking a few breaths, drumming, or even ringing bells or clapping hands. On the other end of the spectrum is the ceremonial cleansing and clearing of a section of land to hold rituals. Claiming the intention to dedicate, defend, and designate an environment, place, or space as sacred makes it sacred. That is the power of the energy and magic. Remember, this is an invitation to explore what it means for you. Where do you feel safe, protected, and able to access energy and do magic? That's where you set up sacred space and do so in a manner that makes sense to you.

Further readings are suggested in the back of the book if you'd like to explore the vast array of sacred space creations. In my practice, I've been able to carve out a small room in my home where I am centrally creating magic. But I also consider my entire property a sacred space, even a sanctuary.

Additionally, I maintain a couple of altars inside and outside my home. Altars can be both permanent sacred spaces and temporary working spaces, and they are an easily accessible way to carve out a special spot to do your magical mixology.

Altars to Drink

Where sacred space can be metaphysical, an altar is very much physical. Laura Tempest Zakroff explains it in *The Witches Altar* when she wrote that "an altar is a specified structure that a sacred activity takes place on or is focused around" (Mankey and Zakroff 2018, 10). Most Witches I know have at least a couple of different altars. I'd like you to consider that any drink spaces can be an altar, too.

Designating the spaces where you create magical drinks prompts the mind, body, and spirit to recognize that you are crafting magic. Let's take a look at a few examples.

Hydration Altar

As a nod to the most important drink you drink each day, consider creating a small hydration altar, something that coincides with a morning water ritual. Have lemons and a juicer all ready at your fingertips. Perhaps have a special salt container with a special spoon. Keep a special water pitcher there as well, if you like. Make it a destination space in the corner of the kitchen that makes sense—perhaps below the glass cupboard. Alternatively, this could be something you set up the night before so it's ready for you in the morning, and everything gets put away after you finish the morning hydration.

In that space add anything else you'd like. Much like a spiritual altar, this hydration altar might feature a candle representing the spark that water alights in the body when consumed. Add statuary of a deity or saint as a reminder to hydrate or to whom you'd dedicate this hydration practice. A simple toast may work as a consecration. Such a toast could be "I dedicate this practice for a moon cycle to Freyja; may she bless me with health!" or "Holda, give me strength today as I complete my tasks" or "May the protection of Brigid keep me healthy!"

Tea or Coffee Altar

Where we turn leaves into tea or beans into coffee may be an altar, too. Perhaps consider keeping water, coffee, and tea all in the same space. A small corner of the kitchen lets you be uninterrupted while fixing morning water, mid-morning coffee, and afternoon tea. Everything you need to make the coffee or tea and refill a water glass throughout the day is found in one place. Again, make it a place that brings you joy, helps you ground and center, and focuses on the gifts that the brown bean water and green leaf water give you. Perhaps you'd keep a raw clear quartz on the coffee maker. You might like to keep a bit of volcanic rock near the tea kettle. Both align with the energies of these devices. If you enter my kitchen, you know immediately where you will find a drink, almost like a magical attractant. It feels intentionally special. Set the mood. There will be more information on using crystals with drinks in the tools section in chapter 4.

Witch's Brew Altar

Some sippable spellcraft takes more time to create. Naturally, a space or altar where you brew, store, and maintain infusions, shrubs, cordials, and tinctures is necessary. As you are brewing these potions, you'll need to access them frequently and keep them in a cool, dark place. Perhaps this is in a separate cabinet that is shielded from direct sunlight and allows easy access to all the concoctions. I have hung bindrune charms (such as the one pictured) in my own brew cabinet to protect all these brews while they ferment, infuse, and transform. Consider adding more crystals or specially blessed vessels to elevate the magic and make a brew altar all the more sacred.

An Altar of Spirits

The last suggestion for you to consider as you begin this path of sippable spellcraft is to consider an altar where alcohol or cannabis is prepared and consumed. Whether it's a canna lounge or a home bar, having a place where all the adults-only magic happens may be appropriate. Like all the suggestions above, it can be what you need and desire. A vintage shelf, cart, or cupboard works; an altar of spirits showed up for me in the form of a bookcase where I could sit nearby and sip a nightcap. Again, it is treated like any other altar, featuring symbols and elements that align with solar or lunar energies. Allow intuition to be the guide. On mine you'll find a large selenite ball in a prominent spot to provide protection and clarity for all the pieces and parts of mystical drinkmaking.

Maintain the Vibes

As with any altar, maintenance happens regularly with the change of the seasons, weekly cleansings, full moon purifications, and the like. This habit along with ritual clearing and cleansing are necessary for any sippable spellcraft altars or sacred spaces. Regularly throughout the seasonal moons, Witches will energetically charge and cleanse their tools. Personal drink altars might include coffee grinders, a tea kettle, bar tools, and ingredients. For instance, if the coffee has tasted bitter, it's time to clean all the components. Working with cosmic energies helps prompt such maintenance. A new moon charge can help begin something new, such as a morning hydration ritual. A full moon easily warrants the release of something. Beyond the moon, as many astrologists will tell you, there's the influence of planetary movements.

A quick example is that you might want to rebalance the machine during a Libra new or waxing moon. Water sign moons allow us to give special attention to all the liquids we drink. We'll dive deeper into the influence of the zodiac in chapter 8.

Dedicate Time and Space

Regardless of your altar setup, you will want to create an energetic environment to make what you're doing something special, something spiritual. The suggestions above are not an exhaustive list by far. Allow yourself the space, place, and time to explore and play with what speaks to you. Compose with intention; get to know the ingredients you'll be working with through repeated energetic connection and layer magic into all drinkable liquids. This process can be transformative. Make it as magical as you would a personal spiritual altar. The mindfulness of dedicating time and space to this practice feeds into the energy you put into all the drinks you consume and supplements their properties. And, let's be honest, it tends to be that much more powerful whenever you do something with great purpose and direction. If you need permission, I'm here to invite you to do so and have fun with it. Make it yours.

Storage Solutions

If you brew cordials or dry herbs or fashion ready-to-go garnishes, you'll need to consider where and how you'll store these things. Any of these suggestions can be turned into sacred spaces or altars.

MASON JARS

These are a great multipurpose tool for all the drinks you brew. Having them in various sizes—from 4-ounce glasses to the half-gallon size—will facilitate everything from brewing to storing and drinking witchy concoctions. Mason jars are available at the local grocery, hardware, and farm feed stores. The half-gallon size is a serious workhorse for making and storing infusions and shrubs. The quart size is great for canning broth, which I consider a fundamental magical brew, given you've intended to make something more from all the scraps. It's an abundance of magic in practice. The pint and half-pint sizes are great for herbal tinctures, teas, and other brews. There are a variety of lids for these jars. There are different styles for storage, canning, freezing, brewing, leakproof lids, etc. They are all interchangeable on the various sizes of jars and come in two sizes: regular mouth and wide mouth. I especially appreciate the fermentation kits that come with a vented lid and a giant spring to help you make the best sauerkraut, kimchi, fire cider, or whatever other fermenting or infusing projects you desire. You may want to invest in a canning funnel to get things into jars. It helps keep things neat. Magically, it carries the energy of smooth movement and forward progress.

LABELS AND A LABELER

There is nothing more frustrating than reaching into a brew cupboard and finding a jar that is unlabeled or labeled poorly. I once thought I was reaching for dandelion syrup, only to find after I had added it to my drink that it was a vinegar infusion. Stock some labels or a label-printing device to avoid encountering mysterious or stale ingredients. Use painter's tape and a permanent marker, blank printable labels, or even a label maker. There are online "print your own" programs from a couple of blank label makers easily found at office supply stores.

DARK, COOL SPOT

Depending on what you're brewing, you will likely want something akin to a root cellar or wine cellar . . . in this case, a Witch's brew cellar. Creating one can be done in a variety of ways, and all it takes is a little intention and invention. Perhaps you might take inspiration from my creative setups. I have a couple of spaces I use for brewing. Some are unconventional. I took an enclosed bookcase that I got free off of Craigslist, covered the glass with some material that matched the color palette in the house, and it became a space to store things that were brewing. Another active brewing space is in a small corner of my kitchen. It's a natural spot for it because it gets zero sunlight, and between the ceramic backsplash and granite countertops, it stays pretty cool. Many bottles of raspberry rum have matured in that corner. I've also employed an entry bench that hosts a cupboard below it. The bench gets no sun where it sits, as it occupies the northeast corner of my house. It stays fairly cool and unbothered there, and things like fire cider, four thieves, kimchi, and pickled eggs find a home in that space. Yes, that dark corner or cupboard in your home is a good place to start.

REFRIGERATION/FREEZER SPACE

At some point, you may need to store rum-soaked berries, broth, purees, oleo saccharum, and even moon water somewhere colder than that dark, cool spot. Even when I lived on my sailboat, there was a section to keep the brews safe—especially my seasickness tincture. Designate a shelf, drawer, or cabinet only for magical mixology goods. That way, there is a spot where you can easily find what you're looking for when it's time to brew up some magic.

THERMOS

Especially if you must take magical potions while away from home, a good solid thermos is a worthy investment when completing a magical mixology kit. Getting in a good hike to forest bathe and then being able to uncap some warm tea, coffee, or even a libation sweetens the activity all the more.

ALL THE
WITCH'S
cups

In this book there are dozens of spells and recipes for all sorts of liquids. No matter what space the Witch mixes drinks in, something to pour them into is needed: you must fill a cup. While filling that glass, mug, or other special chalice, understand that this vessel may represent an element, thereby adding another layer to the magic being generated.

The cup is a symbol of magic across many cultures and faiths. For many dedicated occult practitioners, it represents the Goddess. It is often associated with the concept of the divine feminine, embodying qualities such as nurturing, abundance, and receptivity. In the Wiccan religion, as detailed by Scott Cunningham's *Wicca: A Guide for the Solitary Practitioner*, the cup used in rituals and ceremonies represents the Goddess's womb and the element of water

(Cunningham 1990, 33). In the tarot, the cups symbolize situations and events in our emotional world as well as the element of water and "understanding through love, inspiration, and imagination" (Dugan 2012, 81).

Then there is the case of the various cups used by Norse and Northern Germanic tribes. According to a group of Danish experts, these cups played an important role in various social and religious rituals (Bro-Jorgensen 2018, 47–54). These drinking horns and traditional cups were originally made from horn bone or wood. Specialty artisans would carve, burn, or paint traditional Nordic knotwork, a key and traditional feature of such drinking vessels. The symbolism of the drinking horn often represents the interconnectedness of all things. It is also associated with the weaving of humanity through everything that shapes our lives. In short, when they drank, they did so with the understanding of the intention they raised while imbibing, making it magical.

Pertho, one of the twenty-four Elder Futhark runes, also represents the cup; in particular, it is often said to symbolize the casting cup. It appears like a cup on its side, the lots already cast: ᛈ. Known as a divining tool by today's Witches (myself included), the casting cup was historically used to get divine guidance from the gods as well as choose leaders and settle disputes and the like.

These Nordic and Germanic peoples had stories of magical drinking vessels, too. The first story from the *Poetic Edda*, "Lokasenna," which means "Loki's quarrel," is an excellent example. Loki crashes a party of the gods and begins insulting or accusing them of ungodly actions and highlighting their weaknesses. In order to keep Ragnarok from starting at the party, Sif, Thor's wife, offers Loki a drink.

She tells him, "Hail to you, now, Loki; take this drink I offer you of our good old mead. Do this rather than find fault with me, alone among all the gods and goddesses" (Crawford 2015, 111). She's telling Loki to chill out and have a good time with all the other gods. But Loki is the trickster he is, and he provokes the gods in attendance at the party. It doesn't end well. A magical bowl has to be used by Sigyn, Loki's wife, to catch a

serpent's poisonous venom that drips on a restrained Loki's face as pun-
ishment from the other gods for his crimes. Sigyn holds the bowl for as
long as she can, but she has to empty it occasionally. When she does, the
venom drips on Loki's face and causes him great pain—so much so that the
entirety of the universe shakes (earthquakes here in Midgard/Earth). As
often as earthquakes happen (the large ones that we notice), the bowl held
an epic amount; some would even say it was a magical amount. This bowl
that Sigyn held is a symbol of her love and devotion as well as a symbol of
pain and suffering.

The *Poetic Edda* further relates the story regarding the Horn of the Mead
of Poetry belonging to Odin. The Hnitbjorg Crystal is a magical cup that
appears in the story of the goddess Freyja's journey to acquire the necklace
known as the Brinsingamen. This pure crystal cup was said to have the
power to bestow wisdom and insight to those who drank from it. Freyja
was a boss babe and snatched that powerful vessel up.

Then there is the concept of the Holy Grail, and I'm not talking about
the lore of the Last Supper's cup—although that's another story about a
magical cup. Rather, I'm referring to a more ancient holder of liquid. The
first notation of the Holy Grail comes from the ninth-century poem "Per-
ceval, the Story of the Grail" by Chrétien de Troyes. In his work, the grail
is a magical cup, almost described as a cauldron, that provides everlast-
ing sustenance to its possessor, including a liquid that can bring the dead
to life. Chrétien likely wrote his stories based on the ancient tale of Brân
the Blessed (of Raven King lore) in the *Mabinogion*, a collection of medieval Welsh tales. According to an article by Sioned Davies, a professor at
Cardiff University, "The stories are rich in pre-Christian Celtic mythology,
international folktale motifs, and medieval historical tradition" (Davies
2012). Although there wasn't a written compilation of the tales until the
twelfth and thirteenth centuries, its impact on the mythology throughout
the British Isles is significant. It's about honoring the magic our ancestors
held for centuries around drinking and the vessels they used to brew up
and gulp down sippable spellcraft.

Choosing Your Chalice

There's a long tradition of having magic in your cup. It can be an extra layer of intention and fun. Can you imagine being able to have a pure crystal cup? You absolutely can. It may not look like a hollowed-out wand of selenite (as I imagine Freyja's cup looks like), but rather more like what you find currently in Waterford, Ireland. Being intentional about what you're putting into the cup as well as also what cup you're pouring that drink into is where we want to focus our attention now.

What you put that liquid magic into can layer more power—energy—into any working you're doing with coffee, tea, juice, or spirit. Get as deep into the weeds with this as you like or keep it as simple as you like. I prefer most of my beverage containers to be made of other earthen elements. For instance, I have long curated real crystal glasses for my adult beverages. The crystal reinforces the magic I want to achieve for all these potions. Using a real glass for drinking water and juice or one of the crystal rocks glasses when having a nightcap becomes another tier in the magic. The container becomes a partner in the workings. Stone mugs for coffee and tea lend grounding. I am not a fan of drinking from plastic, even choosing to sip with reusable glass or metal straws instead of plastic ones, and that's because I primarily get negative energy from using plastic when consuming. What the cup is made from and how it was made are other layers to consider when making choices.

The design of any drinking glass is not purely for show; rather, it has much to do with the drink and the best way to drink it, according to beverage-industry reviewers (Spence 2017, 32–44). I have a friend who doesn't like to drink "mug water," meaning drinking water from a coffee mug gives her bad vibes. When you think about it, if that's all there is to drink water out of, you will do it. But if you want to make the experience magical, you will be more intentional about what holds the drink. Studies have demonstrated that the shape and feel of what we hold as we drink can influence our perception of the taste/flavor of the contents, so it's not just drinking snobs or Witches asserting that; science believes it, too.

Look at some common drinkware and their purpose, shape, and energies. This is not an exhaustive list; it's only what we'll use for this book's spellcraft.

BEER MUG

With every drink geekdom, different drinkware is used for different drinks. Beer is no exception. There are glasses for pilsners and hefeweizens; pokal glasses; krugs, also known as tankards; and the lidded, stoneware-made steins. American root beer is often served in a beer mug. We only use a beer mug or pint draft glass in the workings here.

COFFEE MUG

The classic coffee mug holds at least 8 ounces of liquid but can hold up to 14 ounces. Typically they are made of ceramic with a sturdy wide handle so you can wrap a hand around the mug. You likely have a favored one that fits well and gives you enough heat transfer to warm your hands comfortably. Mine has motifs of the sun, moon, and stars, and it reminds me to be intentional.

Collins Glass

This vessel holds roughly 12 ounces and is used primarily for the Tom Collins cocktail. This glass is ideal for many cocktails with high carbonation served over ice and tropical drinks, whether frozen or on the rocks. A few ounces smaller than a collins glass, the highball glass is sometimes mistaken for a collins glass.

Cosmo Glass

This glass is very distinctive, with a shallow bowl holding 4–6 ounces. Some have long stems, some short. These are mostly used to serve "up" cocktails, or cocktails served without ice.

Coupe Glass

A favorite of craft cocktail users, the coupe is often used economically for margaritas and martinis. It has a wide, shallow bowl and a stem and is a popular choice for serving sparkling wines.

Espresso Cup

You may know an espresso cup by its French name: demitasse. These are simple cups, and their top capacity is 3.4 ounces of liquid. They tend to be thicker walled than their classic coffee mug counterparts. These often have a flat, ring-shaped handle to allow a finger to slip through and balance the cup in one hand.

Flute Glass

These long-stemmed skinny glasses are ideal for champagne, sparkling wine, or any carbonated cocktail without ice. Its shape lends itself to preserving the bubbles in champagne. Mimosas look so fancy in these.

Latte Mug

This mug looks like a small bowl with a handle but is smaller than the flat white cup or French *bol* that a cafe au lait comes in. A latte mug will serve you well to brew a latte, flat white, au lait, or even a cappuccino. As with a classic mug, it's typically made of ceramics. But like the classic coffee mug, you sometimes find designs on it, unlike the unadorned espresso cup.

Nick and Nora Glass

Made to hold neat cocktails delicately. These glasses got their name after lead characters Nick and Nora Charles in the 1934 film *The Thin Man*. Also known as a mini martini glass, it holds about 5 ounces and is high sided, bowl shaped, stemmed, and narrow mouthed. Its shape is meant to help prevent spills and make it easier to imbibe without spilling on clothes or furniture.

Pint Glass

This glass is also known as a draft glass and is very versatile, not only for beer. These are my favorite to chill in the fridge to serve cider, smoothies, or any mixed drink with a carbonated beverage (e.g., rum and cola). These are different from the handled beer mugs and steins. Lemonade, especially with pretty garnishes, also works well in this glass.

Punch Bowls and Party Mug

If you plan to host a crowd but don't plan to be in the kitchen or the bar the whole time, this is a lovely way to make sure that everyone can top off their glass—or matching punch mug—with ease. Many punch sets include seasonal colors and symbolism that can up the magic with whatever you brew. Most punch sets come with a ladle, which is a must-have to serve

guests. Magical energetic sharing happens when the host serves from this punch bowl.

RED OR WHITE WINE GLASSES

The white wine glass has a slim bowl to preserve the temperature of chilled wine or cocktails; the red wine glass is balloon shaped to allow the wine's aroma to release, or breathe. In a pinch, they make great offering glasses for an altar; those with cat familiars may need to do a risk assessment first.

ROCKS GLASS

Sometimes called a lowball glass, this ideally holds 6 ounces of liquid. I like to drink a neat scotch nightcap in one of these, especially if they are crystal. A rocks glass is often slightly wider at the top and slightly tapered at the bottom, giving it a nice stability that feels very comfortable in the hand when sipping whiskey on the rocks.

SHOT GLASS

A quick gulp and done—found in varying sizes between 1½ and 3 ounces. These are great replacements for the jigger that bar Witches use for measuring cocktail components. Also use this to hold brewed espresso or a daily shot of kefir.

TEACUPS

Teacups are smaller than coffee mugs and come with a saucer and handle and can be made of china, ceramic, or glass. This is considered the British teacup. However, there are different teacup styles from around the globe, including original Chinese teacups, Japanese teacups, and—one of my favorites—the Arabic teacup known as an *istikan*, which is tulip shaped, often handleless, and holds about a half cup of tea (and sugar) and has a saucer as well. Regardless of the type of teacup chosen, the tasseomancy is optional but oh so fun.

TRAVEL TUMBLER

If you commute or regularly travel for a job, you likely own one of these tumblers. The whole purpose is to retain heat for a long time. Investing in a good one can be pricey but worth it so the beverage stays warm longer. Some are made specifically for coffee; others, tea. I appreciate my stainless steel one with a ceramic exterior. It's not dishwasher safe like an all-ceramic one, but it is more durable and keeps things hot for a long time. It's worth the handwashing.

TULIP GLASS

The bulbous body and flared lip of this glass capture the aroma and flavor of beer, but it's also fabulous for all sorts of cocktails. The short stem is great for swirling, which enhances the beverage's aroma.

Sippable Starts

Please know there is no expectation for you to have all of these mugs, cups, or glasses. I don't own all of these glasses. There are no Nick and Nora glasses or coupe glasses in my collection. A rocks glass serves to host red wine in a pinch. No one needs all the glasses to do this magic. However, having a dedicated pair of good glasses for whatever preferred magical mixology lends itself to does magnify the energy.

I have slowly procured a crystal set of bar glasses over the years, prompted by a lovely gift from my friendly and well-missed Romanian neighbors when I lived in Waldorf, Germany. However, a plastic cup from my local convenience store held the magic before that. With my bartending background, I can't neglect that the choice of glass will lend itself to a more appealing experience. After all these years, my base collection includes collins, rocks, wine, flute, shot, cosmo, and beer tumblers. They have provided a good foundation and many years of entertainment and magic.

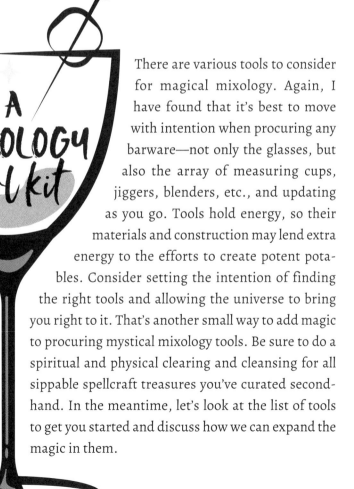

A MIXOLOGY tool kit

There are various tools to consider for magical mixology. Again, I have found that it's best to move with intention when procuring any barware—not only the glasses, but also the array of measuring cups, jiggers, blenders, etc., and updating as you go. Tools hold energy, so their materials and construction may lend extra energy to the efforts to create potent potables. Consider setting the intention of finding the right tools and allowing the universe to bring you right to it. That's another small way to add magic to procuring mystical mixology tools. Be sure to do a spiritual and physical clearing and cleansing for all sippable spellcraft treasures you've curated second-hand. In the meantime, let's look at the list of tools to get you started and discuss how we can expand the magic in them.

SUNWISE FROM LEFT:
COCKTAIL SHAKER; FINE MESH STRAINER
(AKA CONICAL STRAINER); BAR SPOON

Tools of the Trade

The following list, while not exhaustive, is meant to familiarize yourself with all the basics. You may encounter miscellaneous items, consumables, or equipment as you walk this path—things like parchment paper, syrup bottles, reusable drinking straws, timers, spatulas, whisks, funnels, and aprons. Don't stop learning about sippable spellcraft because you don't possess a spice grinder. Find a workaround and stay flexible. If you believe in magic, you've creatively solved gaps in other spells. This is no different. Many of the hand tools have served potion masters through the ages. They are always a good place to start. Don't forget that everything in a magical mixologist's kit is an opportunity to consider extra layers to the spellcraft work. Those items hold energy and correspond to magical properties. The more you walk the path, the more you'll understand those energetic differences and how they lend themselves to individual practice.

BAR SPOON

Some drinks should be stirred, not shaken. This long-handled spoon stirs and even layers drinks. It has a long, twisted stem designed to achieve a smooth and consistent stirring motion, which, like the shaker, ensures the drink is well mixed and properly diluted.

BASTING BRUSH

Needed for some of the slow-drink workings here. A clean paintbrush works as a stand-in.

BLENDER

A blender will get a lot of play for sippable spellcraft. In a pinch, use a shaker bottle and add a workout to your drink creation. If you have a food processor, that's also a good substitution. You might need to adjust the volume of ingredients. When using the blender, magically associate the energetic blending occurring during the work.

CHERRY PITTER

You may use a paring knife to do this, but a proper cherry pitter is great when you're making garnishes or drinks that need more than a half-dozen pitted cherries. They come in various types and sizes, from handheld to electric. My favorite is a device designed to go on top of a mason jar, which catches the pits.

COCKTAIL SHAKER

Every bar Witch has a shaker they prefer. Some like stainless steel shaking tin sets, and others like to use a metal shaker bottom with a beer tumbler to create drinks. I prefer a cobbler-style cocktail shaker, which means it has a built-in strainer in the lid, allowing you to easily double strain the cocktails or mocktails with the addition of a Hawthorne strainer (more on that later). A shaker, whichever you choose, is useful for making adult beverages magical and when mixing nonalcoholic drinks and any concoction where aeration or dilution enhances the drink. A shaker ensures all the flavors are evenly distributed and helps chill beverages.

COFFEE GRINDER

Grinding the beans just prior to brewing makes the best fresh-brewed coffee. This grinder can also do spices, but if you do lots of hot peppers, get yourself a dedicated spice grinder and keep the coffee beans away from it.

COFFEE MAKER

Within the workings in this book, you'll need a coffee maker of some sort, whether it's electric, a pour-over system, or a stovetop coffee maker. Most folx opt for an electric one, whether a percolator, no-nonsense drip, or a combo that grinds and brews for you.

COOLING RACK

Some of the garnishes in this book will need a space to set and cure before you serve them in a drink. A cooling rack is perfect for this.

CUTTING BOARDS AND KNIVES

As a magical mixologist, you will cut up many fruits, especially citrus. You'll want a small cocktail knife, a paring knife, and a channel knife. To accompany those basic knives, you'll need a cutting board. Knives can hold a magical association like swords in the tarot—cutting away, tempering, and acute accuracy. The materials these are made of will hold energetic properties, too.

Electric Dehydrator

If you dive deeply into being a Witch of cups, you may want to invest in an electric dehydrator for making candied citrus and other mixology ingredients. Air drying or using an oven on low works, too. For me, the ease of dehydrating large batches of things outweighs the additional noise of an electric dehydrator. The basic variety is sufficient for what is done within the spells here.

Electric Frother

If you're big into the espresso workings here, you may want to invest in an electric frother. There are plug-in kinds and battery-operated types. I prefer the latter.

Fireplace Lighter

Such a fire starter has a nice long handle and neck, allowing you to be well away from the flame. This could also be put in the magical tools category, and if you're a Witch, you may already own one.

Freezer-Safe Pan

I include this because nothing is better than pouring a home-brewed drink (cider, beer, mixed) into a chilled glass. Keeping those glasses safe in the freezer is helped by a pan to hold them steady, especially with a drawer-type unit. In a pinch, use a cardboard drink holder procured from a favorite coffee stand—a small reward when it's time to grab the drink orders for your mates. If you make ice molds, this pan can also partner with the molds in the freezer.

French Press

The low-tech way to make drip coffee and espresso is classic. There are even mobile versions of modern materials that would fit in a backpack, also known as a manual hand press. These are typically a tube shape, not the pot shape of the traditional French press.

SUNWISE FROM TOP LEFT:
HAWTHORNE STRAINER, JIGGER, MUDDLER,
MORTAR AND PESTLE, MULLING BAG

Garnish Skewers and Cocktail Picks

These small sticks secure garnishes in cocktails or appetizers. They are created in various ways, sizes, and shapes well beyond the ubiquitous umbrella. Garnish skewers are typically longer than cocktail picks and hold multiple garnish items, whereas the picks are used for single garnishes like a cherry.

Grater or Microplane

Found in most kitchens as well as the bar, these are used to shred or grate spices, fruits, and nuts. They can have single or multiple sides, have a handle or be a box, or even be a handled rotary style.

Hand Juicer

Also known as a manual juicer, this solid old-school tech fills a definitive need in the magical mixologist's tool kit. Whether you opt for a classic handheld squeezer, a manual citrus reamer, or a countertop reamer, you'll need at least one.

Ice Molds

Modern materials allow us to get more than the cube, crushed, or chunked ice. Make the ice look like brooms, skulls, or flowers, or choose one giant cube or ball in the middle of a rocks glass for having whiskey on the rocks. They also inspire ice made from fruit puree or juice. A punch bowl looks delightful with ice that echoes seasonal decor. A ribbed baking tray under the ice molds is handy, too, so there's no spillage mess.

Jigger

Used by bar Witches to measure precise amounts of alcohol, jiggers can be hourglass shaped and come in all kinds of materials, but a shot glass can do in a pinch. I enjoy using a jigger because you're not wasting anything, especially while creating a craft cocktail with many ingredients.

Kettle

Whether a stovetop, electric, or microwavable kettle, a drink weaver will reach for it daily. It's useful for making everything from tea to hot cocoa and coffee. Magically, the kettle is much like a cauldron with its womb-like look and feel, and it has longtime correspondences for intuition, health, and people care.

Liquid Thermometer

This is a sealed narrow glass tube with colored alcohol and a scale for temperature readings inside something liquid and hot. It's very useful if you need to make sure the liquid is heated to a specific degree. Magically, thermometers help with intuition, scrutiny, and discernment.

Measuring Cups and Spoons

From tiny ⅛ teaspoons to multiple-cup measurers with spouts or lids, these will be a staple in a sippable spellcraft kit. Magically, these correspond with assessment, appropriateness, and vigilance energies. Again, the materials they are made with have their associations.

Mixing Glass

This was an item that I hesitated to get for my home bar for quite a while, but I have since learned that it is an essential part of a tool kit. This is an extra-large clear vessel, often with a pouring spout, where a cocktail is stirred in before being poured into its serving glass. This is often used for drinks that are served "up," or without ice, like a Manhattan. A large measuring cup with a spout works, too.

Mortar and Pestle

This simple tool is essential in various cultures and culinary traditions for grinding, crushing, and mixing a variety of ingredients. The mortar is a bowl made of something very strong, like stone, wood, metal, or ceramic. The pestle is a blunt, rod-shaped hand tool that works against the mortar to break down solid ingredients.

Muddler

It looks like a wooden weapon for the Witches of yore. It's used to pound out oils and juices from herbs and fruits to add depth, flavor, and texture to your drink. It's great for getting frustrations out, and in mixology it is a fine act to connect with the ingredients and add your intention. Crushing the ingredients more or less allows the Witch to control the intensity of the flavor and the aroma of the cocktail. A muddler is used when you need to add flavor fast instead of infusing or steeping ingredients.

MULLING BAG OR CHEESECLOTH
Both mulling bags and cheesecloth are made of loose-weave muslin or cotton. Cheesecloths are simple squares of fabric that can be purchased in various sizes either by the yard or in pre-cut sections. Mulling bags have small drawstrings or ties to hold spices or fruit in liquid, much like a tea bag. Both can be used for straining and clarifying ingredients for drinks.

PEELER
Used to remove the outer skin of vegetables or fruits, peelers are common in most households, featuring a handle and blade. You'll use this to create strips of citrus peel for use as garnish or to make oleo saccharum (citrus syrup).

PITCHERS
Used to mix, store, and serve beverages, having a variety of styles and functions will serve any witchy mixologist in many ways. You'll need one with a lid for some of the workings included here. Pitchers are like giant cups, so there are emotional associations and magical health, wealth, and uplifting correspondences.

SLOW COOKER
This is a convenient and popular device for preparing warm drinks for a crowd. Like a punch bowl with heat, some sippable spellcraft can be "fix it and forget it."

STRAINERS AND SIEVES
In mixology, strainers and sieves are reached for often. These tools help achieve perfect textures and clarity in drinks by separating liquids from ice, pulp, or solids. In this book, I especially use a large fine mesh strainer. This tool features a wide, bowl-shaped mesh with fine metal wires. It fits

nicely over bowls, large measuring cups with spouts, or even over a mason jar with the help of a canning funnel. You'll find this strainer often in the kitchen supply section. The fine mesh ensures small solids (especially seeds) are filtered out. This type of strainer may be echoed in a smaller shape, and its size neatly fits over a glass. After using a sieve to create ingredients, when creating drinks there are three other types of strainers frequently used.

Conical Strainer

As the name implies, it is cone-shaped and used for clarifying large batches of drinks to ensure a smooth consistency. It's much like a fine mesh strainer but is cone-shaped instead of bowl-shaped.

Julep Strainer

Originally designed to create the mint julep, the all-the-rage nine-teenth-century drink, this is a spoon-shaped strainer with holes, traditionally used to strain stirred cocktails, like a Manhattan, from a mixing glass.

Hawthorne Strainer

A flat, perforated strainer with a spring that traps ice or solids, perfect for staining shaken cocktails like mojitos. Most are stainless steel for easy cleaning. Be careful of those that are not. They will not last.

Strawberry Huller

Another hand tool that helps you make strawberries look pretty without their hull and leaves, especially for garnishes. A paring knife will do the trick, too.

Teapot, Strainer, or Infuser

You must decide how to brew tea. A pot is for a crowd, a strainer for a cup, and the infuser can be used within a teapot to keep loose teas contained yet still allow brewing.

Wooden Spoon

Great for stirring, cooking, and making magic. What a spoon is made of and how you came by it adds to the magical mixology used for this humble tool. In a pinch, it's a great wand.

ZESTER

A zester is different from a grater or microplane. It is handheld and has a curved metal end, resembling a miniature rake or single-rowed grater. It is mostly used with citrus and delicately grazes the peel, avoiding the pith and creating tiny ribbons of zest.

Magical Supplies

Throughout the workings, a few supplies will be referred to for use in the spell. Below are the magical items included within the text. Again, I invite you to feel free to expand or adapt any of this to your preferences. For most Witches, these are common items, but they're included here so you're ready for the next part of this path.

CANDLES

Often a symbol of fire, they can hold and amplify our magical intention and raise that power. The color of the candle can correspond to additional meanings and energies. For many practitioners, candles represent the direction of south and the element of fire. Please practice candle safety and do not let one burn unattended.

CAULDRON

A cauldron is useful and magical, whether you use a small one as a burn bowl or a big cast-iron Dutch oven. It will be used as both within this text. There are whole books written about the Witch and their cauldron. If you want to learn all about this magical vessel, you may want to check out *The Witch's Cauldron* by Laura Tempest Zakroff.

CRYSTALS

Many workings included here call for the optional use of crystals. Again, there is energy within these stones that amplifies any magical working. Invest in a book that explains these magical items more deeply. As a drink weaver, understand minimally that many crystals are not for putting in any liquid. Crystals ending in -ite are generally unsafe for water, such as selenite, fluorite, etc. Do not put iron ores or crystals that contain copper (e.g., pyrite) into a drink. When in doubt, leave it out! Putting a crystal near liquids in the same space as where you're working is sufficient and safer. The energy is there.

HEAD COVERINGS OR VEIL

Although included here, not every Witch or Pagan practices the practice of veiling; however, there are some, myself included, who use it for a variety of reasons due to spiritual beliefs, preferences, and traditions. For me, it is an empowering choice and energetic protection. However, it can also honor specific deities, ancestors, and rituals. Materials, colors, and symbols included on the veils may lend themselves to additional magical correspondences.

INCENSE

Often used on Witch's altars to symbolize the east or the air element. Within this text it is used as such, as well as to provide an offering, create a calming atmosphere, and enhance the practitioner's focus, in addition to being used for its energetic properties. If you need more information on the correspondences of incense, refer to *The Complete Book of Incense, Oils and Brews* by Scott Cunningham.

JOURNAL AND FAVORED WRITING INSTRUMENT

Not just part of the workings in this book but also a key part of most Witches' practice because it's our record of what we have brewed, or, as I like to say, "stewed." Ivo Dominguez, Jr. says in *Casting Sacred Space*, "Magickal journals are one of our best shields against forgetfulness and lethargy" (Dominguez 2012). Make it fun and meaningful. You can even turn a discarded composition or spiral-bound notebook into a spellcraft companion.

COMFORT ITEMS

Items like a yoga mat, pillows, blankets, and even the dog, who thinks you're her emotional support human, are considered comfort items and often come into play within the included spellcraft. Understand what those are for yourself, and when the recipe calls for comfort items, you'll know that includes fuzzy slippers that look like unicorns.

MUSIC

If you play an instrument, it is likely already a part of your practice. For dancers, this part may also come easily. For the rest of us, having music ready to move energy through our body and around it may take a bit more doing. Find what works for you and whatever helps you achieve the energetic state you need for working the Craft.

OFFERING PLATES AND BOWLS

It's especially helpful if these offering vessels are fireproof for burning bits of herbs, paper, and incense. Whether the work is for honoring the divine, connecting with energy, or other magical practice enhancement, these will be present in spells as well as on altars and other sacred spaces.

STATUARY

If deity devotion is in your practice, including such statuary within the workings is appropriate. These can be a conduit for other energies, like my own effort with Black Madonna Czestochowa in late summer for a season of gratitude. Witches might even craft one as a symbol of the energy they are raising or honoring.

YOUR HEAD, HEART, AND SPIRIT

The most important tool for any spellcraft is what you already possess. You will need a clear head, a willing heart, and a mindful spirit. You'll likely need to set aside space and time for those things. Setting time aside for yourself to attend to spiritual practices is self-care. Stronger magic happens when the Witch is strong. Prioritizing activities that maintain the most important vessel in this spellcraft, the Witch, is a key foundation to being our truest selves and living our best lives. Carve, block, and protect when caring for mind, spirit, and body. Again, make it as simple or creative as you like. Set a timer. Keep the time sacred and let yourself connect with the universe for no purpose other than connecting. Allow yourself the time and space to meditate, play, and create magic.

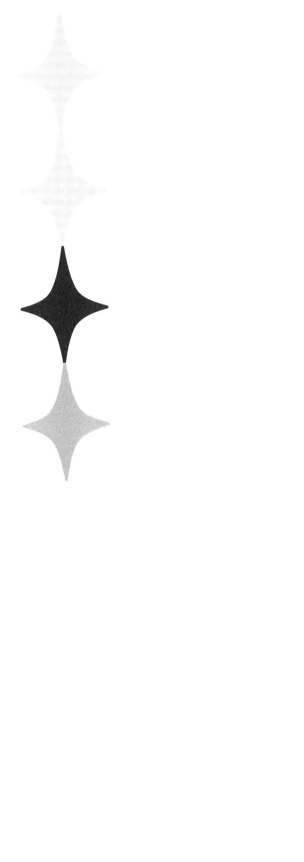

BREW MAGIC *techniques* *&terms*

Hang around a pub or sit at any cafe observing long enough and you'll learn another language. The same goes for a coffee roastery, the kitchen of a Michelin star restaurant, or the tea and spice shop downtown. Sippable spellcraft and magical mixologists have their jargon as well. Here are some terms to familiarize yourself with what will be used frequently in any mixology circle (magical or otherwise) and certainly within this book.

BITTERS

These are neutral alcohols infused with other natural ingredients from spices, roots, fruits, and herbs. Most bitters have from 35 to 45 percent alcohol and are used sparingly. They are sold or maintained in very small bottles, often with droppers or dash dispensers, since a scant ⅛ teaspoon is the usual dosage in a mixed drink.

BUILDING AND LAYERING

These terms refer to different ways of making cocktails. Building a drink adds all the ingredients to a glass in the order they are called for in the recipe. Layering adds ingredients to a glass in a specific order so they do not mix, such as in a black and tan or a tequila sunrise.

CHILLING

To preserve the quality of ingredients and enhance the flavor and refreshment level of a beverage, chilling a drink is part of the creation process. The brew can be shaken with ice, stirred with ice, or added into a chilled glass to achieve the desired effect. You can chill glassware. This is done by placing the glasses in the freezer for a few hours.

DASH

A dash of bitters is something you may hear a bartender mumble about. Just as in baking, it is a unit of measurement traditionally considered to be about ⅛ teaspoon. A dash of this and that can help add flavor, complexity, bitterness, or a little bit more magic.

EXPRESSING

This has nothing to do with speed; it means to squeeze the rind of a citrus fruit to release its oils into a drink. This is done by holding the fruit over the drink and using a bar spoon or other implement to twist the peel back and forth. The oils are released in a fine mist, adding flavor and aroma to the drink.

FLAMING

This has nothing to do with troll wars; rather, it's a bit of fire magic for creating theater while preparing a drink. High-proof alcohol is floated on top of a cocktail and then ignited.

GARNISH

Garnish adds flavor, color, visual appeal, and even more aroma. It is also used to identify the cocktail type being served. Everything from a martini's olive to a mojito's mint sprig helps with the presentation and the flavor. For Witches, it's additional energy to use in mixology.

INFUSION

Steeping tea leaves and herbs in hot water to extract flavors. Occasionally, you may hear someone call it a tisane or herbal tea.

POURING

This is measuring and pouring a specific amount of liquor into a glass. This differs from drafting, which is filling a glass directly from a tap or barrel.

RIM A GLASS/RIMMING

This means to coat the rim of a glass with an element such as salt or sugar by way of using juice or syrup as an adhesive. Think of the salt on a traditional margarita. That glass has been rimmed.

RINSING

This does not mean cleaning a dusty glass but rather coating the inside with a thin layer of liquid, such as liquor, bitters, or other spirits. Again, like many of the terms in this section, it is about adding flavor or even an aroma—and, for Witches, magic.

SHAKING

This is when those tumblers pushed together—cobbler-style or otherwise—are used to chill, dilute, or aerate a drink. This method creates a more frothy and effervescent drink.

Slapping

This is a technique where fresh herbs like mint are hit, clapped, or slapped in a hand to release the aromatic oils before garnishing a drink.

Steep

Much like infusion, a solid is put into hot or warm water to slowly release its desired elements, like in brewing tea, making herbal remedies, or adding a flavor while preparing drinks or food.

Stirring

This is another method to chill or dilute a beverage. Stirring is a softer way to mix a cocktail, unlike shaking. Stirring is preferred when you do not want a lot of air in a drink. Stirring creates a more balanced drink. Often a bartender will use a weighted long-stemmed stirring spoon for this procedure, known as a bartender's spoon.

Straining and Double Straining

This happens when you don't want that muddled blackberry at the bottom of your cobbler shaker to be in the drink, only the flavor of it. Straining, especially double straining, removes the solid ingredients from a drink before serving. The mixture is poured through a strainer, which catches the solids and allows the liquid to pass. We talked about the kinds of strainers and sieves mixologists use in chapter 4.

THE
ALCHEMY
of
intention

At the root of Witchcraft is working energy intentionally. Our intention holds big magic. There's an old witchy adage about where attention goes, energy flows and results show. The energy is not only in actions but also in thoughts. It's in the words you use to speak and write. This understanding of energy is the most powerful tool at a Witch's disposal, regardless of personal gnosis. Living in such a way—intentional, mindful, consistently striving to be better than yesterday—allows us to be blessed and to bless in return. However, that tool of intention doesn't work alone. Adding concrete tasks via our spells, rituals, and magical crafting of special teas, juices, or cocktails furthers those intentions and the ripples (sometimes waves) of energy that return to us.

It is here where I wish I had a Doctor Who-like phrase like "a big ball of wibbly wobbly, timey wimey stuff" to explain how that feels. When Witches talk of standing in their power, it is part of the return of doing a spell and getting exactly what you intended. Once you feel it, you will want to experience it deeper and deeper. Soon enough you will need to tangle with the balance and harmony of said energy. That's a bit more work. But through the vessel that is our daily cup, we can make that work an integral part of our practice toward being our truest selves, living our best lives, and having some fun while we're at it.

Magic In, Magic Out

Right now, I invite you to look at what's in the cup not as liquid or a mixture of beans, leaves, or fruit but as something that can fuel dreams and desires. I invite you to see the invisible that is there but is below the surface, which most people don't register. This is an opening to see the energy, the properties, and the magic of what you're about to drink. Curating the skill to see the energy, understand that energy, and work with it is a skill many Witches cultivate. Every cocktail, glass of juice, mug of tea, cup of coffee, or sip from any hydration flask is a chance to practice that skill. You may practice that skill by moving with intention and working with the seasons in everything you drink. It's liquid mindfulness often. At the core of all this sippable spellcraft is the magic of the ingredients, how you combine them, and you. When you put magic into something, you're going to get magic out. But make that connection first.

EXERCISE

MAKING A CONNECTION

Let's practice seeing that invisible energy right now. Get yourself some water. Put it in any vessel of your choosing. I would encourage you to choose one that provides you with some positive energy or complementary energy. If you awake on the grumpy side of the bed, perhaps a mug matching the mood is what you need. It's nice to have an ally to listen to us crank through why the sun rising at 4:30 a.m. is a blessing and a curse. As Witches, a lot of what we do in practicing our Craft is to work through emotions, use them for our highest good, learn, grow, and move forward. That does not mean that we dismiss things. No, we do the work.

One note here: everyone has different levels of senses. Use what is available to you. My eyes don't work great without my glasses; I'm half deaf. My energetic connection, however, has only grown stronger throughout my life. We all have the ability to connect and move energy. Of course, that has variances of ability as well. And ability is like everything in life: it ebbs and flows. We start where we are and work from there. Approach this with kindness and love.

We do this exercise with water because water makes up so much of our physical composition. The connection will be easier to feel, even for the Witchling just learning about energy connection. We'll go through all the senses and this water.

Start with sight. Look at the water either through the glass or down into the mug. I want you to connect with the energy of the water. It's there. Use the eyes to look at the water. Does it glisten in the light from the window? Does it seem muted and matte against the ceramic mug?

Remember that
Witchcraft is a practice.

Use that sense of smell. Yes, water still has a scent, even if it's coming from a municipal tap. There may even be an absence of smell or you may detect the scent of minerals. Get to know it.

Swirl the water around in the cup, mug, glass, etc. Let its sound connect within you. The noise it made whirling around—what thoughts, scenes, or feelings does that bring to you? Note it in the mind.

Put the water down, hold your hands a bit away from the glass, and give energy to the water. Can you imagine the invisible connection of the energy from you to the water's energy? It's there. Observe. Let whatever thoughts come to you without judgment. Did you feel that energy? What does it make you feel? Focus to make the connection stronger, then quiet it down again. Energetically hit the gas again, sending the energy to the water and letting the water's energy come to you. Hit the brakes and soften the connection. Quiet the mind and shield yourself from the water's energy. This part may be harder. Take the time and keep doing it until you feel it.

Remember that Witchcraft is a practice.

Do this exercise throughout a moon cycle, a little each day. Take five minutes. I also invite you to keep a journal about the experience. This helps create some easy reconnecting in our minds, bodies, and spirits when we're ready to mix up some magic. Ask yourself what it felt like to connect with water and write about it. Was one sense stronger than the other? How might you balance it out? How might you connect faster, stronger, etc., compared to how it worked for you this first time?

When I do this exercise, it feels like the water sees the water in me. My stomach gurgles as if I had guzzled a lot of water, even though all I'm doing is connecting. My ears might prick up and remember the sound of the ocean. You may smell that salt air or the scent of the backyard pool or vacation hot tub. There are no wrong answers here. It's all about connection and feelings. This energetic connection will be a great skill as we learn to have magic in our cups daily.

Referencing the Energy Inside

For those who have practiced the Craft in one way, shape, or form for some time, you recognize that energy is pulsing through everything. Like people, our drinks, food, and everything we come in contact with has an energy. Knowing what magic or energy something holds off the top of the head takes a hot minute. I've studied the Craft for more than forty years. I still pull out good reference books to double-check myself or learn something more deeply. Do not think yourself less of a Witch because you forget that roses—which are edible and used in my rosé margarita—are used to bring happiness, love, and psychic awareness or that nutmeg is also used for psychic awareness, marjoram for love, and marigold for happiness. We all individually will have our go-to concoctions that we turn to daily, monthly, seasonally, or annually that we remember more readily.

Our modern lives are full of information, and having a handy guide at our fingertips is a way to work smarter, not harder, in our Craft. For many practitioners, having a library of books that helps inform the path is smart Witchcraft. This can look different for everyone. My path has been informed by a whole host of books, including nonmagical-focused cookbooks, bartender's guides, field references to foraging, and the history of the people who lived at the forty-ninth parallel before me, as well as books from Margot Adler to Scott Cunningham and Starhawk through to Laura Tempest Zakroff. The resources listed within this book inform my own experience practicing Witchcraft. Luckily, now we can have full bookshelves as well as store data on handheld devices. Take these bits and pieces, fill a Book of Shadows, grimoire, or composition book, and allow them to empower your magic. Witches have been doing that forever. Like many a drink, take this knowledge and let it steep, ferment, and mix with how you connect with the collected energies to make new magic.

The Power of Drink

There have been a couple of times when drink magic was so überpowerful that the manifestation, the warding, or the healing was almost instantaneous for me. Sometimes drink magic works more slowly, but it does work. It doesn't work solely by ingredients; it works with the energy of intention. It's important that no matter the drink—water, wine, or tea—understanding its energy and how it combines is an integral part of the workings included here. The hope with this book is that you will have some liquid energies to use with magic making daily, weekly, monthly, and at all points on the Wheel of the Year. It is a regular supply of magic in your cup. The first step is examining the energies inside the ingredients.

Beyond the Physical

There are nods to the nutrition in many of the workings here; however, we'll be looking beyond the physical properties and examining the magical properties of the drinks, sometimes referred to as correspondences. For many Witches today, magic is working with energy. To do that, understanding the ingredients' energy and how that energy presents itself as you work with it and connect with it will be key to success. The workings presented in this book will list energy. However, this is where that reference shelf discussed earlier comes into play. Not all the energies, modalities, and uses will be documented necessarily within the workings here, but they can have more to them than you'll perhaps need for any given drink. Take, for instance, rosemary. In *Cunningham's Encyclopedia of Magical Herbs*, rosemary holds the energies of protection, love, lust, mental powers, exorcism, purification, healing, sleep, and youth.

Meanwhile, in Laurel Woodward's *Kitchen Witchery: Unlocking the Magick in Everyday Ingredients*, rosemary also includes energies toward beauty, communication, friendship, and remembrance. For me, rosemary holds strong protective energy, which is why you will find it planted all around my home. Additionally, to me it holds the energy of abundance. You may connect with rosemary, and it may tell you something else entirely. The point is to know before you go conjuring a cocktail. Learn what others know, connect yourself with the ingredients (as you did earlier with the water), and watch understanding grow. This then creates a stronger foundation to magical workings.

Understanding the Magical Energies

If you read enough books on Witchcraft or hang out with a crowd that's been doing it for more than five minutes, tomes and friends will tell you that you are the most important element in any Craft working. Most Witches understand this universal connectedness within and around everything in our world. Ask any of them; they will tell you it took a minute to be adept at that.

Many of us are still reaching for books on what energies are held within different things—like protection for rosemary or abundance for sugar—to solidify and authenticate our practice. That said, becoming more knowledgeable about the energy within and around yourself first and foremost will set you up for success. Reading that rosemary has protection energies is one thing. Connecting with it and feeling it is another. Do the work. This book is full of options for you to do the work. Doing the work provides opportunities for every Witch to carve more paths to live magically. It's an unending exploration. In short, you exercise that skill regularly. The Craft—being a Witch—is called a practice. Develop these skills and take sometimes very slow steps forward. But forward progress is progress and cannot be denied the title of advancement or growth. This is the permission to move forward. Practice makes the Witch.

You may start with what's been documented here and in other books. It's a natural first step. Can you feel the protective energy that rosemary provides? Perhaps the plant whispers something different to you. Your connection may bring forward another correspondence. Rosemary carries a general amplifying energy when I connect with it. Again, you'll want to trust instinct and gut, or what Witches call intuition. This will be especially helpful when there are different ingredient choices for the workings. For instance, evergreen trees have long-held energies of resilience and prosperity; there's a reason our ancestors chose them as the symbol of hope during winter. I've noted that pine cones from the ponderosa pine have a different energy in my experience than, say, blue spruce pine cones. Both come from coniferous trees, albeit different species. One grows along the Pacific, the other along the Rocky Mountains. The ponderosa cones hold a bit more saltiness to their energy, whereas the blue spruce is the strong, silent type in its presence in any kind of spell. That's my personal experience. However, given where and how they grow and their other distinct characteristics, you may conclude that saltiness comes honestly to the ponderosa, and the blue spruce echoes its Rocky Mountain neighbors. You may find that working with a balsam fir is preferable when creating a spell for any type of support. Again, the input, senses, knowledge, and connection make it magic.

Just Add Witch

Next in the magical formula of drinks is the magic within the maker, the Witch, the bartender, or the barista, if you like. This will always be essential to these drinks, brews, and potions, so it's included here again. It may also impact a Witch's ability to make something magical. Therefore, the most important ingredient in these spells, rituals, and recipes is you, the Witch. Whether it's making a magical cocktail or another working, any magic keeps the worker's energy in mind.

Perhaps there's a time when you're brewing tea, and the intention you need to put into it is something positive, but you're not feeling good or very energetic. It doesn't mean you can't do magic. Instead, you must be mindful. In these situations, you may take it slow, do your best, and perhaps choose an approach that allows for lower energies. Choose some extra ingredients to boost mood or energy. Before these workings, you will want your physical, mental, and spiritual energy to be up to the task. This is more pointedly true when dealing with slow-craft items or tinctures. Whatever the reason or situation, if you are under the weather, consider that and mitigate it however possible before creating drinks magically—or doing any magic, honestly.

Most magical workings start with some sort of grounding and centering step. If you're a Witch, mystic, woo-woo adjacent, or practice yoga regularly, you've learned to ground and center yourself. To return to the body, connect the third-eye mind and the energetic being. Breathwork, recognizing and redirecting our thoughts, putting our feet bare, connecting to the earth, water cleansing, and practicing varied meditation methods are mixed and matched in various Craft practices. All of them alone or combined in various ways can get you to center energy and focus intention.

H. Byron Ballard, author of *Small Magics: Practical Secrets from an Appalachian Village Witch*, dedicates an entire chapter to grounding and the many ways a Witch might find "is the act of deeply connecting with the planet's living energy field in order to achieve a stronger stability" (Ballard 18). That connection includes connecting back to the Witch's energetic field, too. In Mat Auryn's *Psychic Witch*, there are exercises in chapters 6 and 15 specifically for engaging this connection. For me, my grounding and centering practices make me feel like I am a witchy superhero. I am standing in my power. My breath is a force to direct this energy, and I can feel this invisible electricity all around me. I visualize sending this energy all around me like an invisible full-body shield. I quickly assume a mountain pose (tadasana) stance. I take three cleansing breaths to bring me back into my body. I focus on the ground under my feet, feeling the connection between the sole of my foot and the ground, and eventually soul and ground, as this process ups my spiritual and energetic connectedness, or "interconnectedness," as Auryn puts it. Then that focus moves up to the top of my head, focusing on the energy I want: calm, receptive, powerful, etc. Then I work to clear my mind by focusing on the breath and seeing it as positive energy in, stagnant energy out. I know I'm grounded and centered when I feel that connection between my soul and the universe. I often end the session with three claps of my hands, which reawakens that connection. Training myself to do this has taken many years and was not something I found particularly easy. But the more I worked on it, the more I could stand in my power and connect to the universal energies around me. You likely already know what a grounding and centering practice looks like or are exploring one. Continue to study. See what works for you. Before you do these workings, please ground and center however that looks like for you.

Show up to all the magic you want to create as the most powerful you. If you're not grounded and centered, it's a harder path. In my experience, missteps, mistakes, and misused magic all happen when we're discon-nected. You are the most important ingredient in all of this. The Witch's energy, efforts, and personal magic are what make it magical. Under-stand, accept, and respect that, and you're on the way to weaving a world of magical drink.

If any of these suggestions or practices are unavailable to you, mod-ify any or all of the parts to the fullest extent of your ability as desired or required. Creative problem-solving is a core skill in any Witch's tool-box. Any spell, ritual, or rite in this book is a jumping-off point. Add your energy and magic to make it yours.

Choosing Your Magical Ingredients

As a Witch who lives as close to the land as her energy and resources will allow, I use the available things. You may not have raspberries growing near the back door, but maybe the local community produces lots of straw-berries or you reside in an area that has a bounty of potatoes, okra, apples, or even edible flowers. Maybe the neighbor gives you zucchini from their garden each year. Any and all of these scenarios are important to note as you weave drink magic throughout life.

Different plants may contain similar energies. For instance, if you were working up something to amplify the sensitivity of connecting magically, ingredients like daisy, marigold, violet, chamomile, and rosemary all work to develop sensitivity. Perhaps you accidentally killed the marigolds; chamomile will work to bring the same energies. A book like *Llewellyn's Complete Book of Correspondences* by Sandra Kynes can help you keep every-thing straight. You may consider putting favorites into a Book of Shad-ows. I've lost count of how many volumes of my personal BoS contain my beloved rosemary. You might also consider creating a digital collection of articles, photos, artwork, etc., that talks about any of the ingredients of a drink, not just the herbs. However, like any published compendium on magical correspondences (properties), it includes animals, minerals, astrology, preferred deities, and so on. Everything has energy and brings something else to magical mixology.

QUALITY OF INGREDIENTS

When choosing ingredients for any Craft working, the most powerful energy is when the ingredient is in its most natural state before you use it in a brew. This could be fresh from the vine, tree, or plant. It could be freshly roasted or toasted. That does not mean that dried herbs or commercially processed milk cartons are not powerful. As minimally processed as possible is preferred (and not pulled from the depths of a hermit aunt's cupboard). But in a pinch, even though most natural may be the freshest, what is available on hand works. There will be many suggestions for ease and access in all the drink weaving in this book. For instance, I can't understand why anyone would not use whiskey distilled locally for their nightcap ritual—yet, if what is available is an airline bottle of Jack Daniels, it still holds the same magical properties. However, if you live in the greater Lynchburg, Tennessee, area, Jack may be where it's at. You may not vibe as deeply with the far away, yet very fine Woodinville whiskey from Washington State. This is also the case with anything you ingest. Apples grown in the local area are fresher and stronger. As a Witch, we understand the concept of holistic interconnectedness, so those local ingredients hold a stronger energetic connection to us. Think of it as if there are bits of you inside the ingredients.

Local ingredients hold a stronger energetic connection to us.

This is why we follow the energies of our seasons; Wheel of the Year, in-season appropriate considerations will often decide if substituting one ingredient for another is the stronger magic. Fortunately, no matter where you are in time here on earth, the choices are endless. I give you a jumping-off point in this book for a mystical mixology path, but I hope you'll take what I give you, explore further, and deepen the connection to the bounty Mother Nature provides near you. As the connection grows, so too will the energy and magic that can be made with it. Give that connection to ingredients that are the best they can be. They don't have to be fancy, rare, or exotic. Focus instead on the corresponding properties of ingredients, which are sympathetic to the cause and sustainably accessible. When you know the brewer of the spirits you use, the roaster of the beans you grind, the green tea grower of the brand you like, or where the local honey comes from, that daily cuppa becomes layered with more magic. Then you take that energy and create something even more deeply powerful. It's a wonderful circle in a magical life.

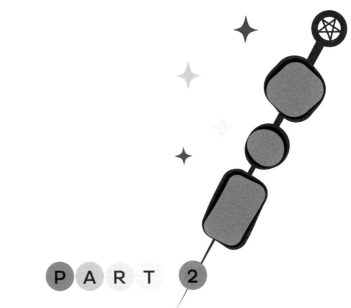

P A R T 2

MAGICAL MIXOLOGY
in practice

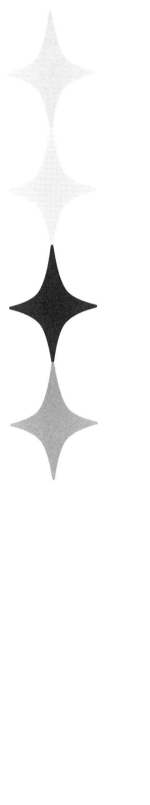

CHAPTER
7

THE
WITCH'S MOST
IMPORTANT
drink

Biologically, we need water. Will the Witch find themselves performing magic with every glass of water? No. What if we offered the universe a nanosecond of acknowledgment as we get ready to sip water—simply the thought of *Thank the universe for this water* or *I hydrate my body to power my goals*? How might that change the day, the body, the mood? Imagine the ripple effect of giving that kind of attention to one glass of water a day.

That effect is what Japanese scientists decided to study almost a decade ago (Radin 2006). They wanted to test the effects of distant intention on water crystal formation, so they conducted a double-blind test. The scientists had two thousand people on one side of the earth send positive intentions toward water samples maintained in California. Different water samples were set aside in different locations as controls. The results indicated that ice crystals formed in the samples where participants focused their energy. The samples from the same source that were also in other locations were also affected.

Like the water connection exercise detailed earlier, our energy can affect the water. The more you connect with the energy of water, the more magical the refreshment. Regardless of its source, turn to water whenever you feel stressed throughout the day. Taking a drink, breathing, and maybe sipping more is like a mini reset button. Talk about some powerful magic.

We are starting with making hydration magical because it is an essential and often overlooked component of our ability to do what we want. According to recent studies, many of us walk around chronically dehydrated, especially children and seniors (Kenney 2015, Porterfield 2019). Nearly everything the body and brain do is dependent on water. According to the Mayo Clinic, we lose nearly ten of those eight-ounce glasses of water we are supposed to drink daily to support an average amount of activities (Pruthi 2022). If you are not drinking at least eighty ounces of water daily, imagine how that affects anyone's ability to function. Our mind is our most powerful tool when it comes to magic. The body supports the mind. Witches want mind, body, and spirit at their best. This state sets the foundation for strong magic.

A meta-analysis of thirty-three studies regarding dehydration and cognitive function uncovered a corresponding lack of brain power in dehydrated subjects than those fully hydrated (Wittbrodt 2018). They found that the average person must consume fifteen eight-ounce glasses of water daily to hydrate fully (that's 120 ounces). That is many trips to the bathroom, at least initially. Once the body expects the hydration level it needs, it tends to level off, and the rest responds appropriately (Pacheco 2023). It is easy to see that it would be hard to be a potent Witch if one were dehydrated.

As Witches, many of us are fully committed to consistent self-improvement. The strongest magic is always that which we weave within ourselves. Therefore, what if we drank the water our body and brain required for optimal functioning? How would that look? Could we approach it from a spiritual, energetic point of view? If this book guides the reader to proper hydration and makes it part of daily routine, then good energy has just been doubled, and we are both the better Witch for it. If there is one more powerful Witch out there doing good work with themselves and for others, that's a win-win!

If we make hydration part of our spiritual practice, we perform the whole "where our focus goes, so our energy flows" mindfulness. That diligence is significant because it puts the energy of our thoughts behind a daily habit. When we make a daily habit magical, we are living with a level of intention that is unmatched and hard to undo.

Water Source Considerations

How do you make hydration magical? To do this, you do not need to be a Water or Sea Witch. This magic is available to everyone. First of all, you simply need to decide that you want to make the hydration practice magical. Once you do that, you must look at where the water comes from. Because the Craft is often centered on earth and other elemental magic, understanding where the water comes from begins the path to daily magical hydration.

Everyone's water access looks different. For instance, my household shares a well with a couple of neighbors. This type of access allows more control over how water gets to my home. It requires more energy from our perspective as Witches, but that extra work strengthens a Witch's connection to the lifeblood that is water. It is not as convenient, but it can be more consequential. That is not to say that water pumped into our homes from municipal water supplies does not also create a powerful connection. However, indoor plumbing does not necessarily mean the water is safe to consume or use: ask the people of Flint, Michigan, or a vast contingent of places in Texas or Baltimore (Bendix 2020). Wherever the water comes from, you will want to know how it is treated, pumped, and brought home. Ensure what you are putting in the body is as healthy as possible.

Another issue with our modern water connection is the commodification of it. This is not only in opposition to many practices of Witchcraft, but it is hostile to all life on the planet. Do we truly need to buy bottled water for convenience? Supporting that system is baneful magic. We can acknowledge that bottled water saves folx during things like tornadoes, hurricanes, and other disasters, but for daily modern life, it is simply untenable.

If the water in the home is not suitable for drinking, there are other ways than buying bottled water at a retail space. Hit the local food co-op and use their filtered water system to create a more sustainable water purchase. These water kiosks are still offering water as a commodity but provide a more sustainable, eco-friendly, and accessible way. Perfect? No, but as the permaculture principle shows, small, slow solutions are often sustainable. Is there no food co-op nearby? Work with the local corner store to create such access. Alternatively, the neighborhood could work to bring one to the grocery store. As Witches, we understand the conundrum of attempting ethical consumption under capitalism since it's a harmful system. We can try to bring the need for water as close to ethical and healthy as possible, even if it is to be gentler to our budgets.

Years ago, I worked with a woman who bought one twelve-ounce bottle of water and a candy bar daily from the little cafe inside the office building. While on break, she would stop and ask me something about the weather or the significant traffic incident, happily munching a chocolate bar for breakfast. One time, I inquired why she bought the water. It was bothersome then—and this was way before BPA issues, not to mention the oncoming climate crisis we are currently facing. The confusion was caused by the sheer amount of money that one bottle cost. Meanwhile, she complained about her rent going up. Sucks, for sure. She liked her apartment complex, its amenities, and the location. She did not want to move. She was looking at postings in-house where we worked that might give her a bump in salary. I cheered that idea. She said something about eating ramen again to make up for the cost of her rent increase. I pointed at the water bottle in her hand and did the math with her right then and there. She spent nearly three hundred dollars a year on bottled water. Today she could own a BPA-free water flask in a different color for each day of the week for less than that. If she had put the money away, even in a savings account, she would have a nice nest egg to fuel other dreams.

However, the biggest problem is those plastic bottles. Having spent some time living on a sailboat and seeing the ocean from that perspective and the number of plastic bottles in our waterways, they still cause a cringe reaction when seeing them. So much negativity exists in one ubiquitous twelve-ounce (or more) container. Is it less convenient sometimes to have to pack water in a more sustainable container? Sure. Are there access issues? Without a doubt. Can we work as Witches to overcome those barriers? Absolutely. Such activism is very much a part of practicing the Craft. As we examine and inquire about the water system that reaches our mouths, as a Witch, the activism will come step by step. In the interim, perhaps develop a daily water ritual. Water is the most crucial liquid for us. Starting the day with it is a no-brainer.

Morning Water

When we rise in the morning, it is a perfect time to connect with water energy and make hydration a ritual. There are many possibilities on how to do this. One choice jump-starts daily hydration by providing electrolytes. Its acidity is good for gut biome and digestive ease, revs up the body's muscles, and manages the adrenal system. The adrenal glands are essential in how our bodies handle stress. This is where the body produces hormones like adrenaline, cortisol, and noradrenaline, which help it respond to everything life throws at it. Proper adrenal system management helps us avoid things like anxiety, depression, and heart disease. These are all things that plagued many of our ancestors and kindred, but it can be mitigated with disciplined hydration. A neglected adrenal system can make our nervous system overwork, creating all kinds of physical problems, and it is even harder to get that under control. If you want to maintain both, drink water.

Enter the morning hydration ritual. This ritual is like drinking winter sunshine first thing in the morning. In the middle of winter, when many are prone to seasonal affective disorder, the "sunshine" in the cup becomes like medicine. Even in the height of summer, it is medicine, too. Cooling or heating the water is unnecessary because it is first thing in the morning. Cold water can shock the body's systems, especially upon waking, so tepid water is best. Warmer than room temperatures can be pleasant, especially in winter—but, like green tea, warm, not boiling, please; the water should be no warmer than 180°F (82°C).

The recipe below calls for sea salt. Please do not use table salt. Sea salt means minimally processed salt. Himalayan salt is a good alternative, too. However, the cost of pure sea salt can be more affordable. Also, the salt has to be finely ground to dissolve quickly. Do be sure to measure accurately. Too salty is no fun first thing in the morning. Consider including a special salt container that allows a just-the-right-size ritual spoon, which holds symbols of health, to dip into the container and get the right amount.

As for the lemon juice, freshly squeezed is preferred, but bottled lemon juice works, too. The amount of lemon juice per half a lemon squeezed equals around a quarter cup but perhaps use less if using bottled. Experiment and choose. Regardless, there is something comforting each morning in this tiny physical activity of moving the half lemon into the juicer. The sound. The smell. The result. They all combine to turn a little smile on the face. I keep the lemons out on the counter so they are easier to juice; however, the fruit may wither faster in summer. In that case, keep the lemons in the fridge and smartly take out one for the following day the night before. Then it is easier to juice and is also protected from summer's heat. Reserve the unused half of the lemon to do this again in the evening, if needed, or the following morning. An airtight container that remains on the counter works fine. If that is not available, store it on the fridge door, where it will not get too cold, wrapped in some beeswax paper or other sustainable way. The goal is for the lemon not to be too cold when retrieved for the Witch-ade or a morning hydration ritual the following day.

Practicing this daily ritual for a moon cycle can create a habit that will improve your health. Start the day better hydrated, directed, and nourishing the body. Get powered up with the water that's needed. It is the most important drink of the day.

WITCH-ADE
FOR MORNING HYDRATION

SERVES
1

EQUIPMENT

Glass that holds at least 14 ounces

Spoon or single chopstick for stirring

Manual juicer

INGREDIENTS

12 ounces filtered room-temperature water

Half an organic lemon, juiced

⅛ to ¼ teaspoon finely ground sea salt

INSTRUCTIONS

1. Into the glass of water add the freshly squeezed lemon. Stir.

2. Add the salt and stir until dissolved. Do thirteen turns with the spoon sunwise to represent incorporating the salt into the potion, and then thirteen turns widdershins to represent the salt's dissolution into the potion.

3. Pause here, place hands over the glass, and set an intention for the day. Something positive. Something actionable. "I choose joy today" or "I am strong" or "I am a patient Witch." The choice is yours.

4. Drink the potion all the way. It is not necessary to guzzle. Sip and journal or plot out the day. Pause and take a few minutes to drink this. Do not have tea or coffee before finishing this. Drink the water first—all twelve ounces. Try to do it within fifteen minutes.

Consider using electrolytes after an intense yoga session, long hike, or any other situation where extended exertion occurs. Switch up the lemon for another citrus; simply keep the measurements the same.

Water and Ice to Aid Dream Work

Beginning the day with water and ending it with water has many benefits beyond hydrating the body. Physically, it regulates heart rate and blood pressure. Emotionally, it stabilizes the mood so that we are ready for bed. According to the Sleep Foundation, a nonprofit headquartered in Seattle, WA, drinking water before bed can help stop many problems. Primarily, it continues the excellent hydration throughout the day, supporting all the systems in the body that help us sleep.

Some may think drinking a bunch of water before bed ensures waking up in the middle of the night and using the bathroom. Such disturbance in sleep is likely from underhydration during the hours before bedtime, not overhydration. It is not a problem when beginning the day with a morning hydration practice. Instead, this water becomes an anchor for better sleep, more dream messages, and better dream recall. The key to avoiding sleep disturbances because of hydration is to actively manage your intake throughout the day, every day. This includes considering anything that impacts your hydration, like caffeine or alcohol consumption. Then you're mitigating as many barriers as possible to provide for a good night's dream work.

Dreams are an often untapped source of guidance for our lives, even within the percentage of the population who declare they do not remember dreams. This particular working of sippable spellcraft allows the body to have muscle memory and the brain to have an anchor in the waking world. It gets the Witch tapping into another energy source to help be the most authentic self and live the best life.

Unlike the morning hydration practice denoted above, this drink of water will be cold. Its base is ice cubes. That cold will prompt consciousness, brain, and body to help recall dreams. Add the Witch for it to become a spell anchored in reality. As detailed in the book *Why We Dream* by Alice Robb, "reality tests" are vital to recalling dreams, allowing the mind to know when it's dreaming, and retaining the dream in waking life. This particular working is a reality test with a witchy bent. Use it to begin to sharpen your dream recall. Practice regularly recalling dreams before mixing up the Off to Dreamland Tea as a partner in lucid dreaming in chapter 12.

Cool Dream Recall Water

EQUIPMENT

- Insulated or thermal cup that will hold at least 8 ounces
- Bedside table and coaster
- Notebook and pen
- Ice molds (optional)

INGREDIENTS

- 1 cup ice cubes or large cube
- Drinkable water to fill glass

SERVES
1

INSTRUCTIONS

1. About 15 minutes before turning the lights off for bed, fill an insulated cup with ice. Then pour enough water to fill about half of it. Drink the ice water and say three times, "I easily recall my dreams." Say it quietly or as loud as feels comfortable, but do say the words. Drink the cold water in the glass. Leave the ice cubes.

2. Put the insulated vessel by the bed with a coaster under it so as the ice melts overnight, any condensation is captured and does not ruin furniture or floor. Go to sleep.

3. When waking up at night or the next day before getting out of bed, sip the cool water the ice has left behind. Get ready to recall the dreams. In the reserved journal, write down those dreams when you first wake up. This allows recording each bit of the message from the dream. Repeat this throughout a moon cycle to heighten dream recall.

Consider having larger-sized ice cubes if living in a warmer area. Ice molds of fun or magical shapes, like a whiskey cube, can be used. Consider also dedicating or consecrating a particular glass reserved for this working.

Every Drink Starts with Water

Next, we examine how water is the basis for every brew. Much of the beer-making, cidermaking, and winemaking from our ancestors was because clean drinking water was often hard to come by, especially as humans began dwelling together in larger and larger communities. When making water more magical, we may have to wait until night because we need the moon as our accomplice in this brewing process.

CHAPTER 8

Making moon water and working with the moon's energies is undoubtedly a foundational practice for many Witches. Since the moon is the heavenly body closest to our planet, it is unsurprising that many cultures have witnessed its effect on nature, most notably the sphere of water around the planet that holds the tides.

Of course, the moon is not the only heavenly body that Witches pull energy from for our drinks. The sun is there, too. How many reading this have made sun tea at the summer solstice? Although making solar water happens from sunrise to sunset, the creation of it is similar to moon water. Why, then, is the moon so significant for Witches? The moon is closest to us

MOON
WATER
magic

and holds the sun's energy in its light, which is how we see the moon from earth. The light comes from the sun itself. Unless it is the heat or some potent stimulation and zeal needed in Craft spells, like sun tea, I find that moon water also holds solar energy. That is why so many Witches work with moon water: it holds the energy of two heavenly bodies. As energetic influences go, ingredients created to infuse them with moon energy are something Witches recognize and use to stand in and raise their power.

There is also the fact that for Witches, the moon symbolizes the Divine Feminine. It is a representation of the Goddess's energy. Like a woman, the moon and many of the stories of feminine deities move through cycles of maiden, mother, and crone, waxing and waning. The moon's cycles hold different energies that ebb and flow, much like the movement of river water—constantly changing but still moving. It is a powerful connection, and using the moon to create magic in a cup is an obvious choice.

Making Moon Water

Moon water is simply water charged with the moon's energy. Depending on phase and astrology transit location, our dear moon imparts its energy and properties into the water, whether it be protection, healing, or cleansing. It is used in various ways in any Craft practice but can be incredibly potent for brewing magic in your cup. It is easy to see how including moon water with tea, coffee, and other brews layers on more magic. It's like a daily gift.

The great thing about moon water is that even when a Witch feels unable to perform a spell or ritual with the new or full moon (or any moon, for that matter), there is moon water. On any lunar cycle, sometimes called *esbats* in Witchcraft circles, water bottles are lined up along the windowsill, looking like colorful glass soldiers standing at attention in front of the moon. This collection of particular colored containers provides visual clues about what energy the water holds. It can be visually appealing, too. Use whatever vessel wanted in order to make some. Maybe all-black bottles are preferred; maybe only a crystal goblet will do. Find something that has personal meaning, minimally. Have the intention that this will be a vessel to hold a sacred liquid after the moon has finished blessing it. The point is to hold the water, but utility, aesthetics, and intention are considered in tandem.

Moon water is a great way to infuse tea, coffee, Witch-ade, or a cocktail with extra magic. Even making ice cubes from moon water is a great way to strengthen the energy and make drinking much more special. Making magical moon water is one of the first things many Witches learn to do in their Craft. A quick internet search reveals thousands upon thousands of articles, blogs, and books devoted to turning water into something magical under the light of any given moon.

In many of the spells in this book, the list of ingredients to be used may note "moon water." Water straight from the pitcher, tap, or carafe is fine. The infused moon water adds another magical layer to the brew, spell, or ritual, but plain water suffices. Remember, the practitioner is the most dominant part of any magic conducted.

Knowing when the moon is rising and falling is fundamental, but it generally tracks the same way in the sky as the sun, so a south windowsill is prime. For instance, in the Pacific Northwest in the middle of May, the moon rises in the middle of the night and sets in the middle of the afternoon. Times also vary at any given location. The moon does not always come up at sunset and set at sunrise. Finding this information is simple for us modern practitioners. Do a quick internet search, use various apps, or go old school and get a farmer's almanac or astrological ephemeris.

It is time to make moon water. The following may be done on an outdoor altar or a windowsill where the moon will shine on the water vessel.

The Witch is the most dominant part of any magic conducted.

ANYTHING BUT BASIC

M O O N W A T E R

EQUIPMENT

Any clean container that holds water: glass, bottle, or jar

A chosen night with the moon

INGREDIENTS

Drinkable water

INSTRUCTIONS

1. Fill a container with water. Place in a spot where it will be exposed to the moonlight for at least eight hours.

2. Pause and put your chosen intentions into the water. Allow your hands to hover over it. Close your eyes. See, feel, and connect with the moon's energy, then do the same with the water, and then yourself.

3. For example, say, "May this water accept the energies of the new moon and infuse in it the energy to start fresh toward my goal of [insert desired goal here in as specific terms and steps as possible; e.g., easily finding the right career path and excitement in my work]. All of this or better. So it is."

4. Collect the water after the moon sets and use it in any magic working.

Drink it. Bathe in it. Make soup with it. Make tea with it. Make ice cubes with it. Hydrate the body or plants. Cleanse the home or the body. Use moon water in any water-use capacity!

Drinking Lunar Energies

Understanding what energies the moon imparts into the moon water created will also inform how it's applied. Many Witches make moon water for houseplants. Any water source can be "blessed" by the moon. On our covenstead we make willow tea, which is some young willow cuttings in a five-gallon bucket full of water that sits out under the moon all the time. However, this Witch works energetic connections and intentions with this water source on a new or full moon. The plant needs to release and renew itself monthly, like the moon and like us. Targeting specific energies for certain drinks, spells, or rituals makes magic more dynamic.

As Witches, we have lots of prerogatives when making moon water. Consideration of the moon's energies is necessary. The next step is understanding how to incorporate the phase of the moon as well as its astrological transit placement and its effect on the water. Working moon magic has many choices! Don't fret. This section details many ideas on using moon water and which one might help a particular working. Regardless, a Witch could spend a whole year doing moon water magic exclusively.

Moon Phases

First, let's talk about the moon phases and how they affect making moon water. The moon, the heavenly body closest to earth, goes through a cycle of phases as it orbits our planet. That takes approximately 29.5 days. Each phase corresponds to a changing position of not only the moon but where the sun and earth are as well.

Using moon water within a ritual, spell, or working instead of plain water means a Witch understands the additional layer of energy caused by the moon phase and how it will deepen the work. Does everything created at the bar or on the stove have moon water in it? Of course not; that's hardly a reasonable expectation. Could it? Yes. Should you? If you desire. Remember those layers of magic discussed? Witches understand a spell ingredient that was made magically boosts everything else in that spell. Let's look at each phase and how it may impact your sippable spellcraft.

Dark Moon

This moon phase happens right before the new moon. It is the waning crescent phase, also called the balsamic phase. It can last between one to three days. Consider creating dark moon water within the first twelve hours of the moon and sun conjunct one another. This is the time when the moon is unseen in the sky. This energy is significant for transformative inner work. Use to release anything blocking a Witch from a goal. Within the following chapters, dark moon water is used in Revelation Tea and Start Fresh Coffee.

New Moon/First Quarter

The energy with this moon phase is all about moving forward, setting goals, and dreaming the most illustrious dreams possible. Moon water created at this time is all about manifestation, attracting abundance, and starting anew. Witches might use this water for Witch-ade or Gin-Cin Comfort Tisane.

Waxing Moon/Second Quarter

The seeds of dreams (or actual plants or tinctures) were planted during the new moon. Now, with the waxing moon, it is time to grow and leave our comfort zone. Fortune Favors Boldness, Positivity Tea, and Afternoon Delight Latte all use moon water created during this moon phase.

Full Moon/Third Quarter

While working on a goal from the dark or new moon through to the full moon, Witches move forward, meeting a benchmark toward their objective or even accomplishing them. Perhaps progress toward said goal has stalled a bit. No worries—it's time to reflect on what's working and what's not, to double down on what is and release what's not. Look at the full moon as a time of rest; moving more slowly and trusting our gut becomes paramount. This is when Witches are permitted to take things easy, especially a Witch who feels a particular moon's energy even more strongly, where suddenly we're sleeping less or more, or other patterns we've noted are impacting our lives. Moon water made during the full moon is used in Rosé Margarita Punch or Celebration Cider Punch.

Waning Moon/Fourth Quarter

This is the best time to do Craft workings that remove something from life. The energy is waning; it's taking away. This is a time of completion. There is much potential with the waning moon, and I feel like it's not used enough by many modern Witches. This is a great time to edit energy and remove the drama llamas from the fields of life. Moon water created now is splendid for making Weed Out the Weary Tea.

Astrological Influence

Next, we look at not only the consideration of the moon phase, but the energies and correspondences of the moon's position within the zodiac. We're layering again. There are layers of energies based on planetary influences, seasonal influences, and elemental energies. Only one or all may be chosen. There are no rules, only what calls to the Witch. The moon and astrology are the easiest ways to add layers to magic. Adding energetic layers makes Craft workings weightier. Let's look at how we apply astrology and moon watermaking together.

Each zodiac season will feature a new moon in that sign. The full moon in that sign will correspond about six months later. For instance, a new moon in Cancer will come in the Cancer season, which falls between June and July. The full moon in Cancer comes sometime between December and January. Tracking the progress and incorporating appropriate drink magic is an excellent exercise in seeing progress from setting intentions on, say, the Capricorn new moon and then reflecting, renewing, or releasing come the Capricorn full moon, which typically happens six months later.

In the meantime, as we practice magical mixology there is a massive opportunity to raise the energies within our Craft workings with each moon transit. Look at the underlying qualities and usefulness in each moon's astrology and how it boosts magic by working with the movements of the planets. If a Witch wants to understand how astrology affects magicmaking, many books can start on that path, with many layers to explore. After I incorporated astrology into my spellcraft, I experienced a new level of energetic power in my magic.

Each astrology sign imparts different energies into the moon water created. Each sign has modalities, elemental and physical correspondences, and ruling planets, which, when considered together, create an overall energy. You'll use that energy to provide further intention in whatever spell or ritual is performed, but especially within drinks since, as noted above, they all start with water.

The following is a more detailed look at each sign and how its energies might be used in spellcraft.

Aries

A moon in the cardinal sign of Aries is ruled by Mars energy. This fiery moon helps break through barriers toward goals. A new moon in Aries gets much attention, especially on how it seems to ignite a fire inside the body to do any physical activity we might want. Conversely, an Aries full moon imparts abundant assertive energy. Need to be done with that ex? Use that full moon in Aries. Moon water created under an Aries moon can help up the passion and excitement, release obsession, or get a person unstuck from negative patterns or thought processes.

Taurus

A moon in the sign of Taurus is ruled by Venus energy. Using the fixed earth energy of this moon for mixology reinforces the loyalty, beauty, and persistence of any working. A new moon in Taurus sets the stage for creating stability and sustainability in life and general self-care. Taurus moon water may help us boost finances, lean into sensuality, or reinvest in the relationship with self and nature. Simple fennel tea made with Taurus moon water and a small amount of local honey brings out the earth mother in all of us.

Gemini

A new or full moon in Gemini will bring lots of heady and intellectually focused energy. Ruled by Mercury, it may be used for learning new things. Its mutable air modalities create a moon water that makes a fantastic base for a good chat over tea. It is used to combat the capricious nature of the

Gemini moon and avoid malicious gossip. If you are taking coffee to go, use Gemini moon water and enhance that cup with more inspiration and creativity.

Cancer

Shown as a crab in astrology symbolism, the moon rules Cancer, and a Witch may consider making extra moon water at this time as it focuses on emotions, family, and home. As the cardinal water sign, Cancer energy often washes over folx unexpectedly. Harnessing that excess energy and creating harmony via magic and drink can help the Witch attract compassion and repel the need for control. Off to Dreamland Tea—a lucid dream tea infused under a Cancer moon—is excellent for leveling up dreamwork.

Leo

The hot stuff of the zodiac, a new or full moon in Leo brings out all our self-expression and fun. Need the fiery energy of the sun? You get the moon and sun all in one when making moon water under a Leo moon since Leo is ruled by the sun. The exciting thing is that shadow work and manifesting are encompassed all at once with the fixed Leo energy inside this moon. Washing hair or doing a vinegar rinse with Leo moon water infused with this sun- and moon-powered liquid will likely make a Witch's mane look the best. Don't forget the fun, too. Share Leo Season Luscious Lemonade with the coven or besties and let the good times roar.

Virgo

This mutable earth sign has a particular way of getting us to focus on the practical. Virgo energy brings healthy habits toward us or helps us release unhealthy habits. Need to get organized? Want to help? That Virgo new moon can help set intentions to do that. Watch out for the less desirable aspects of this moon, specifically perfectionism. Virgo moon's energy heightens critical thinking. Don't become a critic. Instead, begin your morning hydration ritual under or with Virgo moon water. Using it in spells regarding serving the community is so Virgo.

Libra

When we feel like the world is all work, work, work, the Libra moon comes along and gives us balance and harmony and reminds us of our relationships, including the one with self. If improving artistic abilities, whether art, music, or fashion, use Libra moon water (ruled by Venus) in whatever working, brew, or beverage. As the cardinal air sign in the zodiac, Libra's energy is all about making peace with self, kindness, and community. Libra moon water will heighten the effects of Ice the B.S. Coffee.

Scorpio

As the fixed water sign in the zodiac, Scorpio energies deal with emotions, the subconscious, and the soul. Need to realign intuition? Ready for a change? Need to flood some intimacy or privacy into life? Use Scorpio's new moon water. Ruled by Pluto and Mars, setting up and defending boundaries is good work with Scorpio's full moon water. Use this precious fixed water energy in a Day-Zees Tea.

Sagittarius

Pack those bags for a new or full moon in Sagittarius because expanding horizons, adventure, learning, and meeting new people are likely happening during this time. These mutable moons direct magic toward shifting directions, creating ease, or motivating us to do something new. Ready that thermos with Cackling Round the Fire and head somewhere a Witch can feel the breeze on their face—maybe somewhere high up in the mountains? A star-gazing trip where learning new information about Jupiter, the ruling planet of Sagittarius, might do the trick.

Capricorn

As a cardinal earth sign under Saturn's influence, the moon's energy in Capricorn on water is all about being a Witch with a plan. Capricorn energy knows when to set goals, make the plan, take action, wait it out, and celebrate success! Moon water created under this sign can help with discipline, discernment, and determination. Want to be the head Witch in charge? Channel that Capricorn energy. Swift Witch Hot Cocoa Mix brewed with Capricorn moon water is the bomb for manifesting boss energy. I save a gallon of Capricorn moon water yearly to make our traditional wassail.

AQUARIUS

Making moon water under an Aquarius moon will lend its fixed air energy to the water. Uranus, the planet of innovation, technology, and sudden change, rules this sign. Need to find some independence? Want to work toward social justice or uncover a new path to fix a problem? Aquarian moon water is all about progress. It's also an all-purpose energetic amplifier. Party Hearty Punch is a good use of Aquarius moon water. On the covenstead it is consistently used for brewing cider and beer.

PISCES

Ruled by mystical and dreamy Neptune, Pisces moon water brings mutable, powerful energy. Need to make dream work more acute? Use the energy of a Pisces new moon. How about honing intuition or artistic abilities? Pisces full moon water is good for that. Pisces moon water enhances any psychic Witch exercises. When balancing out some fire energies in a brew, pull in water charged under a Pisces moon, especially if turned into ice cubes.

· · · · ·

Many of the drinks we enjoy as Witches can be augmented and created even more magical using moon water instead of plain water. It's also possible to bless and infuse any batch of drink brewing—not just water—under the moon. When our covenstead brews cider, we consider the moon we're making it under and the energy that may be imparted to the process. I wouldn't recommend leaving a gallon of milk under the moon, however. Employ good food safety knowledge in this process accordingly.

Hydration is required for any Witch to be at their best. Plain water can be a drag some days. Infusing cold water with fruit, herbs, and even spices gives any magical mixologist and their kindred a healthy alternative to chemical-laden commercial soft drinks. Infused water can also help with weight loss because the items infused in the water provide nutrition that boosts metabolism. Also, infused water provides an increase in daily fiber intake, which improves digestion. When a Witch is hydrated and takes in extra fiber and nutrients, it is immunity-boosting because the body receives extra antioxidants to help protect cells from damage and fend off illness. Besides, infusing water or moon water can augment the taste, benefits, and magic.

A Witch might want that boost right about the middle of the afternoon or with lunch. Plus, it adds to

THE REALM
beyond
WATER

our continued hydration efforts throughout the day. Infused water is at our service.

The following potions feature things easily at one's disposal. As mentioned before, with emphasis on encouragement, explore what is available easily to you and what properties those ingredients hold magically and physically. Don't forget taste. If it's not pleasurable, you won't drink it. Keep trying new combinations until you create your next favorite drink.

Flower Medicines

I discovered elderberry—*Sambucus nigra*, or specifically its predecessor, elderflower—when I first arrived in the Pacific Northwest. A local businesswoman sold elderberry syrup, which was in heavy rotational use in our household during cold and flu season. Having children in school always meant someone had a cold. There was a noticeable drop in our suffering with regular doses of elderberry syrup, which made that elderberry syrup absolute gold. That local cottage industry entrepreneur earned a regular customer. Her spring offerings received extra excitement as she would make elderflower cordial—if a Witch were lucky enough to get some. The cordial had this subtle vanilla-meets-tropical-note flavor to it, and it always went fast.

I always say thank you when I compost.

Both the flower and the berry have excellent medical properties. Elderberry's uses include being an immune booster, an anti-inflammatory aid, and an antioxidant. To make a cordial, which is sweeter and has some alcohol, much like you might find in kombucha, a large amount of elderflowers—like dozens—is needed. If you are interested in the elderberry's goodness and can only access a few flower heads, treat yourself with seasonal elderflower-infused water. Right about the time sourcing elderflowers is possible, the citrus belt in North America is making sure we can have limes in our kitchens. This is a special drink and is something where the intention is the anchor. It must be made soon after picking the flower heads. Some farmer market vendors may carry them, and if you are keen to get this and don't have a bush accessible, you'll need to have a rapport with that vendor or find a Green Witch friend. Be careful of bees in the elderflower heads. I often find them still asleep inside the flowers.

Magically, the elder plant, including its flowers and berries, provides protection and healing. I've even seen some mentions in various Witch circles of the elderflowers' hex-breaking energies. For our purposes in this brew, it will be all about protection. Lime's magical properties revolve around purification in this working. Simple syrup is optional; it gets into cordial territory if added. However, if you need a little extra love, add it in. These instructions are more detailed because handling the elderflower is likely foreign to many of us. Take the time. You won't be disappointed.

When you're finished, consider composting the solids. I always say thank you when I do the discarding—another point of positive energy exchange.

Springtime Protection Infusion

EQUIPMENT

- 2 pitchers (1 for mixing, 1 for serving)
- Wooden spoon or bar spoon for stirring
- Fine mesh strainer
- Drinking vessel of choice (I recommend a chilled draft glass)

INGREDIENTS

- About 1–1½ cups elderflowers without stems (about 4 to 5 heads), fresh only
- 4 cups cold water (options: Pisces, Libra, or Scorpio)
- 2 limes, juiced
- 1 teaspoon lime zest
- Lime wheels for garnish (optional)
- Simple syrup to taste (optional)

SERVES
4

INSTRUCTIONS

1. Be sure that the elderflower heads are fresh. Make sure the tiny buds have opened, and use them the day they are picked. This is important because the flavor can go bitter instead of sweet and floral.

2. Do not wash the flower heads; look through them gently and carefully to not bruise them. Remove any unopened buds and anything that is not fresh. You do not want the taste to be spoiled. This is a central and intensive step.

3. Zest lime. Juice limes. Set aside.

4. Add elderflower heads and then the juice into a pitcher. Stir well. Add cold water. Stir well. Cover the mixture.

5. Hold hands over the covered pitcher and say:

    I am protected.
    I am protected.
    I am protected.

6. Visualize an image of physical and spiritual safety.

7. Refrigerate the pitcher for at least four hours or up to a day. Serve within about twenty-four to thirty-six hours (otherwise the flowers could turn bitter).

8. Strain the water through a mesh strainer into a second pitcher. Compost solids.

9. Add simple syrup and lime wheels, if desired.

10. Serve and enjoy.

Be aware of areas in life that need better boundaries or warding. After drinking this infusion, ideas and inspiration about where to focus protection energy may arrive.

Fruits of Summer

Using what is available locally is part of the magical mixology exploration as it's the most sustainable. Will we sometimes have exotic ingredients? Yes; coffee doesn't grow within 150 or even 350 miles of this Witch. I still use it. However, the Witch must fully understand the ingredients' energy when procuring items outside the local, political, geographic, or even hydrographic area. You will learn that working with energies close to where personal energy resides is more robust. Simply put, there is more energy for which to connect. Repeatedly, I've found that the closer to where you are in time and space, the stronger the energetic connection. You may find energetic connections work differently for a variety of factors. Understanding this variability doesn't deter intention or capability. Witchcraft sometimes requires unexpected extra work. Don't shy from it; lean in and learn.

We find these connection variables easily with food and drink. Raspberries, known to grow in the back yard or be readily available at the local farmers market, can differ greatly from grocery store raspberries that have traveled many miles to get there. Both will hold the correspondence of raspberries, but the energy level may feel different when the Witch connects. No matter where the Craft path takes the practitioner, those connections with our energies differ depending on many factors. The Witch's energy makes it equitable.

Don't shy away from extra work; lean in and learn!

Raspberries are featured a few times in this book and are prominent in the following working. The flavor of raspberry is likely beloved because it reminds folx of foraging in the early summer and plopping berries into their mouths in the sweet sunshine. The job of this working is to promote happiness magically. The drinker may be focused on at least that moment of happiness while sipping raspberry and mint-infused water. Simply add the Witch to make it even more magical.

The mint in this recipe helps bring some crispness and coolness to the juxtaposition of the berry's sweetness and tartness. This recipe calls for a bunch of mint. I've always asserted that the amount is equal to what I could grasp in my hand or to my preferred taste. Professionals like exact measurements. For mint, a bunch would be equal to about a quarter cup prepared. The correspondence of mint, for those with magical eyes, is all about abundance, specifically with money. This drink weaving leans toward more good fortune and taking it easy on a lazy summer day. However, it requires double-straining, an investment in time. View that investment and the energy the practitioner pours into it as laying the foundation for some time to recover from whatever summer is throwing at you. Enjoy the fruits of your labors and the labors of our lovely earth.

Fresh berries are preferred, but frozen works well, too. These berries' energetic properties are abundance, healing, and protection. All three correspondences play in the next infusion. Dried mint leaves do not impart the same flavor, so go clip that potted mint that's on the kitchen sill or grab a handful from a local grocer. Dried mint's energy is not right for this working.

Do note if doing this working while front-porch sitting or out on the balcony in the line of sight of others, they may comment about you seemingly praying to the glass. Smile and say, "Your drinks don't talk to you? Oh, too bad for you." Keep sipping. Consider it a bonus: an instant boundary spell.

SUMMER REFRESHER &
R E S T E L I X I R

EQUIPMENT

2 pitchers (1 for mixing, 1 for serving)

Mesh strainer

Wooden spoon

Water glasses or chilled draft glasses

SERVES
2

INGREDIENTS

2 pints fresh or frozen raspberries

1 bunch fresh mint

4 cups water, chilled (options: Taurus or Sagittarius)

INSTRUCTIONS

1. Put the raspberries and mint into one of the pitchers. Gently mix them to combine. Some of the raspberries may break up; this is fine. Go with the flow here. It is all part of the process for this infusion.

2. Pour cold moon water over it. Get ready to stir sunwise and chant over the pitcher, following the intention's instructions:

   Circle once, then circle twice.
   Refresh, restore, and then once more;
   Circle last for rest to the Witch's best.

3. Tap the wooden spoon three times on the pitcher's side and say, "So be it."

4. Refrigerate the pitcher for at least two but no more than six hours.

5. Remove the pitcher from the refrigerator and strain the solids from the water. Repeat two times. Each time it has strained, visualize a scene that inspires feelings of refreshment, relaxation, and rest. Include a scene of conquering the next challenge on a busy summer day. Remember, this is an investment in yourself. Compost solids.

6. Pour into a chilled draft or water glass. While pouring, revisit step 5's conjured scene, then close your eyes and feel the energy inside the glass. Connect. For the first sip, visualize that scene again.

7. Finish the refresher in one sitting. Take moments to be in between sips. If you are called to do so, do breathwork. Sit and drink.

8. When finished, clean the glass and gear. Snap three times and then say, "So it is."

You may experience a spike in energy after this working. There is no need to go full throttle again. Ease back into the day's responsibilities and flirt with the corners of the mouth turning up. Know you've got this.

Fruit and Herb for In-Between

There is much to love about watermelon, the fruit that lets us eat fluids with sweet succulence, as it is more than 90 percent water. This next drink gives watermelon hydration and energy without the work required from an agua fresca.

This witchy work is good for when the Halloween decorations are coming into the markets but work has been slow or you've been burned by the sun or someone. Whatever chafe Witches deal with before the autumn relief, this watermelon-basil combo helps us move through that liminal period. Watermelon is healing not only because of its physical properties but also its magical energies. It represents humanity's need to be free and eradicate oppression. Basil is love.

Healing and love let us move through weird, odd, or otherwise off-kilter spaces. It's not quite summer, but it's not fall, either. Whatever liminal space Witches find themselves in, choose this drink. When we accept ourselves into the liminal—whatever it is—we connect to intuition, guides, and ancestors more easily. If there is trouble connecting, I recommend turning to watermelon-basil and a small amount of movement.

Before making the following drink, shake the body. Yep, shake all the restlessness, anxiety, and dread for the present away. Put on music and dance if you prefer. Dance party in the kitchen! But start from head and move through to shoulders, then hips, and Charleston your way through the knees and ankles if necessary, then let the whole body shake and wiggle and move. Let that inner child out. Do this for at least three minutes—about the length of one song.

Seasonal Shift Watermelon Refresher

EQUIPMENT

2 pitchers (1 for mixing, 1 for serving)

Wooden spoon

Large fine mesh strainer

Water glass or chilled draft glass

Small ritual bell

Skewer for garnish (optional)

Music (optional)

SERVES
2

INGREDIENTS

2 cups watermelon chunks, with a few extra small cubes
for garnish, if desired

1 bunch fresh basil, plus some reserved for garnish, if desired

4 cups cold water (options: Scorpio or Gemini)

INSTRUCTIONS

1. Put two cups watermelon and a bunch of basil in the pitcher,
   then pour the moon water over them and stir with the wooden
   spoon thirteen times. Watch the fruit and herbs spin and
   circle in the water while stirring. Allow it to become almost
   meditative. Refrigerate the pitcher for at least four or up to
   twelve hours.

2. Pour over the strainer from one pitcher to another. Compost
   the solids. Wrap a basil leaf around a reserved watermelon
   cube, skewer it, and then cut a sliver into the skewer to reside
   on the glass. Make sure the chunk is manageable (think small
   bite).

3. Drink with the toast:

   *May I truly appreciate and understand the life between
   the day and night and night and day, between winter
   and summer and dry and rain. Give me courage and grace
   to face this [insert your space/time/trouble here]
   with a generous spirit and unshaken love.*

4. Clean the glass and gear. Ring the bell and say, "So mote it be!"

Shielding Relationships

Relationships can be complex and complicated. We must conscientiously maintain them. Sometimes the cabin fever of winter creates a little friction. Living the life of a Witch may often mean that we are working on being the best versions of ourselves. Conflict can arise during that growth and progress—or, as some in our community call it, operating at a higher frequency or vibe. One drink is not a balm for all relationship troubles. However, the situation may require, at minimum, a heart-to-heart. The next working helps when seeking a truce, a compromise, or even a reconciliation.

If you've ever visited a cranberry farm, you may have sensed its protected and idyllic energies. They do the same thing inside the following drink. Magically, cranberries correspond to protection, like a little Mars warrior in a glass to energetically shield. Feeling psychologically protected when we feel vulnerable in the face of conflict is necessary for everyone to express feelings, ideas, and needs safely.

Rosemary is often an herb we might lean on heavily in the Craft, understandably so since it's such a powerhouse for magical workings. Holding the energies of protection, healing, love, and that whole "vibe higher," it's no wonder it's a staple in any Witch's tool kit. Notably, this is why so many Witches grow rosemary.

In this infusion, we use the power of winter via ice. Also, because cranberries are tougher than raspberries or watermelon, the ice helps extract good protection energy from the cranberries. Working this spell toward a winter's truce, little bits of icy goodness form around the cranberries, symbolizing how prickliness can lead to goodness.

Plan to make ice cubes from some solar water ahead of time. Solar water is used instead of moon water here because it is winter. Most of us could use some extra sunshine in winter, especially in northern climes. Complement the energies or balance them however you prefer. Add a little Taurus and Scorpio energy to this work as ice cubes, then complement it with Libra or Aries moon water for the water part of the recipe. Need air energy to cut through nonsense or fire energy to bolster passionate expressions? Embrace the choice.

The "spell" part of this working is the toast you create. A toast, for all intents and purposes, is a spell, so go into this working with that in mind.

One word of note: one of the pitchers must have a lid of some sort. I dig the old-school Tupperware mixing pitcher that seals liquid tight, but using a mason jar with a leakproof lid works, too. No lidded pitcher? Use a wooden spoon to mix things vigorously. However, shaking things for this drink is part of the magic. It's like aerating and loosening soil so plants can grow better. Set the stage for a productive conversation or a reconnection session with someone important. Shake it up, then watch things get rooted deeper.

A toast, for all intents and purposes, is a spell.

HOARFROST CRANBERRY
INFUSION

EQUIPMENT

2 pitchers (1 for mixing that has a lid, 1 for serving)

Wooden spoon

Large fine mesh strainer

Water glass or chilled draft glass

SERVES
4

INGREDIENTS

2 cups fresh cranberries

1 bunch fresh rosemary sprigs

2½ cups ice (options: Scorpio, Taurus, solar)

1½ cups nonchlorinated water (options: Libra, Aries, moon)

INSTRUCTIONS

1. Put cranberries in mixing pitcher; cover with half of the ice. Secure lid and shake cranberries and ice vigorously. Envision the soil of the relationship being made ready for new growth.

2. Add the rosemary to the pitcher and then add the other half of the ice to cover the rosemary completely. Secure the lid and repeat the vigorous shaking as before.

3. Pour water over the ice, cranberries, and rosemary. Ensure there is enough space in the pitcher to shake vigorously again. Don't forget the visualization here. See yourself working joyfully within relationships.

4. Refrigerate for at least a day. Check after a few hours, when the ice has melted, to ensure enough water covers the infusion elements. Add additional water if necessary.

5. The next day, strain from mixing pitcher into serving pitcher.

6. Because the remains of what is strained can be a headache to clean if you leave it for later, take the time now before serving to clean your equipment. Add a sprig of rosemary when serving, if desired. Toast to deepening the roots of relationships and fostering an environment where it is safe to come together to problem solve, apologize, and generally get the winter out of said relationships. End the toast with, "All this or better. So it is!"

Winter Blessings in a Cup

As a constant gardener, the deep winter is about rest and planning. If we allow nature to mirror us, we can learn about ourselves. This is why many Witches see this season as a time of introspection, as we humans mimic what nature is doing—resting and saving resources to burst into new growth come spring. Through this stage some anxiousness for spring can begin; be mindful that it is okay to slow down and have a think—or, as a friend says, "Put that in a tumbler and see if it shines." This infused water lets us tumble through winter and hopefully come out on the other side polished and ready for spring.

The ingredients in this infusion are all about comfort and support. It's like a big ol' hug from a warm blanket beside the fire. The good thing about warm water is that this infusion is drinkable sooner. Regardless of temperature, pouring this into a favorite mug to wrap both hands around and have a little daydream session is one of the best winter activities.

The orange brings love into the infusion, the foundation for all peace. Meanwhile, including ginger brings abundant patience and notes a pattern of comfort and ease, much like the blanket above. The cinnamon not only tastes scrummy and balances the acid of the orange and the ginger's heat, but it also intensifies our intuition and brings wealth (not only money, honey). A garden that produces nourishment is wealth. That means the physical garden or the metaphorical one.

In the winter, it can be challenging to find fresh ginger. If that is the case, substitute candied ginger, which increases the amount in the working to one tablespoon. Those possessing a healthy sweet tooth may prefer this to fresh. Regardless of fresh ginger or candied, this infusion is nice with molasses cookies, apple cake, or other winter treats.

Gin-Cin Comfort Tisane

SERVES
2

EQUIPMENT

- Kettle or another way to heat water
- A favorite witchy mug
- Large (4 cups or better) heatproof pourable measuring cup with spout
- Dish towel
- Zester
- Bar strainer
- Teapot or carafe

INGREDIENTS

- 2 cups moon water (options: Capricorn, Pisces, or Cancer)
- 1 whole orange
- ½ tablespoon chopped ginger or 1 tablespoon candied ginger
- 1 cinnamon stick

INSTRUCTIONS

1. Bring water to 170°F (77°C), which is the lowest warmth for most steeping, and add to measuring cup. Gather the rest of ingredients.

2. Zest the orange into the water. Peel off the pith, cutting it off if necessary. Put the orange sections into the water on top of the zest. Gently stir. As you do, think about what love means to you. See it in action in life. Giving. Receiving. The people. The places. Where is love in your life? Again, visualize it in action.

3. Add the ginger. Gently stir again. Over the stirring liquid, say:

> *I am ready to accept comfort*
> *and support into my life.*

4. Next, break the cinnamon stick into two. It might take a bit of doing, but this is also an exercise in knowing personal strength, not primarily physically but mentally and emotionally. If you tell yourself to snap it in two, you will. Trust, Witch.

5. Add the broken cinnamon stick to the water and gently stir. Say:

> *I clearly hear, feel, and understand my intuition*
> *and the communications the universe provides.*

6. Let it steep for eight minutes. Dedicate this time simply to be. Feeling energetic? Meditate. Consider preparing a fire and a favorite blanket for sitting and sipping.

7. Strain the infusion into a teapot or heat-tolerant pitcher. Serve in a favorite mug next to a winter-hearty baked good. Watch the ease and comfort roll on in.

Trust, Witch.

Whenever there is fruit juice, my mind often goes right to seeing if I can make cider. When it comes to vegetables, I want to make all the juices! Vegetables such as leafy greens, carrots, and even beets create juices I adore for their health benefits and general nutrition. As the seasons change and shift, what ends up in juice differs, amazingly bringing the right amount of needed nutrients exactly when we need it.

After living off potatoes, onions, cabbage, and squash all winter, when the first kale, mustard, arugula, and spinach pop their heads up in late winter or early spring, we are ready for them in all our meals. By the time summer arrives, cucumbers, carrots, and celery are ready to be harvested. The body is ready for the beta-carotene and minerals these veggies bring to juice, especially helping protect the skin from the summer sun's rays.

JUICING
THE
magic

Creating juices as part of a Witchcraft practice has a magical simplicity. Find the magical properties—also known as correspondences—of favorite veggies, herbs, and fruits; whirl them in the same mixture; and drink up. Our ancestors are probably looking at us with our modern blenders and thinking we are potionmaking demigods. Pick a focus in life where you're seeking improvement. For example, health—grab some celery (health), cucumber (healing), grapefruit (purification, and it holds the growth the sun gives), and some watermelon (healing and sweetwater element). Together, these not only provide incredible magical correspondences, but they give good hydration and taste remarkable. It is hard to beat the convenience of all the juicing concoctions and subscription box services of the latest health juices where you just add water. However, truly knowing what is in the glass and adding your witchy intention and positive energies is where you'll find more magic. I recognize not everyone is on a path like mine, growing the food our kindred and community eat. However, any Witch can get the freshest ingredients. The local farmers market and even the produce section of the local grocery market hold the magic to becoming a juicing queen.

This is not promoting a diet of strictly juice. That falls outside the "everything in moderation" theme of sippable spellcraft. However, a day of detoxing with juice now and again can be a healthy reset. Please do so after consultation with healthcare professionals. I've been known to spend a weekend drinking nothing but liquid nutrition, and a juicing repertoire is certainly helpful then. It is likely (but not necessarily) under a Leo full moon, and there is much intention around it. The best time certainly depends on personal energy. Again, this is a situation where the wise Witch practices everything in moderation.

Later in this book, we will consider creating dehydrated green juice on-the-go packets. No subscription service is required. However, there is some equipment to discuss for the go packets and all the juices.

Fresh vs. Ready-Made, Juicer vs. Blender

With juicing many recipes are completed quickly, whether with fresh-squeezed elements or ready-made ingredients. It is the Witch's choice to use fresh, frozen, or canned; the magical energies are the same, regardless of whether the choice is one cup pineapple chunks or six ounces pineapple juice from a can. However, using whole ingredients whenever possible is encouraged. It is a more encompassing energy. Please also recognize that creating juices becomes much more important and exciting with the current added interest in mocktails. Get the blenders ready, and make some juicy, witchy magic.

In the following workings, I denote the ingredients needed for both a juicer and a blender, with the latter coming first. Juicing machines can be budget breaking and a pain to clean. There is less prep with juicers (depending on the brand), but their cons can stop magic in its tracks. Nevertheless, it does not have to block you. Truly, do not let it stop you. Especially in summer, when greens, veggies, and fruits are overflowing and it feels too hot to eat, a nice juice blend can give you what you need right when your body needs it.

And now a quick note about blenders from my inner treasure-hunting queen who wants to tell you not to spend a ton. Scouring online shopping sites or hitting a local thrift shop or even a weekend garage sale could net you a high-end blender for a fraction of what you would pay for a brand-new one. Look for ones with an all-metal drive; from my experience, those made with plastic never hold up.

Sun in a Mug

There is something extraordinary about watching a sunrise. The entire planet feels fresh, hopeful, and peaceful. Meditating as the sun rises and rewarding yourself with this next beverage is a treat. Along with sunrise watching, this drink helps wake up a Witch's intuition, connect with Mama Earth, and gives the body so much goodness. This was inspired by the need to fall in love with life again. If that is you, starting the day at dawn with this drink will bring into focus all there is to love in life.

As noted before, oranges bring love, but they also bring cleansing. Peppers amp up desire. Lastly, there is love, especially self-love from the strawberries and carrots, which help us connect and remove negativity. Feel free to adapt this recipe to your taste preferences. Note in this working you'll want the strainer to nest neatly into the large measuring cup or bowl.

It makes an excellent replacement for the morning hydration ritual (Witch-ade), especially on those yummy slow-start Sundays. Make it the night before for a more leisurely morning. Shake before serving. Perhaps set the intention to simply have a great day. When having a long weekend with a beloved, this is a great recipe to find the way back into bed—wink, wink.

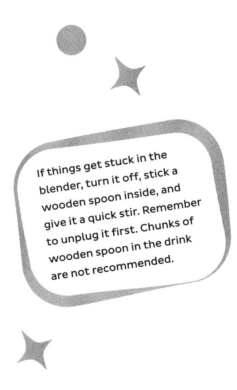

If things get stuck in the blender, turn it off, stick a wooden spoon inside, and give it a quick stir. Remember to unplug it first. Chunks of wooden spoon in the drink are not recommended.

HELLO SUNRISE
J U I C E

SERVES
1

EQUIPMENT

Blender or juicer

Spatula

Large fine mesh strainer

Large pourable measuring cup or bowl with spout

Conical strainer

Rocks glass

INGREDIENTS

1 orange, juiced (blender) or peeled, divided into smaller sections (juicer)

12 medium strawberries, hulled, sliced in half

1 to 2 orange, yellow, or red bell peppers, halved, seeds removed

3 ounces ready-made carrot juice (blender) or 3 medium carrots, trimmed of tops and cut into thirds (juicer)

INSTRUCTIONS

1. Chop the ingredients well. This helps the blender mix the ingredients quickly. The larger the chop, the longer it is until it is ready. Put the orange (juice) and strawberries on the bottom. They are juicier and help the blender do its job more efficiently. Then add the peppers and carrots. Repeat the following until all the ingredients are in the blender: "Without, within, in joy we rise; hello sunshine, this day's a prize."

2. Blend, beginning with a low speed that is slow and steady. Increase speed slowly after fruit moves to a more liquid and creamier state.

3. If things get stuck, turn the blender off. Unplug it. Stick a wooden spoon inside and give it a quick stir.

4. Set the mesh strainer over a sizeable measuring cup or bowl. Pour the juice from the blender into the strainer and press it with a spatula to extract additional juice. Allow it to strain naturally at first, then occasionally with help from the spoon.

5. Compost pulp and rinse the tools.

6. Take a conical strainer and run the juice through a second time, pouring the juice into a rocks glass. Drink under the rising sun and have a perfect day.

Hold the Caffeine

Many people love their coffee in the morning. Sometimes coffee can give many of us a mid-afternoon slump in energy. Also, a cup of coffee at 2 p.m. can be a recipe for a sleepless night. Enter this juice. However, this is not only a tipple for the mid-afternoon slump. It can help with a mid-project slump or may be good company while reading an engaging book.

Within this juice is lettuce, which holds the energy of peace necessary to focus and remember goals. Only a handful of lettuce leaves are needed, around five good-sized leaves. It represents the power of the stars and the symbolism of the pentagram.

This juice also includes parsley, which holds the energy of protection. Protecting the peace to remain motivated is essential to the success of this working. Also, kale brings abundance, and the abundance we want here is the healing away from the malaise of the mushy middle. The cucumber provides the healing to help us refresh our physical and mental energy to continue our tasks.

The pineapple adds sweetness to this juicy working and lights a little energetic fire under us, as it is ruled by the sun. Alongside the cucumber, it is healing and protects our physical and mental energy. The harmony that the pineapple and pear bring, zapped with the acidic juice of a lemon, holds the correspondence of happiness. Do not skimp on the pear, ruled by Venus and one of the longest-fruiting trees in the world. Some can bear fruit for eons. Pears may be the fountain of youth right in our backyards. This potion brings stamina, so following the rest period where we consume this juice, we can return to our tasks with extra energy.

Mid-Anything Pick-Me-Up Juice

EQUIPMENT

- Blender or juicer
- Spatula
- Fine mesh strainer
- Large pourable measuring cup or bowl with a spout
- Conical strainer
- Collins glass

SERVES 1

INGREDIENTS

- 6 ounces pineapple juice (blender) or 1 cup pineapple, chopped (juicer)
- 1 pear (the riper the better), cored, sliced
- Juice of 1 lemon (blender) or 1 lemon, peeled (juicer)
- 1 bunch (at least 5 good-sized leaves) romaine lettuce, chopped
- 1 bunch parsley, chopped
- 2 to 3 kale leaves, chopped
- 1 small cucumber, chopped

INSTRUCTIONS

1. Chop ingredients well. Put the pineapple, pear, and lemon on the bottom. They are juicier and help the blender do its job more efficiently. Then add the lettuce, parsley, kale, and cucumber. Add a personalized intention/spell or feel free to use the one below. Repeat until all ingredients are in the blender.

I want to rest and rest assured

The time is now for work and earn.

Give me strength; energy returned

Boost this fuel to give motivation stern.

This or better; so it is.

2. Blend using a low pulse at first and then slowly increasing speed. After the chunks of fruits and veggies begin to break down, slowly increase the speed.

3. If things get stuck, turn the blender off; stick a wooden spoon inside and give it a quick stir. Do not do this if the blender remains plugged in. Chunks of wooden spoon in the Pick-Me-Up Juice are not recommended.

4. Set the strainer over the large measuring cup or bowl. Pour the juice from the blender into the strainer and press it with a spatula to extract it. Nice and easy, put renewal intentions into the straining of the juice. This may take a few minutes; continue with intention while focusing on breath.

5. Dispose of the pulp and rinse the strainer.

6. Strain a second time using your conical strainer into a collins glass. Like your fine mesh strainer, you'll want to rinse it right away for ease of cleanup.

7. Consider having this juice on a break, under a tree, or somewhere else outside, in nature. If the weather is less than stellar, minimally aim to see some plants and the sky.

Take a rest while drinking this. Expect the energy increase.

When Things Are Rocky

Despite the many joys of our world, it is not without its negativity. When kindred or community members are not okay, hand them a glass of this juice. It is in these times when the restrictions, oppressions, and utter seemingly physical assault the world is whipping up can have us so anxious and muddled in our thinking that we end up feeling like a gerbil on the wheel. When walking into a room and forgetting why, recognize the need for Chill Witch Juice. The time it takes to create this is short, and unlike some of the other juices, the straining is super quick. This is a great tool to whip out of the coping box when we need to practice some de-stress tolerance.

Candied ginger is in this recipe. Its magical correspondence here is for grace and abundance. It helps balance out the tart from the cherries but is also a root that promotes calm. It is rich in antioxidants and anti-inflammatory compounds. It is an excellent digestive health spice and one you'll find stuck between tooth and gum of many sailors to mitigate motion sickness. It also activates cognitive functions and memory, alleviating confusion. Add powdered or minced fresh ginger, decreasing the measurement by half, for a less sugary version.

Blood oranges are an extraordinary variety of citrus. If unavailable, use any variety of orange. Blood oranges blend and highlight the cherry without making it too tart to drink. All citrus corresponds to strength, so use what is available, but lean toward something sweeter or accept involuntary duck lips when sipping this juice. Consider bottled blood orange juice to replace the freshly squeezed option.

Make sure the strainer nests well inside the large cup or bowl. If fresh cherries are unavailable, check the frozen section. All the pulp leftover from this process is exceptional for the compost. Rocking in a rocker while sipping this adds to this spell's soothing nature.

Another tremendous consequence of this drink is that the juice is super hydrating, and often when we are frazzled and anxious, there is a chance we are dehydrated or tired. Again, this is the perfect time for this juice.

CHILL WITCH
J U I C E

SERVES
1

EQUIPMENT

- Blender or juicer
- Spatula
- Large fine mesh strainer
- Large pourable measuring cup or bowl with spout
- Bar strainer
- Collins glass

INGREDIENTS

- 1½ cups watermelon chunks
- 1 cup pitted tart cherries
- 2 tablespoons candied ginger, diced
- 1 cup fresh red kale
- 1 cup red lettuce
- 2 blood oranges, juiced (blender) or peeled (juicer)

INSTRUCTIONS

1. Gather the ingredients. Take a moment to bless them and intend to seek proper rest or, at minimum, momentary relief from the pressures and stress of modern life. Speak the intention aloud three times. Example: "I am strong and capable and at peace with myself" or "I am grateful for all that I have" or "I am safe. I am taking a deep breath."

2. Chop ingredients well. This helps the blender get to the juicier stuff. Put the watermelon into the blender first. Layer the cherries next, followed by the ginger. Add the kale and lettuce. Lastly, pour the blood orange juice on top (blender) or the peeled oranges last (juicer).

3. Blend or juice until solids turn liquid.

4. Set the mesh strainer over the large measuring cup or bowl. Pour the juice from the blender into the strainer and press it with a spatula to extract the juice. The activity of pressing the pulp to extract even more juice can be very therapeutic at this

moment. Focus on the task and let the rest of the world fade away while working on this juice.

5. Dispose of the pulp and rinse the tools. Do not let this sit to get crusty in the sink. Clean as you go when making juice. Again, let the mindlessness of rinsing the strainer be the focus.

6. Take a bar strainer and run the juice through a second time, pouring the juice into a collins glass. Rinse the bar strainer right away.

7. This juice was made for sitting on the front porch. If necessary, set a timer for when you need to return to work afterward. Center your attention on sipping, rocking, or quietly sitting. Do not be surprised if the solution to that problem descends.

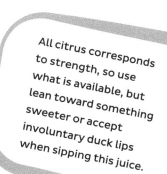

All citrus corresponds to strength, so use what is available, but lean toward something sweeter or accept involuntary duck lips when sipping this juice.

Taming a Tumultuous Tummy

There is a point after an episode of flu or food poisoning where the stomach is tender yet hungry. Working slowly to nourish and aid healing is essential here. The following drink helps settle that queasiness. Again, take it slow.

Unlike some of the other workings in this book, this one uses store-bought. And if you're feeling really sick, hopefully they are on hand or they can be delivered by a friend or a commercial service. Regardless, it is designed to be easy on the body's systems, especially the stomach. That tummy will start feeling better before anyone says Green Around the Witch.

The ingredients seem odd, but the taste is reminiscent of a cherry cola. With its antioxidant properties, the red grape helps soothe the throat, which is essential when feeling queasy. Magically, its energetic properties are about creating fertile ground for healing. Moreover, the kola syrup—make sure you get the stuff from the kola nut and not high fructose corn syrup and sugar—is well known for calming a gurgling stomach. Yes, yes, the science types will say that is malarkey. However, West African herbalists have been using the kola nut to keep a healthy digestive system for eons. Witches know better. Available at most beverage and grocery stores or in the holistic area at the local pharmacy.

Lemon is optional, but it helps bring about purification as its correspondence—to help rid the body of the nastiness making it ill. Also, the scent is often known to help make people feel less stressed. The lemon wheel is also some additional aromatherapy, so do not be shy about adding it.

The red grape juice in this is ready-made. Juicing grapes to get enough at home is a bit over the top, but the benefits of red grapes are excellent when feeling poorly.

Green Around the Witch Juice

EQUIPMENT

- The mug in your cupboard that cheers you up
- Measuring cups and spoons
- Knife and cutting board
- Spoon for stirring

SERVES
1

INGREDIENTS

- 2 teaspoons kola syrup
- 1 teaspoon ground cardamom
- 4 to 6 ounces red grape juice
- Lemon-flavored sparkling water (optional)
- ½ lemon, sliced into wheels for garnish (optional)

INSTRUCTIONS

1. Pour the kola syrup and cardamom into a mug. Mix it well until the spice begins to dissolve. Look into the cup and visualize feeling better.

2. Add the juice and stir until the cardamom dissolves. Say over a favorite cheery mug: "By nut and seed and fruit of vine, health shall be mine!" Repeat three times, then close with the traditional "So It is."

3. Top the beverage with sparkling water to taste and a lemon wheel if desired.

4. Sip slowly, returning to the visualization of health, the mantra, or both within the mind with each drink. Be well, Witch.

Magic on the Go

Many health companies are making green juices to go. However, these ready-made green juice mixes have some unappetizing chemicals in them, like thallium (a metal), goitrogen (a disrupter of our thyroid hormones), and oxalate content, which are known to cause kidney stones, the latter of which is unsurprising because our bodies already naturally produce oxalates as a waste product. Not only that, but many of them contain, on average, 33 grams of sugar, and often more than that. Too much of a good thing feels like baneful energy. No, thank you. Aim for receiving the nutrition and not the pollutants.

This Go-Go Green Juice to Go has the convenience of those portable liquid meals without harmful chemicals. The fun part is that personal choice decides what the green is. Keep drying veggies throughout the summer growing season and add to the next Go-Go Green Juice to Go batch.

This is some very slow magic. It may take a whole growing season to create enough to have a half-dozen green juices. It is considerably slow magic, including the time it takes to grow the vegetables. However, as slow as it can be, these veggies hold some personal energy when home-grown. Nevertheless, it is simple to speed up the process. Grab kale and other vegetables from the farmers market or the local grocery store.

Dehydrating still takes an investment of time. That also means there is much time to continue putting personal energy and intentions into the drink powder. There is some special equipment involved that makes creating this so much easier, specifically a food dehydrator. They sell dehydrators often in places that sell food preservation supplies. The plain low-heat ones without temperature control or other bells and whistles are affordable; no professional level is needed. Using the oven works, too, provided it can go down to 140°F (60°C). Some modern ones do not register below 170°F (77°C). Alternatively, use a combination of oven and dehydrator if making a large batch.

Air drying is possible, yet it takes a reasonable amount of time and can be fiddly. Screened shelves are a must to allow air circulation or hang the ingredients for drying. Few people I know have the kind of room for drying the amount you need for creating this dried juice mix. Many veggies are used to make this powder, so a dehydrator is the way to go if space is an issue.

When storing this powder, include a small packet of food-safe desiccant to keep the powder dry and free from spoilage. These packets are found where retailers carry food preservation supplies—if canning jars are on the shelves, desiccant packs will likely be nearby.

This juice powder is a clear self-care heightener that brings deep-rooted magic into the physical body. Greens are all about abundance. Lime purifies. Coriander corresponds magically to love, especially self-love. The apple juice mixed with it is all about health and making it sweet. The working focuses on bringing the earth's energy into the body. It is potent, giving the drinker a healthy glow. Do not let the ingredients intimidate or frighten you. This is positive and accessible magic.

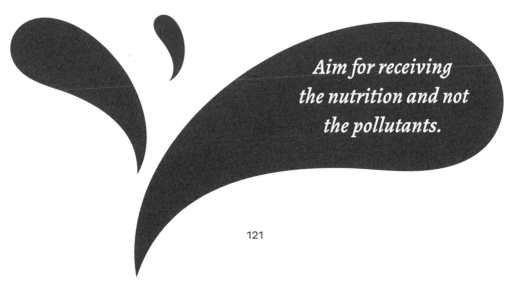

Aim for receiving the nutrition and not the pollutants.

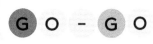

GO-GO

GREEN JUICE TO GO

EQUIPMENT

Cutting board and knife

Extra-large bowl

Hand juicer

Salad spinner or a couple of folded dish towels

Electric dehydrator or low-temp oven

Baking sheets if using oven method

Food processor or spice grinder

Sterilized quart-size or larger storage jar and dessicant packet

Blender or shaker bottle

INGREDIENTS

1 bunch kale

½ bunch arugula

1 bunch spinach

1 lime, juiced (about ¼ cup)

1 small to medium-sized zucchini, sliced into wheels, patted dry

1 tablespoon coriander powder

6 ounces apple juice per serving

INSTRUCTIONS

1. Wash all the greens (kale, arugula, spinach) and remove anything that is not fresh. Sing or play music that aligns with the intention of this green juice batch.

2. Put the greens into an extra-large bowl and sprinkle with the fresh-squeezed lime juice. Mix the greens well in the juice. Set aside.

3. Be sure that zucchini is patted dry before putting it in the dehydrator on the lowest level.

4. Use the salad spinner or put greens between two dish towels to ensure they are not actively holding liquid (water or lime juice). Use the remaining trays to fill with the lime-juiced greens. Be sure that the greens are not overlapping so air

can circulate. Add the trays of greens on top of the trays of zucchini. Set the dehydrator to 140 degrees for eight hours.

5. More than one round in the dehydrator may be necessary if the vegetables are not dried enough after the first eight hours. Start next with a four-hour round of dehydrating.

6. Once vegetables are dry, put them into a food processor and pulse until finely powdered. Multiple batches are possible, depending on how large the processor is. Alternatively, use a spice grinder. However, a food processor has more capacity.

7. Pulsing, say: "Once for happiness, another for health, and every other one abundance and wealth." This is an all-purpose intention/spell for the to-go juice. Feel free to create a personal spell. Watching the dried veggies whirl in the food processor can be very meditative. Be ready to receive divine downloads or messages from ancestors.

8. Store the powder in a sterilized mason jar with a desiccant packet.

9. To make the juice: Depending on taste, take 1 to 2 tablespoons of the powder and add 6 ounces apple juice inside a blender (or shaker bottle). Blend to mix well. As the blender incorporates the greens, sing again.

10. Pour from the blender into a drinking vessel. Drink to health.

Alternatively, substitute apple juice for water. Options for this are the Witch's choice between moon or solar water and any zodiac sign.

BUT FIRST,
COFFEE

Coffee is present in about every culture worldwide. The Swedes have *fika*, where coffee (along with pastries) is enjoyed with friends and family and viewed as a relaxing activity. Turkey is well known for their robust and unfiltered coffee, served in small cups and heavily sugared. Go anywhere in Turkey and they will likely offer coffee; please accept. Italy has its espresso, enjoyed as a mid-workday pick-me-up or dessert. More famously, the coffee ceremonies in Ethiopia start with roasting the beans over an open fire; the grinding happens in specially made clay pots. The cups are small and held without handles. Such formality or extravagance is unnecessary for our magical mixology purposes, but we will be mindful. We will fully understand this ingredient and continue the energetic connection you proved with water and juices.

Some studies suggest that coffee reduces the risk of type-2 diabetes, Parkinson's, liver disease, and some types of cancer. Given that all of those maladies exist in many of our ancestors, it certainly seems worth any risk of potential adverse effects from drinking coffee. However, some people find it increases their anxiety and causes sleeplessness. I have a friend whose blood pressure situation cannot abide coffee. Drinking coffee when taking iron supplements can block some of its absorption. Plus, its most well-known component, caffeine, does not always play well in the sandbox of prescription medications. That may preclude using coffee for everyday magic. Do not worry if this is a concern; there are alternatives to explore. Trying it once is encouraged, and doing so as a magical practice may serve up goodness.

If you are new to coffee, try different ways of drinking it to find the path to working with its magic, even once a week. While exploring, understand that Mars rules coffee and holds the energy of the fire element. Its energies are for mindfulness, awareness, and understanding. We will be playing off that throughout this chapter in various coffee drinks, including some that are not coffee, a nice choice for those who find *Coffea arabica* untenable.

Drip, Drop, or Press

The first time I drank coffee was with my father. He was adamant that coffee was best black. No sugar and cream allowed. Coffee with cream or sugar was polluted in his eyes. How to drink it was ritualized, too. He also insisted that coffee must be drunk before it reached room temperature. Further, Pops demonstrated that coffee must be smelled before drinking. His ritual, one many coffee drinkers share, incorporated the scent of it. Practicing this brings an understanding of the aromas different coffee blends give. Soon you will ascertain the notes that coffee aficionados spout, like fruity, chocolatey, or earthy. You will also learn to discern the components of coffee's flavor: body, acidity level, and aftertaste. "Coffee, like life," my Pops used to say, "can be full, tangy, and surprising." He wasn't wrong. Come find how it is for you.

THE BASIC DRIP

Let us ensure we get the basics down for traditional drip coffee first before finding alternatives. Coffee has many varieties and ways to grow and harvest. We focus on the basics as they apply to magic and practice the Craft. This is simple drip coffee. The most accessible way to make drip coffee is with an electric coffee maker. Almost any coffee maker on the market will do the job. It is a bonus to have a combination machine that includes a grinder. Grinding fresh beans expands the energy of any coffee experience. It brings back the "energy in and energy out" principle. Here are a few tips that will set the Witch up for coffee success.

Make sure the coffee maker is clean, physically and energetically. Clean it regularly.

Use fresh, cool water. Please do not pour hot water from the tap in the drip machine.

Use filtered water if possible. Non-chlorinated is good, too. If using a municipal water supply that uses chlorine for water purification, fill a pitcher with water and let it sit for twenty-four hours. After that day, most of the chlorine will have evaporated. Boil the water and let it return to room temperature, then refrigerate it before putting it in the coffee maker. Remember, coffee is an excellent use for moon or solar water. Feeling too heady? Get some Taurus solar water in the coffee maker. Feeling uninspired? Gemini moon water will have all the ideas flowing. As with other drinks, adding evaporated tap water, solar water, or moon water helps heighten the energy.

Look for sustainable filter choices. Although unbleached paper filters are accessible and more earth-friendly than bleached paper filters, a reusable metal filter basket is cost-saving and makes a cleaner brew. Paper filters may impart some paper flavor into the coffee during filtration.

Get to know the electric coffee maker. Newer ones allow for the change of strength to light, medium, or strong. That owner's manual is a friend. If purchased secondhand, it may be possible to find the owner's manual online.

Please note that the spellcraft in this book with coffee relies heavily on an electric coffee machine. Make adjustments within the instructions for the preferred method of brewing coffee.

BEAN CHOICE

The quality of the coffee bean is important. The Witch will want mindfulness to rule the working here, too. That doesn't mean you need to be as particular as Ludwig van Beethoven was. He started his brew each day by counting out sixty beans and then used a "glass contraption of his own design" (Stilwell 2021). Fortunately, we can still be particular without being peculiar (unless that's your thing—then by all means count the beans). Regardless, there are some easy guidelines to ensure a good-quality bean.

The roast on the coffee beans looks uniform in color, shape, and size. Look for glossy beans that smell delicious when the aroma hits the air.

Support fair trade and small growers (and roasters) with bean purchases whenever possible. Fair trade coffee means putting our planet and the people who tend to it first.

Pick out small sample sizes while exploring the different methods of roasting as well as all the distinct varieties. Have them ground unless grinding them at home. Many roasters will sell the whole beans and happily grind them immediately before purchase. Brewing the coffee right after the beans are ground is so delicious that it may be hard to stop doing it that way. I find that the energy connection happens more efficiently and substantially this way.

If brewing drip coffee, the beans are ground to medium coarse.

There are many good quality beans available. Perhaps the grocery store brand is okay for workdays, but use a higher-quality one for Sunday brunch and pull out the hand grinder and French press.

COFFEE MAGIC

Now everything is ready to go: the water, the coffee maker, and the beans ground to medium coarse. It is time to get to brewing magic. The three things to consider are the quality of ingredients—the beans and water—and the coffee's preparation, which makes coffee even more deeply magical. It begins with making a solid connection with the water and beans. Coffee is always a way to travel to a distant place, feel its energy, and give a little loving energy back. The first time I connected with the energy of coffee, my senses transported me to a fertile-smelling earthscape where unfamiliar birds sang. Mountains were all around me. It was a brilliant psychic flash, but so clear and telling. Each sip can give you the energies of that temperate mountaintop on which it was grown as well as the loving hands that grew, picked, and perhaps dried or likely roasted it. That is a solid energetic connection.

If the preference is coffee with cream or sugar, feel free. Adding cream or sugar brings extra energy to the brew. Understand that sugar's magical correspondence is love; cream is about higher spirituality.

Coffee makers typically have filter baskets. If you use paper filters, rinse them with hot water to eliminate the chance of them adding a papery taste to the coffee. Reusable filters are more sustainable than paper filters, especially the bleached ones. Carving a sigil or bindrune on the reusable filter basket as an extra layer of energy is also an option.

Once the coffee is brewed, you may feel called to connect with an ancestral coffee lover, as I do with my father. Drinking coffee often allows me to feel him cheering me on and giving me good energy. If you don't have an apparent coffee-loving ancestor to connect with using this ritual each day, don't fret. Give coffee grounds to the houseplants or gardens, and you've just connected the coffee to the land around you. Also, know one day it might be you who cheers someone on from beyond, giving them some energy they need to succeed.

Start Fresh Coffee

Equipment

An electric drip coffee maker

Filter (reusable or disposable)

Tablespoon-sized measuring spoon

A carafe/thermos (optional)

Ingredients

Medium-coarse ground coffee of choice

Cold water

Cream or milk (optional)

Sugar (optional)

SERVES 1

Instructions

1. Be sure filter basket is clean and ready for the grounds

2. For every six ounces of water, use two tablespoons of ground coffee. A standard pot of coffee is about four cups of water. If using a carafe or thermos, ensure the amount of coffee brewed will fit.

3. Add the cold water to the coffee maker's reservoir.

4. Put the coffee in the basket and turn on the coffee maker. Brewing usually takes about five minutes. Take that five minutes to ground and center. Do neck hygiene or finish the morning Witch-ade.

5. Add sugar or cream to coffee, as preferred. Stir sunwise and bring in the energy wanted.

6. Where would daily focus or actions move you toward your goals? Choose that mantra, such as:

I am enough.

Today I choose happiness.

I love myself and my body.

7. Take a moment here to hold the cup in both hands and take a big ol' inhalation to get all that coffee aroma into the senses. Let the smell align itself with the mantra. The scent is one of the most vital senses, so making it a part of the magic has unique power.

8. Next, look into the mug, and in the reflection of the liquid, visualize with the mind's eye the outcome, action, or support needed to align with the mantra (e.g., see yourself unstressed, laughing, or feeling super confident in your body).

9. Take a moment and blow the intention into the mug by blowing on the coffee as most do to cool the liquid. Make it audible. Be mindful of that connection, that intention.

10. Take a drink. Let all that goodness, energy, and magic inside. Drink before it reaches room temperature so all that energy is present.

11. Clean the equipment and cups when finished. Compost coffee grounds.

Take a drink. Let all that goodness, energy, and magic inside.

A Spell for Sweetness

A little sweetness to counteract the not-so-pleasant parts of daily life is necessary occasionally. We do our best spell work when we are feeling our best. If you are not feeling solid, reach for a small amount of cocoa, powdered sugar, and instant milk. Homemade cocoa mix lasts in the cupboard for up to three years; however, it likely will be used up well before then. From when those cold morning fogs roll in during late autumn and even through moments in spring, it is easy to reach for Sweet 'n' Frugal Witch Mocha a couple of times a week.

Chocolate is a quick, tasty, and magical way to sweeten the day. Energetically, it carries the properties of gratitude, happiness, health, longevity, love, luxury, and riches. In this spell, the focus is on health and riches. Adding it to the coffee gives all the benefits of clarity and stimulation. Lastly, this is a spell that a Witch may reach for frequently.

First, mix the homemade hot cocoa; you may skip this part and use a favorite commercial variety. However, if these ingredients are in the cupboard already, take the opportunity to try them out. Take a chance; making it magical will produce beneficial energy all around you. Plus, it is cheaper than store-bought.

Regarding the milk portion of the cocoa mix, I'd recommend whole instant milk. The extra fat in the milk protein particles in this makes for a better texture in the cocoa. However, again, this can be a specialty item in some areas. Instant nonfat dry milk is an acceptable base here. You may substitute powdered coffee creamer for the dry milk, as well. Or even a combination of both. Perhaps try it with half powdered creamer and half instant milk. If you are vegan, there are vegan soy powder mixes that work well as a replacement for the milk. They do not have the same texture. However, once added to the coffee, it is indistinguishable. Another replacement could be coconut milk powder; however, the coconut flavor can be too much, depending on the producer.

Lastly, use an amethyst crystal for the storage part only. It helps put more love into this mix. Consider charging this crystal on the Capricorn New and Full Moons. Then, it goes right back into the cupboard with the hot cocoa mix.

Be alert when sweetening the mood without going overboard. For many of us, the mix alone will be sweet enough. Mini marshmallows are optional but add another layer of magic. Find the kind made with better stuff than corn syrup and cornstarch. However, ensure they are not substituting the fat or thickener for something less food-like. Being aware of what we put in our bodies is part of the magic of mixology. Ingredients preferred include marshmallow root—powder or extract, depending on the recipe—water, gelatin (or vegan replacement), honey (maybe sugar), vanilla extract, and some probiotics. If the store-brand made the 1970s way is the only thing available, use it. Lastly, feel free to substitute the water for warmed milk—careful not to scorch it.

The following is the recipe for homemade cocoa mix, followed by a follow-up working for the mocha. They go together like magic and the Witch.

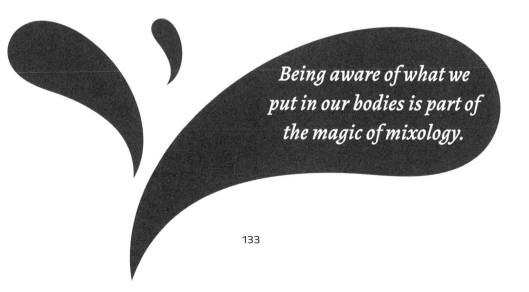

Being aware of what we put in our bodies is part of the magic of mixology.

133

Swift Witch Hot Cocoa Mix

EQUIPMENT

Medium mixing bowl

Measuring cups and spoons

Whisk

Jar to store finished mix in

Canning funnel

Amethyst crystal (optional)

SERVES
20

INGREDIENTS

1 cup powdered sugar

1 cup cocoa powder

½ cup instant dry whole milk or coffee creamer

1 teaspoon sea salt, finely ground

INSTRUCTIONS

1. Combine all the ingredients in a mixing bowl and whisk until combined. Be sure to stir sunwise to bring sweetness and love to the mix and, thereby, the drinker. "Sweeten the cup, sweeten the Witch, may all be wise and make the switch" is what I say when stirring mine.

2. Using the funnel, transfer mixture to a jar or airtight container. Store in a cool, dry cupboard with an amethyst crystal on its lid.

SWEET 'N' FRUGAL WITCH

M O C H A

SERVES
1

Equipment

Favorite coffee mug

Measuring tablespoon

Electric kettle

Stirring spoon

Ingredients

4 ounces heated water (options: Leo moon, Cancer solar)

2 tablespoons Swift Witch Hot Cocoa Mix

¼ to ½ cup brewed coffee, hot

Mini marshmallows (optional)

Instructions

1. Add two tablespoons of Swift Witch Hot Cocoa into mug. Heat water to 200°F (93°C).

2. Add hot water and mix until completely dissolved. Turn spoon widdershins thirteen times to begin the dissolution process and push away any moodiness keeping you from being your best. Then stir it thirteen times sunwise to bring in soft smiles and coolheadedness.

3. Top with brewed coffee. Stir three times widdershins to remove sourness from the day.

4. Look into the mug; slightly turn up the corners of the mouth and think: "No one can steal my sweetness. I store it up and share it fairly."

5. Add mini 'mallows here, if desired.

6. Sip. Taste the coffee, taste the chocolate, taste the sweet. Turn those corners of the mouth up again slightly after that first sip.

Keeping Coffee Cool

Although most morning coffee ritual drinkers may find the five minutes to brew a large pot painfully slow, some of the best coffee takes way longer. Generally speaking, brewing with coffee is a methodical process that takes mindfulness and planning. Cold brew is brewed without electricity and makes some of the best iced coffee. It does, however, require patience, which can be something we all struggle with while living in the age of instantaneous entertainment, communication, drink, food, and seemingly everything. Part of that patience is also prior planning, which requires being present. That mindfulness is some powerful energy.

Like the last two entries, we have one brew that can make two different types of magical drinks. Again, the foundation for both is patience. Cold brew takes about twenty-four hours and can sit up to a few days. It is a go-to for folx who are boating, traveling, or camping. A jar with the ground coffee in the suitcase without much hassle. Then, make it in the hotel room instead of being resigned to that stale disk of coffee of suspect origin that guest services provides.

There are cold brew to-go tumblers with built-in strainers and some fancier cold brew coffee pitchers. Strainer lids for mason jars allow straining from one jar to another, making the process more efficient. Take care that it is a fine mesh strainer for this process unless chunky coffee is preferred. Remember, plants treasure coffee grounds. Compost devours coffee grounds. If you can keep them out of the landfill, please do so.

Magically, this brew deepens the correspondences that coffee, water, and time create. Use cold brew in offerings to deities, to speed up manifestation spells, and, of course, to ground with a keen focus and boosted energy.

Practicing Patience Cold Brew

EQUIPMENT

Sterilized quart-sized mason jar with reusable leak-free lid

Fine mesh strainer

Second sterilized mason jar, carafe, thermos, or pitcher for storage

Blue lace agate or other patience-improving crystal (optional)

INGREDIENTS

1 cup favorite course ground coffee

3 cups cold, non-chlorinated water

INSTRUCTIONS

1. Put coffee grounds in a mason jar. While pouring it in, connect with the coffee. Feel its energy. Connect with it.

2. Pour water over coffee. Feel how the energy of the water shifts and changes the energy of the ground coffee.

3. Put on the lid. Give it a little shake. Alternatively, gently stir. Set an intention to approach everything with patience, calm, and wisdom.

4. Put it in a cool, dark place or refrigerate (although it does not need to be) for twenty-four hours. Place a crystal that helps with patience, like agate, on top of the jar.

5. Strain coffee through a fine mesh strainer into another mason jar. Compost grounds.

6. Refrigerate cold brew until use. Stays fresh for about a week.

Use cold brew in offerings to deities, to speed up manifestation spells, and, of course, to ground with a keen focus and boosted energy.

Shields Up

In the stream of any given day, we can deflect much negativity being lobbed at us directly and indirectly. Five minutes with an Ice the B.S. Coffee can shift the energy and mood. We cannot control everything in our lives, but we can take five minutes while drinking this brew and not let anything bother us.

Remember, since this working calls for cold brew, it is also an exercise in patience. This working pairs well with a small amount of breathwork. Returning to our breath is powerful magic that affects us quickly and physically. If you practice yoga, apply a lion's breath (simhasana) practice here.

Returning to our breath is powerful magic.

ICE THE B.S.

COFFEE

EQUIPMENT

SERVES
1

- 12-ounce glass of choice (e.g., draft glass)
- Stirring spoon
- Sustainable drinking straw (optional)

INGREDIENTS

- Ice cubes to fill drinking glass (options: Virgo solar, Libra moon)
- Vanilla syrup (optional)
- ⅓ cup whole milk
- ¾ cup cold brew coffee

INSTRUCTIONS

1. Take a moment to take a deep breath. The coffee will wait.

2. Fill the drinking glass with ice cubes, recalling what negativity to deflect. Hear the ice hit the glass; as it does, it smashes annoyance away.

3. If using the syrup and milk, add them now, giving them a quick yet gentle stir while thinking kind thoughts.

4. Add the cold brew coffee to the glass. Watch as the dark liquid mingles with the milk and syrup. Imagine all the irritations fading away. Take the opportunity to stir the milk and coffee together while focusing on the breath. Embrace stillness. Breathe. Let it out audibly. Watch the liquid swirl as you mindfully breathe for a minute.

5. Allow your breathing to return to normal and drink while looking at something pleasant. Do not doom scroll—no screens during this time. Look at the sky. Look at the trees. Sit in a sanctuary. Change the view from what you usually see. Keep looking at new scenery while drinking.

6. When done drinking the Ice the B.S. Coffee, set a small intention for the day: e.g., "I put my best self forward." One more deep breath, then say, "So it is."

7. Clean up supplies.

At Home Cafe

As much as I love coffee, I have never owned an espresso machine. Early in this espresso-love relationship, I learned to have that same experience without the entire kitchen counter disappearing. You might eye one at a local thrift store, but using a manual coffee press, moka pot, or French press is easy and stores in a reasonable amount of space. A milk frother helps make a wider variety of coffee drinks using one of those manual makers, turn it into espresso, and mix up an Afternoon Delight Latte.

I encourage you to grind the beans right before use. Purchasing ground espresso coffee from a favorite local roaster works well, too. Making espresso at home without a machine is all about creating a space to sit over a cup of strongly brewed, bold coffee—since that makes espresso different—and connecting with someone, especially if there is something important in need of expression. Espresso is a great way to catch up, tackle tribulations, and dream together for the future in a safe, loving, and supportive environment.

A manual coffee press is a favorite espresso method because it easily creates the pressure needed to brew it. It is simple to use and brews the perfect serving of espresso.

Express Yourself Espresso

SERVES
2

EQUIPMENT

An electric kettle with temperature control

A coffee grinder (if you are not using pre-ground coffee)

A manual coffee press with filter

A measuring tablespoon

Stirrer or bar spoon

2 small demitasse cups

INGREDIENTS

High-quality dark roast or espresso-specific coffee beans

Water (options: Leo, Virgo, or Scorpio; solar or moon)

Organic sugar cubes (optional)

Sugar or butter cookie (optional)

INSTRUCTIONS

1. Fill the kettle with water and heat to 200°F (93°C).

2. Place the filter inside the drain cap. Lightly rinse the drain cap and filter inside the compartment of the press. Place the press onto the cup on a stable surface.

3. Prepare two generous tablespoons of coffee beans in the grinder until a medium-fine grind exists. While grinding, think about what needs to be expressed. Query for the path toward thoughtful, honest, inspirational, nurturing, and kind words.

4. Pour a half cup of the heated water. Stir the coffee, then press down on the plunger swiftly. Be decisive in this expression over espresso. Put that intention into action. Besides, the espresso brews during this plunger movement, so make it full throttle.

5. Repeat this process for a second cup. Serve in an environment conducive to connection. Put one or two sugar cubes in it, if desired, but optimally this is sipped without milk or sugar. Optionally, serve with a sweet treat like a sugar or butter cookie.

Don't Skimp on the Fat

Once again, this drink features espresso but layers it with milk. The working calls for whole milk to bring the energies of satisfaction and nurturing. Again, there is a prompt here to look for locally produced milk. Like honey, dairy produced in the same region will be nothing but extra beneficial both at the nutrient and more significant environmental levels. If the milk is less than 150 miles away, that is a better carbon footprint.

Beyond that, there is the taste. Local milk is fresher; therefore, its taste is at its prime. This also directly benefits farmers, who can create jobs in their communities. Employment can be a purpose that produces resiliency, allowing for better care of one another. See all that energy connected by the intention of doing what is best for our planet? Powerful stuff.

That whole milk with espresso is delightful and creates the right energy in the Express Yourself Espresso working. Two shots of espresso with steamed and frothy whole milk? Whatever the afternoon has lined up—I hope it is fun-based—partnering with this energy is incredible for adding pep and confidence. Look at it as an anti-frustration spell.

This working employs breath. Taking a breath and taking that time to renew energy and drink some of that magic that is espresso and warm, frothy milk is simple magic. When it helps the Witch solve problems, that is still powerful. Consider using that magic to connect with a partner or teammate. Maybe there is a problem you've been working on together for hours and are making little to no progress. Latte it up. A latte and twenty minutes will not change an entire life, but it will shift the energy of an afternoon.

This recipe does not require having an espresso machine with a steamer contraption. But a way to make espresso is necessary, as described previously. For this drink, we will feature and instruct using a French press. Because the milk is heated, a spouted pan is recommended. Lastly, an electric frother wand is ideal, but if you've got a hand mixer with a fine whisk attachment, use that. The electric frother wand is one of my favorite kitchen gadgets because every time I make a latte, it pays for itself.

As for the French press, this again is a method that produces some concentrated brew. It will be less punchy than making it with the manual immersion blender coffee maker. Coffee aficionados say that French press vs. manual repeatedly shows that the coffee made with the French press can feel more oily in the mouth. Its design allows for brewing more than one latte base, however; therefore, it is the better choice for this working. The following makes two double-shot twelve-ounce lattes.

See all that energy connected by the intention of doing what is best for our planet? Powerful stuff.

AFTERNOON DELIGHT
LATTE

Equipment

An electric kettle with temperature control

A coffee grinder (if not using pre-ground coffee)

Measuring cups and spoons

French press

An electric frother

Saucepan with spout

Two mugs that hold at least 12 ounces

Espresso "shot" glass

SERVES
2

Ingredients

High-quality espresso roast

2 cups heated water (options: Aries moon, or Sagittarius or Capricorn solar)

1 cup whole milk

Instructions

1. Put kettle on to heat water to 200°F (93°C).

2. While the kettle heats, grind at least two tablespoons of beans per "shot" (1½ ounces) to fine. Make the tablespoons healthy scoops. Depending on the grinder, a couple of batches may be necessary. Let the scent released as the beans grind distract thoughts away from the day's stress and turn toward delight.

3. Add the coffee grounds to the French press. Set aside for a moment.

4. Add whole milk to a saucepan over low-medium heat.

5. Bloom the coffee. This means adding a splash of hot water from the kettle to the French press and letting the grounds soak for about thirty seconds to a minute. Do not do it longer than that. This is a great time to connect with the espresso quickly.

6. Pour the rest of the water over the grounds. Close the lid and allow the coffee to steep for about four minutes.

7. Pull warmed milk off the stove while the coffee steeps, and carefully use the frother to double its volume. Let it get nice and foamy and frothy.

8. Press the plunger down halfway using slow, steady pressure after the coffee has steeped. Raise it to the top and then plunge using the same even pressure.

9. Stop and say a short incantation of gratitude (e.g., "Praise the energy of this coffee!" or "Coffee is life!") while holding your hands over the French press and sending connection to the liquid inside.

10. Pour a scant ½ cup of coffee into each mug. While pouring, visualize the ideal finish to the day.

11. Give the milk one more quick thirty seconds of frothing and pour over the coffee in each mug, making sure to get as much foam as milk into each cup. If the saucepan has a pour spout, try foam art here; perhaps get fancy and make a sigil, other magical symbols, or another meaningful image.

12. Drink, sipping the foam alongside the espresso and steamed milk.

13. Take twenty minutes to sip and be with the coffee and teammate/partner.

Choose quiet or chatter, but no work conversation—anything but.

Not Into Caffeine

As promised, the following recipe is for Witches who choose to avoid coffee's caffeine. There are alternatives to the traditional cup of joe and still reap many benefits. Of course, there will be magic to do with it as well.

This working includes chicory root (*Cichorium intybus* L.). Although native to Eurasia, chicory is tolerated and labeled as noninvasive in most of North America. Brought from Europe as a coffee substitute to the United States, consider using it as an ancestor offering because many may have used this root. It often grows where soil has been disturbed and in large meadows. Chicory is also known as cornflower, the blue sailor flower, coffee weed, or Italian dandelion. In traditional folk medicine, chicory treats constipation and indigestion and was used as a liver cleanse. Energetically, it holds a lot of air energy and is used magically for love and protection.

Dandelions are part of this working, too, using the root. Like chicory, dandelion is used in folk medicine for liver health and as a digestive aid. It is very rich in vitamins C and A, potassium, and iron. When we use the flowers in syrup making, the energy held in the root is the same: psychic awareness. When trying to do an energetic reset, you will need that all-important equipment in the Witch's arsenal: intuition.

This brew also has chaga in it. This is a type of fungus that grows primarily on birch trees in the northern climes. Chaga is not only tasty but has all kinds of physical and metaphysical benefits. It is rich in antioxidants and provides immune-boosting support because it contains beta-glucans, which modulate the immune system. It is classified as an adaptogen, helping the body beat stress and maintain balance. It has a soothing effect on the digestive system and has been used topically to promote healthy skin. Magically, Witches lean heavily on it for its nourishing of psychic awareness. Because it grows on the side of birch trees, it is associated with the Germanic Great Mother Goddess Nerthus (Hertha), whose energy the rune Berkano holds: ᛒ. Primal creativity is in this brew.

Foraging and processing all these items is possible. However, they can be found at many markets focused on bulk foods, teas, or health foods. Try your local food co-op.

The universe may do something like shift us away from drinking our beloved coffee, but it always provides something new. When hit with a dreaded streak of "bad things happen in threes," where it feels like you cannot handle another thing, it is time to clear the way and flip the script. This also may be a brew to try when experiencing a Mercury retrograde or Saturn return since the magic is very "purge and splurge." Clear the Way for Abundance Brew is about wiping away what does not serve and filling up your cup with the energy to receive what does.

Clear the Way for Abundance Brew

EQUIPMENT

Favorite way to make coffee

Grinder

Measuring tablespoon

Timer

Journal and favorite writing instrument

Calming music (optional)

Favorite coffee mug

Sugar (optional)

Coffee creamer (optional)

INGREDIENTS

6 ounces water per serving (options: Taurus, Capricorn, or Libra; solar or moon)

1 part chicory, ground coarse

1 part chaga, ground coarse

1 part dandelion root, ground coarse

INSTRUCTIONS

1. Be sure filter basket is clean and ready for the grounds. Grind roots and fungi coarsely. Do it in batches, as necessary.

2. For every six ounces of water, use two tablespoons roots/chaga blend. A standard pot of coffee is about four cups of water. If using a carafe or thermos, make sure the brew will fit.

3. Add the cold moon water to the coffee maker's reservoir.

4. Once the Clear the Way blend is in the basket and the water is in the reservoir, take a quick moment to set an intention; e.g., I am open to receiving all the good that the universe has to offer me; I am grateful for all the blessings that come my way; I am excited to see my future bright and healthy.

5. Turn on the coffee maker. Brewing usually takes about five minutes. Gather a journal and writing instrument, then write worries or list challenges or lessons learned, pouring your thoughts and feelings onto the paper. When the "coffee" is finished brewing, stop writing.

6. Pour a cup of this coffee alternative blend. Add sugar and cream, if desired. For the first three sips, be sure to take a breath in between each. Focus your thoughts on your intention.

7. After those first three sips, continue writing and sipping until the drink is gone.

8. To close your spellwork here, clean up mug and coffeemaking supplies.

Make this recipe for seven days in a row for a deep energetic reset.

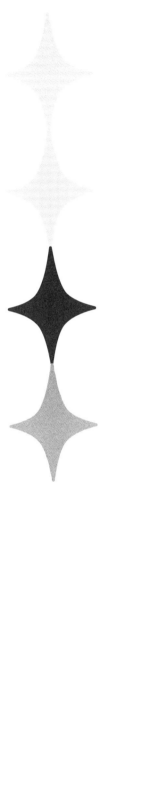

a TEA
for
everything

Humans have been drinking tea for more than four thousand years. Tea drinking reached Europe in the sixteenth century. Portuguese traders then brought it to Portugal from East Asia, where it is a native shrub. According to the Archaeological Institute of America, recent evidence uncovered from tombs in Tibet and Chang'an (now known as Xi'an)—the starting point of the Silk Road in northern China—provides evidence of tea consumption from within tombs more than two thousand years old. Before this new evidence was found in 2016, a Chinese document from 59 BCE was the oldest evidence of humans drinking tea.

Since the birth of the United States, tea was such a sought-after part of everyday human existence that taxes on tea contributed to the infamous Boston Tea Party and the fallout, which galvanized colonists to revolt against the British crown. We can discuss the myths around this story over tea, but we will not explore it further here, only to acknowledge tea's role in American history and culture.

Peruse a metaphysical shop and you'll find dozens of books about Witches and tea, from simple tea witcheries like what is detailed here to reading tea leaves and other herbal magic. There is a good chance the local Witch market is also serving tea. Our metaphysical shops are often prominent places where our community comes together. We may as well sip some tea while plotting the takeover of the world—er, planning the next great witchy event or project.

The magic of tea has remained constant on this planet through the eons. Some references say tea is ruled by Mars and is associated with the element of fire. However, there are others that state it is ruled by the planet Mercury and associated with the elements of water and the moon. It can be both since fire, water, and some leaves make it possible. However, my intuition insists black tea is more Mars and fire, and green tea is more Mercury and watery moons. That is how it is listed here. Regardless, Witches will testify that tea can soothe, awaken, rejuvenate, and inspire. When you add the energies of herbal elements, fruits, and spices, unlimited possibilities exist.

Please Accept the Offer of Tea

If you've been privileged to experience tea and its culture in one outside your own, it can be very eye-opening. When a culture shares its preferred drink with you, it's something special. Be sure to say yes.

One such experience came the first time I tasted Kurdish chai in the mountains of Iraq during a humanitarian aid mission. The taste of that tea, the faces of the people who made it, and the smell of jasmine in the air all rush back to me when I think of that moment. I'm still chasing the taste of that first sip of Kurdish chai. I've come close to re-creating it, but it's only second best.

That doesn't mean it's not still yummy and magical. To get that memorable Kurdish chai flavor, you will take a black tea and amend it with the flavors of bergamot, jasmine, orange, cardamom, and cinnamon. Together, they are steeped for five minutes using boiling water. Served with a heavy side dose of sugar—at least two cubes or spoons of sugar in the tiny clear glass called an *istikan*, "teacup" in Arabic. An istikan is a tulip-shaped glass, often with gold around the rim; sometimes the glass is painted. It is served atop a ceramic saucer that often has some kind of art on it. But making this chai recipe doesn't require that specific glassware. Your regular teacup will do.

Please note that this is different from the masala chai that hails from India and is served with milk in many Western cafes. Also, for many of us, refined sugar is not in our diet, at least not regularly. This is not a drink I would drink daily as the Kurds and Iraqis do in northern Iraq. The tea is pretty darn good all on its own without sugar. But if you want to experience how it is enjoyed in those beautiful mountaintops not far from Mosul, then make it with the sugar cubes first, then the next time add your preferred sweetener (e.g., honey).

Which black tea you choose to amend is up to the Witch. I am fond of a good Assam tea for making Kurdish chai since it seems to have the closest flavor profile to the tea I recall drinking many years ago. But you could choose any variety of black tea. A nice Darjeeling is good. English and Irish breakfast tea is often made with Keemun tea, which is also a black tea. Russian Caravan is a very bold and smoky black tea that reminds me of the open fires they would cook on in the central areas of the villages we visited. As always, I encourage you to use what you have readily available.

CHAI FOR

CLARITY

EQUIPMENT

Kettle

Istikan set or 2 small teacups with saucers

Teaspoons—measuring and flatware (the latter is optional)

Teapot or small saucepan/large measuring cup with a spout

Offering cup for the altar (if in your practice)

Tea strainer, diffuser, or some cheesecloth

Journal and pen, jasmine incense, candles (optional)

INGREDIENTS

1 tablespoon black tea such as Assam, Irish breakfast, or Darjeeling

1 teaspoon dried bergamot

1 teaspoon dried jasmine

1 tablespoon orange zest (fresh is best, but candied may be used)

1 teaspoon whole cardamom

1 stick cinnamon, broken into pieces

2 cups boiling water (options: Aquarius, Libra, or Gemini; moon)

Sugar cubes (at least 2 per serving)

INSTRUCTIONS

1. Ground and center. Set the mood with candles and incense. This may be done alone or with anyone seeking clarity. Gather all the ingredients. Mindfully sum up your objective; e.g., "I want to easily understand my next steps in life with the utmost clarity."

2. Combine all the ingredients, except sugar cubes, into the tea strainer, diffuser, or cheesecloth. Put into a teapot and pour boiling water over. As you do, and if it's in your practice, call in any deities, ancestors, or universal energy to assist and protect you on this quest for clarity; e.g., "Beloved kindred, beyond and within, guide and protect me. Sit with me; sip with me; usher me toward clarity. In love, your beloved, always."

3. Let steep for five minutes. During the steeping time, sit and contemplate. Close your eyes or focus on the steeping tea. Feel free to meditate before continuing, even for a few moments. You may also use this time to be alone with your thoughts, being receptive to the spirit realm. Let the mind focus on being open to whatever divine download may happen. Refrain from expecting; however, do remain open. Direct wandering thoughts back to the focused visualization.

4. Remove the tea solids from the steeping pot and compost.

5. Plop two sugar cubes in each istikan or teacup. Say, "Sweeten the view inside my eyes."

6. Pour tea over sugar cubes. Be sure to leave a small quantity of tea in the pot to provide an offering at the altar for those called upon in step 2.

7. Let the istikan sit for a moment. Look at the tea. Watch how the sugar dissolves. Wait to sip until at least half of the cubes are gone. This takes a little time. While watching, imagine thoughts, events, or relationships breeding insecurity around career, romance, or even what path to walk next. Let those worries or obstacles dissolve within the visualization.

8. Before taking that first sip, mingle the breath a moment with the tea's steam. In other words, give it a gentle cooling breath from the mouth above the cup.

9. Take a sip; allow the more prominent sugar granules to coat the tongue, bit by bit. Talk with a beloved or sit and allow deities, ancestors, guides, or the universe to send messages. Focus the breath. If thoughts return to the things blocking you, repeat the invocation to the spiritual connection preference from step 2. Remember, be open to receive. Keep your body posture open. Stack your spine, then lift your solar plexus to the sky. Take another sip.

10. Journal any thoughts, ideas, inspirations, and notions that arrive during this time.

11. Repeat steps 9 and 10 until tea is gone.

12. Once the tea is gone, provide the tea offering on the altar, being sure to thank the ancestors (deities, guides, or others) as you do. Feel free to stand in silence at the altar to receive any further messages leading to clarity.

13. Clean up the tea equipment; extinguish candles. Be on your way in clarity.

Exotic Ingredients, Different Techniques

Many Americans know little, if anything, about blackcurrants. If you're a reader from another part of the world, you may know the blackcurrant well, but you may not know why the population of the United States is somewhat clueless about it. Blackcurrents were outlawed here in 1911 in order to protect the timber industry. The blackcurrant can be a host to white pine blister rust, so the sale and cultivation of it was banned until 1966. However, many states maintained the ban until 2003. Because of this period of restrictions, blackcurrants are not popular in the United States, and one researcher has estimated that only 0.1 percent of Americans have eaten one.

Those who have spent time in Europe have likely been exposed to this berry as it is very well-loved and consumed there. Blackcurrant is returning to the United States now, and small growers like my covenstead are popping up everywhere. Occasionally, the Witch will encounter red currants or white currants, and those may be called gooseberry instead of a currant, but it is the same plant.

Blackcurrant produces small berries, but they pack a mighty punch. Rich in vitamin C and often used in skincare, tinctures, shrubs, and tea, the leaves are helpful both medicinally and magically. The leaves also contain GLA (gamma-linolenic acid), which is an omega-6 fatty acid that plays a crucial role in brain function (Blue 2022). Additionally, it contains anthocyanins, which are antioxidants (Morris 2017).

Scientifically, the world understands this plant hosts antimicrobial, antifungal, and antiviral properties. Yep, it is a triple threat. The berries have been used for years as a skin salve because they host a specific polysaccharide that exerts an anti-inflammatory effect. For years, European women have been boasting about its internal and external anti-aging effects. The berries contain a particular fatty acid that again suppresses inflammation internally and externally in our bodies.

This plant and its fruit have significantly enhanced my work in the Craft and for healing. Dried blackcurrants are used in place of salt in protection and warding spells. Propagating blackcurrant is easy and lends itself to abundance spells. For healing, I use blackcurrant tea as a way to help stimulate the parasympathetic nervous system to downregulate the stress response, reduce anxiety, and help with pain management. As far as the berries themselves, the taste is tart without being sour, sweet without being cloying, and will surprise many with its yumminess.

Magically, we'll be looking at its impact on the throat and its use as a voice amplifier and throat chakra opener. This tea helps us speak our truths from a foundation of love and kindness. Share this tea with anyone with whom truth must be spoken. There is enough here for a full pot, or about three cups. Alternatively, sip it in front of the mirror if you need to be truthful with yourself. If you are not a tea lover, you may use blackcurrant leaves as a threshold cleanse, in a protection spell to clear auras, or to ground and center while burning in a small fireproof bowl.

Truth-Telling Tea

EQUIPMENT

Kettle

Measuring teaspoon

Tea strainer, infuser, or cheesecloth

Teacup or mug

Timer

INGREDIENTS

1 teaspoon blackcurrant tea leaves per serving

1 cup hot water per serving (option: Libra moon)

Honey (optional)

INSTRUCTIONS

1. Bring water to 180°F (82°C); do not boil water, please, as that would make the tea bitter. Gently steep as with a green tea.

2. Put 1 teaspoon of blackcurrant leaves in a tea strainer; dip into heated water inside the chosen tea vessel.

3. Steep for 7 minutes; set a timer. Meditate over the tea as it steeps, visualizing finding our voice—or, as some say, opening the throat chakra. Imagine an easy truth-telling conversation (or whatever the goal is).

4. Add honey to taste, which is optional, but sometimes truths become more accessible with sweetness and unlock the most tightly closed voice (i.e., throat chakra).

5. Drink and feel the magic unfold. While drinking, continue to visualize the scene as truth is spoken in love and kindness, whatever the situation. Expect to be heard; expect calm responses. This or better; so it is.

Exposing the Hidden

On occasion, we need certain truths revealed to us. Enter Revelation Tea. This tea is designed to reveal what is shrouded from us, strengthen our intuition, and align ourselves. This working uses green tea, another heavy-hitter in the six tea categories. If you dig the taste of green tea and regularly consume it, you are likely in decent health (Xiang 2023). Green tea boosts alertness and improves cognitive functions because of its caffeine, which is lower than black tea. It also contains L-theanine, an amino acid that has calming effects. Green tea has also been shown to have some potential benefits, such as skin, brain, and heart health enhancements, as well as cancer prevention and a boost in metabolism, promoting weight loss.

Magically, it is similar to its black tea cousin and can open up pathways, whether they be energetic thoughts or even one's connection to the Divine and intuition. My experience with this working leaves me astounded by how, almost instantaneously, situations, ideas, or even secrets are divulged. For you, it may have the tarot cards suddenly all pointing to the same thing. Or maybe you are a medium, and intense, new communications are coming in from ancestors and other spirits. It is Revelation Tea. If you need something revealed, then this is the tea for you.

This next brew may be done without the complements of the rosebuds, peppermint leaves, or skullcap (*Scutellaria*). Green tea is mighty for this spell on its own. But if you're one of the folx who struggle with the grassy flavor of green tea, adding some additional energy and flavors may make it not as earthy tasting. Besides, rosebuds bring abundance and love. Peppermint adds lots of luck, like an unexpected check being received. Skullcap has full-on protection properties.

This tea accompanies some deep meditation following its ingestion. Plan to have some uninterrupted time and space to move about since this is a moving meditation. A yoga mat or blanket under a tree works well also.

R E V E L A T I O N
TEA

Equipment

Kettle

Tea strainer, infuser, or cheesecloth

Teacup

Meditation space and time

Comfort items (yoga mat, pillows, blankets)

Tea mug (or travel tumbler) that can accompany the meditation space (indoors or outdoors)

Journal and favored writing instrument (optional)

Ingredients

1 cup water per serving (options: dark moon, solstice moon, Scorpio solar)

2 teaspoons green tea leaves per serving

1 teaspoon rosebuds per serving

1 teaspoon peppermint leaves per serving

1 teaspoon skullcap per serving

Instructions

1. Set the intention that you will divinely discover what you need to know. For example, "All will be revealed to me regarding the missing element in my _____ (e.g., career). As I do so, I will be protected yet open. I walk with the universe (Source/my ancestors/my guides/deity) in safety and grace."

2. Heat water to 180°F (82°C).

3. Gather the tea leaves, rosebuds, peppermint, and skullcap into your strainer.

4. Pour the heated water over the strainer and steep for three minutes. During those three minutes, prepare the meditation space and lay out any blankets or mats.

5. Remove the tea solids and discard them in the compost with gratitude.

6. Set your intention again while looking at the tea inside its vessel.

7. Settle into the meditation space with the tea.

8. Sit comfortably, ensuring the spine is stacked and all the body's energy centers are aligned. Breathe naturally and sip the tea. Do not put the cup or mug down. No need to guzzle. Connect with the vessel and the tea energetically while drinking. Allow thoughts to flow to the focus of this needed revelation.

9. If the mind jumps to something else, be kind to yourself. Simply recognize, refocus, and move to mull over what you need to know. Continue sipping.

10. After consuming the tea, begin the moving meditation. If you practice yoga, tai chi, qigong, or dance, choose whatever moving meditation is in your practice. Don't have one? Rock back and forth while sitting. Stand and gently swing back and forth, letting the arms swing (also known as knocking on heaven's door). Whatever movement is chosen, do so gently and rhythmically. Move with the breath.

11. Continue moving with the breath. Once a rhythm is established, close your eyes but continue to move. Focus for a moment on breath and body movement. Do this for seven breaths, in and out. Do it sincerely.

12. After the seven breaths, continue moving but shift the focus to what you need to be revealed. Keep breathing and moving to the breath (back and forth or in circles or in flow).

13. Do this for at least seven minutes. No need to keep time. Let the body guide you when you are done. There is no need to break a sweat. Be gentle and slower than you think with the movement. If you lose the breath because you are moving too fast or letting the mind's focus jump beyond the body and its breath, simply recognize and return. Refocus and try again.

14. If you've chosen to bring a journal to write down all the downloads, ideas, and further questions to investigate, do so as it comes to you. Try not to spend more than seven minutes in this stage.

15. After recording thoughts, or if you need to return to the day's responsibilities, say a quiet prayer thanks to the universe/ ancestors/deities/guides. Clean up the space. Wash hands. Wash the tea mug. Be prepared for further messages.

Tank the Attitude

Whenever I see that I'm falling back into old patterns, especially the baneful magic of negative self-talk, I redo this ritual. It was inspired by one taught to me early on in my path. A dedicated month to changing thought patterns is powerful magic. On occasion, this is great brew to serve post-ritual as in addition to shifting perspectives, it refills our energetic tank.

Stock up on the magical ingredients because you do this daily for an entire moon cycle. You'll be using black tea, lemon verbena, bee balm (wild bergamot), lemongrass, and dried orange peel. We're pulling in some energies that include that primal fire, strength, as it takes a lot of fortitude to undo a longtime default setting in our thinking, attract positive energy, enhance psychic connections, purify, and love—always love.

Retraining the brain to focus on the positive—to look for the light even in the dark moon nights—is not an easy task. But this ritual takes a whole moon cycle, and it is great to start it with the Aries new moon, but it can be started from any dark moon or new moon.

We all must recognize that toxic positivity also exists. This is when we ignore, glaze over, or generally refuse and dismiss negative emotions. That's not always helpful to our end goals and can shield us from being our most authentic selves and living our best lives. With this working we are not bottling up our emotions. Instead, we're challenging our thoughts and preparing ourselves to be open to the help we seek to improve our outlook.

Positivity Tea

EQUIPMENT

Kettle

Tea strainer, infuser, or cheesecloth

Teacup(s)

Small bowl

INGREDIENTS

1 cup water per serving (options: Aries moon, Beltane solar)

1 tablespoon black tea

1 teaspoon dried lemon verbena

1 teaspoon dried bee balm

1 teaspoon dried lemongrass

½ teaspoon dried orange peel

Honey, to taste (optional)

INSTRUCTIONS

1. Drink this tea daily for an entire moon cycle. Pick a time each day beginning with the dark or new moon, stopping only after the full moon. Spend a few spare minutes drinking and exercising a positive mindset each day. Alternatively, do this from one new moon to the next.

2. Heat the water to 195°F (91°C). Gather the tea ingredients and combine them in a small bowl. Combine well with hands, setting an intention for the month as you do, such as:

I am in charge of my thoughts.

I solve problems when I think positively.

My life improves when I look for the light, the good.

Every day I think more positively.

Today I choose joy and happiness.

My thoughts are powerful, and I am in charge of them.
May I live this as my truth. So it is.

3. Put the "spelled" tea into the strainer. Pour the heated water over it. Let steep for five minutes. As it steeps, think of three positive things in life. Thank the universe, ancestors, or deity for them. Do this aloud or silently. The important part is thinking about the good things for this steeping time.

4. Remove the tea solids from the steeping vessel and compost it.

5. Drink the tea. Allow the mind to wander; if it lands on negative thoughts, mindfully practice changing perspective as you sip.

6. Once you've finished, clean all the teamaking supplies and vessels.

7. Repeat the next day and every day through the moon cycle.

8. On the full moon, offer up an extra cup of this tea to the universe/ancestors/Source/deity, proffering gratitude for the shift in perspective.

9. If you find you are still plagued with pessimistic thoughts, then repeat this working at the next new moon. Sometimes any magical working needs more than once to be successful. Ensure there are no forgotten steps.

This working uses black tea, which is caffeinated, so you may want to do this before 3 p.m. each day of the moon cycle.

When Two Halves Split

At times, Witches struggle with living and straddling the mundane and magical world. It can make you feel like you're split in two. That energy creates lots of franticness in how we move through our days. It's hard for many of us to think clearly when the energy is chaotic like that. Chaos magic is beautiful and often necessary. But sometimes a more methodical approach is better for daily routines and workflow. As Witches, we're pulled back into nature in order to realign that energy when it gets out of harmony. And when we do that realignment, it clears our mind to help us creatively move toward our goals.

Gather a favorite scarf, handkerchief, or other head covering. I like to wear a grounding color or black. However, if something neon feels right to gather personal energy and magic, that's right for you. This head covering acts as an energy shield like you'd wear a crystal for energy alignment or protection. In this working, it's about gathering energy and bringing it all back under one "cover," if you will. Pick a veil you like.

To bring those two halves of life together and gain that calm and clarity, we turn to chamomile as the main ingredient, along with some honey. Chamomile has a unique ability to help us relax, focus, and soothe our nervous system. Medicinally, it helps with tummy issues. Magically, it brings protection, peace, and abundance.

This tea also uses valerian root. Herbalists have been using this for eons for calming anxiety, alleviating sleep issues, and even for headaches and menopause symptoms. Magically, it brings in so much lucidity and readiness. Valerian root can have a strong taste, but it gets mellowed out with mint. It doesn't matter what kind of mint. It is adaptable to taste. Mint brings wealth and luck energy.

Feverfew may be an ingredient that is harder to source. Ask a fellow Witch who gardens. They likely have some and plenty to spare, as it's excellent in propagating itself. Feverfew is another staple in an herbalist's kit as a fever reducer. In Craft workings, it's all about protection.

Juniper berries are there to raise psychic energy and check yourself before you wreck yourself. They are also rich in essential oils and flavonoids that get the body's own inflammation fighters rallied. When we feel good physically, we're more likely to feel good mentally, too.

This tea is good for the body, good for the mind, and the ritual to go with it is good for the spirit. Let's get to it.

DAY-ZEES

T E A

SERVES 1

Equipment

Kettle

Tea strainer, infuser, or cheesecloth

Teacup

Favorite incense, something safe to burn it in,
and something to light it

Favorite head covering

Quartz crystal (optional)

Blanket (optional)

Ingredients

2 cups water (options: Taurus moon, Aquarius solar)

2 teaspoons dried chamomile

½ teaspoon dried valerian root

½ to 1 teaspoon dried mint, to taste

½ teaspoon dried feverfew

A couple juniper berries

Instructions

1. Put the kettle on to heat the water to 180°F (82°C).

2. Put the dried herbs and berries into a tea strainer. Pour the heated water over. Let it steep for eight minutes.

3. While it steeps, focus energy into the cup and visualize returning to clarity and calm. Use an incantation or quietly say, "I am clear, I am calm, I am confident."

4. Strain the tea; compost the herbs and berries.

5. Take the tea to a sacred space to continue the magic working.

6. Be sure to have a quiet, comfortable place to sit. If preferred, sit on the ground to be rooted to the earth. Alternatively, put bare feet on the earth. Connect to the energy as you would when grounding and centering. At minimum, choose somewhere you'll be undisturbed and comfortable.

7. Light the incense. Take some deep breaths while watching the smoke waft. Focus on the breath.

8. Put on a veil, scarf, hat, or other head covering. See in the mind's eye the energy—however that looks to you (light, mist, clouds)—as it radiates down from the top of the head down through the spine into the belly and down to the tailbone, sitting connected through the earth. See the earth's energy coming up through the spine, up to the head, and back down again. Let it circulate a few times.

9. If you're using a crystal for additional cleansing and clarity, hold it. Connect with its energy while listening to the breath. Continue step 3's mantra. Sit in contemplation, pray, or simply be while drinking the tea. Feel clarity, calm, and confidence return.

10. Once finished drinking the tea, thank the ground where you've been sitting for sharing its strength with you.

11. Keep your head covered for the remainder of the day. When you remove the cover before bedtime, pause in gratitude for its protection as you stow, launder, or air it out for use again. When it's an appropriate moon, consider leaving the veil on a dedicated altar to recharge it under the moonlight.

Lucid Dreaming Work

In chapter 7, remembering dreams was the goal with Cool Dream Recall Water. Once a Witch has stabilized such a skill in their practice, they may wish to move toward lucid dreaming. This dream state is a state of consciousness featuring both waking and dreaming. This is also called consciousness during REM (rapid eye movement) sleep (LaBerge et al. 1986). This half-awake, half-dreaming suspension means the dreamer recognizes they are dreaming but remains in the dream state and begins to interact or take control of things happening within the dream—talk about augmented reality! That will be a part of this working, but first let's examine why we want lucidity in our dream work.

Robb again schools us on the importance of dreams for Witches: "Rehearsing for real life, inspiring new ideas, balancing emotions, fostering community—can all be attained through regular dreaming" (Robb 2018, 186). But for those who lucid dream, she adds, "the benefits can be magnified." Mastering lucidity in dreams allows the dreamer to tackle "specific problems, seek answers or insight, stage cathartic encounters, and probe the recesses of the subconscious." Sounds like a form of magic, yes? Minimally, there are equations to divination. Pursuing such divine downloads comes naturally as a Witch; however, no one is a master initially. Sippable spellcraft becomes a helpful aid when practicing such skills as lucid dreaming.

We will employ all our senses before even drinking the tea, and the energy of each brings more of the reality connection, a tether for the dreamer. Prompting the senses teaches our brain and body that it is time for sleep. We'll deal with hearing first via music or sound. My favorite for this ritual is a ten-hour loop of ambient engine noise from a fictitious spacecraft. What sound accompanies this before-bed ritual is up to the Witch. Again, explore here. Another Witch might prefer crickets chirping, frogs peeping, or non-space-influenced white, brown, pink, gray (you pick the color) noise.

We'll also employ sight, but not in the way you engaged hearing. We want to limit our waking life sight. Make the room as dark as possible. Eliminate anything that could possibly wake the dreamer.

Next, find a scent via incense or hydrosol—or, as some Witches call it, spiritual hygiene sprays. Sandalwood is my go-to for this part. Perhaps another might choose copal. Choose an incense that brings the energy you crave at that moment. Check in with yourself when proceeding with each part of this working.

This first step has a prerequisite moon cycle where the Witch will perform a lucid dreaming "reality check" via a rubber band or bracelet on their wrist. Take that into consideration when planning on performing this magic and divination. This is more about triggering the brain and body to distinguish between waking and dream life. When first exposed to this practice, I thought it was a bit much. But it truly works, and I've used it successfully to deal with PTSD-triggered nightmares.

This tea can be sipped multiple days in a row but no more than six days continuously. The working requires a lot of a Witch's energy. Even some experts claim that frequent lucid dreams might disrupt the benefits of doing it. Use discernment. You'll need to rest and recharge from it. Alternatively, consider doing it over a long weekend retreat to dive into a lucid dreaming practice mindfully. Optionally, practice this alongside full moons or other auspicious astrological events/energies for which you want to connect to dreams.

Off to Dreamland Tea

SERVES
1

EQUIPMENT

Kettle

Tea strainer, infuser, or cheesecloth

Teacup with saucer

Incense burner

Device to play music

Preferred sleeping space

Rubber band or bracelet on wrist

Sleeping mask and lavender essential oil (optional)

INGREDIENTS

6 ounces water (options: Cancer moon, Pisces solar)

Choose 1 teaspoon—in total combination—from the following herbs:

CATNIP: Used to enhance psychic connections. Exchange this for mugwort, but please understand any contraindications first.

CHAMOMILE: This herb helps calm the nervous system for rest and sleep.

DAMIANA: This herb is used for visions to help power dreams so you do remember them. Substitute mugwort if damiana is hard to come by.

LAVENDER: Peace and calm follow this herb everywhere.

LEMON BALM: A great herb to reduce anxiety and improve mental connections. Its flavor is lovely and can boost your mood.

ORANGE PEEL: This provides a manifesting boost. Here it helps connect with dreams.

ROSE: This double-duties as protection and boosting divination abilities (e.g., dreams).

SKULLCAP: Used to help promote good sleep. Exchange this for valerian if preferred.

Instructions

1. Combine all or a few of the herbs. Experiment. The properties of the herbs are noted. None of these include stimulants (e.g., caffeine) or anything else that might prevent sleep.

2. Each day for at least one moon cycle before you will prepare and drink this tea, put a rubber band or bracelet on your non-dominant hand. Set an alarm three times a day—morning, noon, and night. When the alarm goes off, snap the rubber band and ask, "Am I dreaming?" Observe surroundings. Use senses. Let the mind decide. Do this in conjunction with step 3.

3. Each night for this same moon cycle, tend to the following senses at bedtime. Put on some music or other soothing sounds. Ring a bell, play a favorite song, or even play an instrument. Whatever the choice, be sure it's calming and is repeated sustainably. Prepare the senses and the mind. This is consciousness training.

4. Light some incense or spray a favorite spiritual spray or hydrosol. Choose something calming. Ensure the sleeping area is comfortable, dry, and secure. Eliminate sleep distractions from the sleeping area.

5. After this moon-cycle exercise of reality checks and environment creation, it is time to brew the tea. Fill tea infuser with chosen ingredients. Pour 180°F (82°C) heated water over the infuser directly into the teacup.

6. Let the tea steep for seven minutes.

7. Remove infuser. Compost the tea solids.

8. As you drink the tea before you go to sleep, keep the thought "I exercise control in my dreams" in the mind every time you sip.

9. Visualize. Allow the mind to see a successful lucid dreaming venture. See yourself asking in the dream, "Am I dreaming?" as in the reality check exercise the moon cycle before this.

10. Leave one last sip in the teacup. Cover it with the tea saucer. Turn off the lights and go to sleep. Sweet dreams!

11. When you wake from any dreams, write down or record everything you recall from your dreams right away.

12. Remove the saucer from atop the teacup and drink what you left in the teacup the night before. Write down anything more that comes to you. Notice where you were in control—where you lucidly dreamed—within the dreams.

13. Perform this ritual for at least one moon cycle (dark to full) or twenty-one days. Schedule seasonal or regular breaks from herbal teas/remedies, including this working.

Rebrew this tea in the morning to help recall or intuit the meaning of your dreams. Write down those dreams to get every detail within its message when first waking.

conjuring
SWEETNESS

Repeated elements in many of these workings are the additions of syrups and garnishes. Both serve to elevate the drink from something familiar to extraordinary—or, in our case, magical. Creating pieces and parts of these magical mixes is quite simple and approachable. A wonderful bonus to creating them homemade is knowing exactly what is going into each cup, namely the energy but also nothing, hopefully, that you don't want.

The Sweetness Connection

All you need is love, or so the famous song is titled. Regarding sippable spellcraft, love is a heavy component of the magical correspondences. That is because many drinks, especially cocktails and their nonalcoholic versions, have a sweet component.

Honey, sugar, tree syrups (maple, date), molasses, and agave correspond to love.

Some of the ingredients have additional correspondences. As you expand practice in the mixology path, compound energies as you need. For instance, honey is also purification, wisdom, and health. Maple syrup works well as a partner in divination, wealth, and luck. Date syrup brings abundance, especially where fertility is concerned. Molasses adds a bit more lust than love, given its threefold boiling done in its processing. Agave syrup, crafted from several agave species, holds the energies of banishing, binding, healing, and nurturing. Recently, the use of coconut sugar and nectar are becoming more popular. While it's not found in the workings here, if you're exploring and experimenting, know that its sweetness holds love, beauty, and clarity. Once the basics are down, you are ready to add all kinds of infusions to the syrup to create different flavor profiles and complements for other components in drinkable potions.

Which sweet source you choose will depend on what energy you seek. Each one has a particular flavor profile. Sugar is seen in many drink-weaver circles as having the right sweetness, mouthfeel, and texture, especially in something you're mixing versus brewing. Agave is surprisingly mild and delicate and is favored by those watching sugar intake. Maple syrup is prized not just for its caramel-like flavor but also for its high antioxidant content. That said, individual tastes and preferences often win out. This is another area where the Witch gets to take side paths and explore and experiment. However, success in sippable spellcraft starts by mastering the simple syrup. Doing so will set you up for all kinds of other magic and the recipe variations that follow. The easy-to-follow recipes take simple equipment and ingredients.

SIMPLE SYRUP

Equipment

  Measuring cups

  Medium saucepan

  Stirring spoon or spatula

  Funnel

  Glass jar or syrup dispenser

Ingredients

  1 cup water (options: Aries, Taurus, or Scorpio, moon or solar)

  1 cup organic granulated sugar

Instructions

1. When making this, take a moment before starting to bless the sugar with the intentions and shared energies of promoting love, and then bless the water with the energy indicative of the water choice (e.g., Aries moon for passion).

2. Heat the water in a small saucepan over medium-low heat until hot: 180°F (82°C). Do not bring to a boil.

3. Add the sugar and stir until fully dissolved. While stirring, visualize the love energy spreading. Connect with it. Feel it. Put any intentions wanted for this syrup in now; e.g., "I easily find myself seeking out the company of my loved ones to reinforce the connection."

4. Once sugar is dissolved, fully remove the pan from the heat and let it cool to room temperature before using or storing.

5. Use a funnel to transfer the simple syrup into a glass jar or syrup dispenser.

6. Label the container with the energy it holds (e.g., Taurus moon water simple syrup) and its expiration date.

7. Store it in the refrigerator for up to three weeks.

RICH SIMPLE SYRUP

The typical Southern sweet tea is made with rich simple syrup, and it is also used in lemonade or iced tea. Additionally, many non-magic-focused bartenders like rich syrup to give their cocktails extra texture and a thicker mouthfeel. This syrup is more viscous than simple syrup. To make it, follow the exact process as a simple syrup but change the ratio of sugar to water. There will be one and a half cups of sugar in the cup of water.

HONEY SIMPLE SYRUP

To create honey syrup, add one part honey and one part water to a small saucepan over medium-low heat. Remove from heat and let water return to 105°F (40°C). Stir until the honey dissolves. Do not put it in when the water is too hot or it will evaporate honey's beneficial qualities. Allow it to cool, and transfer it to an airtight container. The honey syrup will stay on the bar for up to one month and longer in the fridge. When creating this, do so on sunny days when feeling energized and full of vigor.

Base Collection of Syrups

This next section includes syrups within the spell crafts in the next sections. They feature ingredients that are easily accessible. This collection brings a variety of magical energies, too, from wildflowers to weeds. For instance, the dandelion (*Taraxacum officinale*) brings strength to our spells. They are some of the first flowers in the spring and some of the last in the fall, so their endurance energy is incredible. Although many consider them weeds, dandelions also correspond to abundance, strength, resilience, and intellectual and emotional agility. When you need the strength of Aphrodite, Hecate, or Freyja, who are all associated with the dandelion, work with dandelions. There's an earth mama/bee goddess/underworld infinity loop in these associations. Pick a lot of dandelions. You'll need about one and a half cups, which can be more than one hundred flower heads. Be sure to pick from areas that are wild and free of pesticides.

Creating this with local honey gives the syrup some big ol' life-cycle energy. The bees pollinate the dandelions, which feed their kin and help the plant create its seed so it can populate more fields of flowers, which then feeds the new brood of the bees, and so on. Check the note on making it with honey; the directions are slightly different.

This syrup will last up to three months, depending on how finely it's strained. Those little dandelion petals can slip through some sieves. Make sure to use one with a tight weave.

As for the honey-lime or lemon syrup, it is beloved for its brightness and energizing effect. It's like a little cheerleader in the body. "Let's go, Witch! You can do it!" the syrup raves. It pairs nicely with some white tea—spiked with rum or not.

Wildflowers are underappreciated. So many of them are edible and medicinal and help our ever-important pollinators. If I had to choose my favorite, wild violet would be it. Create a wild violet syrup and infuse it with intention or other energetic influences (astrology, sigils, runes, crystals, ritual) and then add a bit to cocktails, iced teas, lemonades, or wherever you need some nice sweet floral notes. However, this little wild thing is a powerhouse of magical energy. Wild violets hold the powers of protection, luck, love, lust, wishes, peace, and healing. They are a nice sweet lift for any brew you might be whipping up. Be aware that these energetic dynamos will take over gardens; frequent harvests slow them down and often make the plant healthier.

Wild violets (*Viola sororia*) are easy enough to find in spring through to the first frost. They like shady, moist, fertile soil. You will find them in understory areas—anywhere they can get a little sun at some point in the day but are sheltered from it the rest of the day. They are easily found dried and preserved, which may also be used in this recipe. Set aside the time needed to brew this up: this recipe takes a day so the flowers' oils can infuse more deeply.

The basil-lavender syrup is about robust and loving protection. The basil is about cooperation, peace, and passion. Lavender corresponds with protection. It also brings a delicate floral flavor and scent to the syrup.

Blueberries are relatively accessible throughout North America as they are one of our native bushes. Nutritionally, blueberries have a high level of antioxidants. The brain and nervous system benefit from consuming these morsels. Magically, they bring prosperity and protection. Use frozen or fresh berries. Cook frozen berries a few minutes longer.

Oleo saccharum, a fancy way to say oily sugar, is created by a lengthy maceration process. Once you learn this, you may find it's the preferred way to add sweetness for drinkable potions. It's made with citrus peels, giving it a super intense flavor. If you want subtle, oleo saccharum is not. Magically, it brings all the properties of any citrus—always cleansing and always energizing—but each has additional energies to consider. In the working below, we focus on lemons, adding confidence to that clarity and purification.

Finally, label the storage jars, including the date made.

NOTE

If you prefer to use honey instead of sugar or agave nectar, you'll need to adjust the heat when adding it so as not to remove the beneficial elements of honey. It will also take a more extended brewing period. Add a slice of lemon to the pot of dandelions and cover it with water. Cover pot and simmer on low for thirty minutes. Let steep for at least six hours or overnight. Strain through cheesecloth. Bring strained liquid to a boil, remove from heat, and let it partially cool. When the liquid is about 105°F (40°C), add a cup of honey. Stir well, allow it to cool to room temperature, and store it as indicated above. Refrigerate at least thirty minutes before use and afterward.

Dandelion Syrup

EQUIPMENT

Measuring cups and spoons

Saucepan

Wooden spoon

Fine mesh strainer

Glass syrup container or sterilized mason jar

INGREDIENTS

1½ cups fresh, pesticide-free dandelion petals

1 cup granulated sugar or agave nectar

1 cup water (options: Taurus moon, Scorpio solar)

INSTRUCTIONS

1. Combine the dandelion petals, sugar, and water in a saucepan. Add in your chosen intention: e.g., "I give this potion my gratitude for love and abundance."

2. Bring the mixture to a boil over medium heat, stirring occasionally. If this working is for future boundary magic, stir widdershins. If this working is for accepting energy (receiving, manifesting), stir sunwise.

3. Once it's reached a boil, reduce heat to low and let simmer for ten to fifteen minutes or until the mixture thickens and the petals lose their vibrancy.

4. Remove the saucepan from the heat. Cool.

5. Strain through a fine mesh strainer into a glass syrup container. Compost the petals.

6. Label and date jar (i.e., Taurus Season Dandelion Syrup 4/26/25, exp. 7/26/25).

7. Refrigerate until and after use. Good for about three months.

HONEY-LIME OR LEMON

SYRUP

EQUIPMENT

- Small saucepan
- Spatula
- Conical strainer
- Large heatproof measuring cup with pour spout
- Canning funnel
- Mason jar and lid

INGREDIENTS

- 1 cup local honey
- 2 or 3 limes or lemons plus peel(s)
- ½ cup freshly squeezed lime juice

INSTRUCTIONS

1. Bring the peels and juice to a boil in a small saucepan. Reduce heat to medium and cook until slightly reduced. Remove from heat and let cool to about 105°F (40°C).

2. Add the honey and stir well.

3. Strain into a mason jar, pressing peels to extract as much oil as possible. Cover and refrigerate for at least thirty minutes before using.

4. On the lid, mark the ingredients and date. Optionally, add a sigil or bindrune to protect the goodness of the brew. Refrigerate after use for prolonged storage of ninety days. It lasts about a month if not refrigerated.

Wild Violet Syrup

EQUIPMENT
Measuring cups

1 quart mason jar or glass bowl

Saucepan

Bain-marie or double boiler

Conical strainer

INGREDIENTS
1 cup violet flowers, lightly packed

1 cup water (options: spring equinox solar, Sagittarius moon)

1 cup sugar or agave nectar

INSTRUCTIONS
1. Gather ingredients. Pause and connect with them. Consider a small prayer of appreciation for the violet's beauty, hardiness, and magical strength.
2. If using fresh, pinch violets off at the top of the stems. Remove the green parts at the base of the flowers. These are the calyxes. This is simply to keep the flavor more consistent. Do this by twisting the petals free. Place the petals in a mason jar and set aside. Compost the calyxes.
3. Bring the water to a boil in a small saucepan.
4. Pour hot water over violet petals in mason jar. Cover. At this point, connect with the water and violet and then say your intention: e.g., "I am resilient as a violet."
5. Let the covered mason jar sit at room temperature for twenty-four hours. Get ready for the gorgeous translucent indigo color.
6. After it sits for a day, pour liquid and petals into the top of a bain-marie or double-boiler on the stove.
7. Add sugar and cook over steam from the bain-marie/double boiler. Stir often until the sugar dissolves.

8. Strain syrup through a conical strainer to remove flower petals.

9. Cool syrup until room temperature. Store in glass jars.

10. Label jars and store them in the refrigerator for up to six months.

If you prefer to use honey for this syrup, follow the method described in the abovementioned dandelion recipe and replace wild violets for the dandelion flowers.

BASIL-LAVENDER
S Y R U P

EQUIPMENT

Small saucepan with lid

Spatula

Fine mesh strainer

Bowl

Small refrigerator pitcher or other container for the final syrup

INGREDIENTS

1 cup water (options: Leo solar or Leo moon water)

1 cup sugar or agave nectar

2 tablespoons lavender flower buds

1 cup fresh basil leaves

INSTRUCTIONS

1. In a small saucepan, combine the water, sugar, and lavender, then stir three times sunwise to mix gently. Think about a favorite summertime memory, especially if it concerns strong women who influenced you. Bring to a boil over medium heat.

2. Reduce heat and simmer for one minute.

3. Remove the pot from the heat and immediately add the basil.

4. Cover and steep the mixture for thirty minutes.

5. Strain out the basil and lavender; compost the solids.

6. Save the liquid in something that pours easily.

7. Refrigerate until ready to make cocktails. It lasts up to one month.

This recipe does not lend itself to using honey because of the subtleness of the basil and lavender. These ingredients need heat. Choose agave nectar if you'd prefer something other than sugar.

Blueberry Syrup

EQUIPMENT

Saucepan

Wooden spoon

Masher utensil

Large fine mesh strainer

Quart-size storage jar

INGREDIENTS

2 cups blueberries, fresh or frozen

1 cup water (options: Aquarius moon, Virgo solar)

1 teaspoon lemon juice

1 cup sugar or agave nectar

INSTRUCTIONS

1. Cook blueberries, water, lemon juice, and sugar over low-medium heat and stir until the sugar dissolves.

2. Use a wooden spoon or potato masher to mash the blueberries as they cook. Think about mulling in extra love and patience while doing this. Simmer for about eight minutes or until the fruit has broken down. As the fruit breaks down, so do the barriers to happiness.

3. Remove from heat and allow the mixture to cool.

4. Pour mixture through a mesh strainer to remove solids.

5. Store syrup in a covered glass container for up to a week and refrigerated for up to four weeks.

Use this syrup in cocktails or teas or make tinctures with it.

OLEO SACCHARUM

EQUIPMENT

- Peeler
- Mixing bowl with cover
- Fine mesh strainer
- Muddler (optional)
- Pint-size storage jar

INGREDIENTS

- 1 cup lemon peels (about 2 lemons)
- Sugar, enough to cover lemon peels: about ¾ cup

INSTRUCTIONS

1. Peel lemons with the vegetable peeler, leaving the white pith behind.

2. Place peels in a covered mixing bowl, add sugar, then massage with the hands until the lemon oil aroma is strong. Alternatively, use a muddler here if you're prone to paper cuts. While massaging, put in the intention of clearing away the nonsense blocking progress or happiness.

3. Let it rest like this for up to twenty-four hours, periodically massaging it more and covering it between massaging times.

4. Strain out the citrus peels, firmly pressing on them in the strainer to extract all the oil. Take a few minutes. Press out the blockages to your happiness or goals.

5. Compost solids.

6. Store oil in the fridge until and after use. The oil lasts for about a week.

Garnishing Goodness

One of the reasons a cocktail at a fancy bar is fun is because the garnishes really can make it an occasion. Taking the time and slicing nice portions of citrus or stabbing some olives with a pretty skewer elevates the magic, not predominantly because it's decorative but because those elements add more energy and particular properties to round out the working. I have shown several ways to work in magical layering throughout the book. Here are several more.

If you have access to duck eggs, I encourage you to try them with these garnishes; however, chicken eggs work fine, too. Eggs are healing and shielding. Duck eggs add a layer of comfort as if wrapped in a down jacket. Ducks also carry the energy of endurance, so sugared basil created with duck egg gives more strength for the working. You'll remember that basil is full of protection, abundance, and love. Add some sugar to double that caring and cherishing. Like many garnishes, this one won't keep but for one day. Only make what will be used immediately.

Herbs used as spears for garnishes have a long history in mixology. They add aroma to drinks, which technically changes the taste. The following recipe for sugared tarragon spears brings the magical properties of expansion. Sugar is love. Use the tarragon spear to stir a drink and slowly add more love and the expansion of said love with this garnish.

Sugared berries sweeten healing workings since they feature fresh blueberries and raspberries. Energetically, raspberries bring abundance, healing, and protection. Nutritionally, they, like blueberries, are high in antioxidants. Best of all? They taste divine.

SUGARED
BASIL

EQUIPMENT

A handled bowl

Whisk

Basting brush

Wire rack inside a baking sheet

Airtight container

Skewers

INGREDIENTS

1 large egg white

1 teaspoon water (options: Aries moon water, Scorpio solar water)

Up to 24 basil leaves

½ cup sugar

INSTRUCTIONS

1. Whisk the egg white with water until frothy. This may take a minute. Be patient.

2. Working with one basil leaf at a time, brush a thin layer of the whisked egg white onto the basil; think of marrying the magic of the egg white to the basil.

3. Sprinkle the basted leaves with sugar.

4. Gently put on the skewer, creating a loose S shape with the leaves.

5. Transfer to a wire rack inside a baking sheet and let cure until dry and dense. Depending on the climate, this could take about an hour or two.

6. Store in an airtight container at room temperature for one day.

Candied Tarragon Spears

Equipment

Dish towel

Wire rack that fits inside baking sheet

2 baking sheets

Whisk

Clean paintbrush

Parchment paper

Ingredients

Fresh tarragon stems (at least 4 inches long), bottom leaves removed to reveal your garnish skewer

1 egg white

1 teaspoon water (options: Capricorn solar, Aries moon)

Ultrafine sugar

Instructions

1. Wash and dry herb stems thoroughly, gently blotting them with a clean dish towel. Lay the herb spears on a wire rack that has been placed inside a baking sheet. Set aside.

2. Whisk together the egg white and water until frothy. This typically takes about three minutes if whisking heartily. Be patient.

3. Using the paintbrush, coat both sides of the herb with the egg wash. Do this lightly. Do not allow egg pools to remain on the tarragon leaves.

4. Sprinkle sugar over both sides of the coated herb leaf. Feel free to re-sprinkle any sugar that lands on the baking sheet back onto the herb spears.

5. When the herbs are well coated, move the cooling rack to another baking sheet that has been lined with parchment paper. Let dry overnight.

6. Store in an airtight jar for up to one year in the fridge.

SUGARED BERRIES

EQUIPMENT

2 small ramekins or prep bowls

Freezer tray or ice cube tray

Freezer storage container

INGREDIENTS

Small handful of fresh raspberries and blueberries

1 tablespoon warm honey

2 to 3 tablespoons sugar

INSTRUCTIONS

1. Pick out at least a dozen berries, about six raspberries and six blueberries.

2. Add a good dollop of honey to a ramekin and zap it in the microwave for about 15 to 20 seconds.

3. Add a couple tablespoons of sugar to the second ramekin.

4. Roll the fruit pieces in the honey and then roll in the sugar. See the honey as love and the sugar as protection.

5. Place on an ice cube tray in the freezer for four hours. Once flash-frozen, remove it from the tray and put it in a freezer container.

6. Sugared berries last about two weeks in the freezer.

TAKING back DRINK

In chapter 1, I covered the history of our ancestors—women and those considered "other" by the overculture—as brewers, distillers, and spirit wranglers, and how their knowledge, livelihood, and more were taken from them. In this chapter, we'll energetically bring the goodness of drink back. Imagine taking the drinking glass out of the hands of the overculture and gigantic corporations and back into the hands of magical people. When we do this, Witches begin to unbind the energy and right the wrongs of so many years ago. Bring that brewing—that knowledge—and the magic back to the hearth and home, back to Witches. As we raise glasses, we heal those ancestral wounds and take back craft brews and the Craft, one drink at a time.

This does not mean that you're pressing apples for cider or required to do any other intensive brewing. My Scorpio sun does not do required; there is no insistence. If you are called and have the means, go for it. Share with fellow Witches. Make friends. Rather, I'm encouraging you to look at ingredients and consider their energy. Is it known how and where they are grown? Is it close by? Supporting the local agriculture community is strong and positive energy. Again, growing it yourself is unnecessary. Simply know the ingredients. Use that deep witchy discernment because you have that energetic connection.

As you do this, be aware of things that can make that healing step backward, namely overindulging in spirits—or Spirit. We're going for balance. With the lowercase spirits, an easy way to prevent accidental overindulgence is eating something when having cocktails. People have long been pairing bits of food—appetizers, hors d'oeuvres, canapes, starters, antipasti, tapas, small plates—when imbibing with alcohol. Doing so slows the rate of intoxication since the longer alcohol stays in the stomach along with all that food, it's not as quickly absorbed into the body (Zakhari 2006). The food acts like a shield to the arrows of alcohol.

You may have already noted the occasional food pairing suggestions. But if you're not a fan of the suggestion, something simple, like cheese and crackers, works. Or some peanut butter and celery. The point is to include a little something in the belly when you're imbibing. Consuming some food that includes carbohydrates, proteins, and a little fat and salt provides a sustained release of energy, allowing more consistent blood sugar levels. Not eating and then drinking means the effects of the alcohol will be faster through the body's systems. Alcohol is absorbed more quickly into the bloodstream on an empty stomach. This can lead to a higher blood alcohol concentration (BAC), which means faster intoxication. Remember, slow magic can be stronger magic. Drink responsibly. Drunk flying broom accidents are not pretty. The world needs you.

Do keep in mind the flavors of the drinks and how the choice of snack blend will enhance the experience and elevate the magic. Many of the cocktails have that conjured sweetness from chapter 13, so perhaps they lean more toward savory options.

If you practice a sober lifestyle, there remain choices here within these spells. The other elements in the drink are powerful as well. Once again, the intention is the energetic foundation of all the workings. Everything else builds on that. Nonalcoholic variations exist for most of the following.

Sweet, Slow Magic

This working happens over a couple of days, as its primary ingredients need to be made ahead of time, including the sugared berries garnish, the blueberry syrup, and the oleo saccharum (the latter three learned in chapter 13). When the Witch needs to focus on the romantic love in life, it's worth the extra planning and time, and it's also delicious. Make lots because you're going to want more than one, but please make sure you're not driving anywhere and that you're practicing moderation. The raspberry gin is readily available at local fine retailers. The labels may say pink or bramble on them. If you're a busy Witch, get store-bought blueberry syrup, too.

Regarding tools, the ease of a cobbler cocktail shaker with a built-in strainer for this drink is handy. If there is a lack of space in the freezer for laying a tray for the sugared berries, an old-school ice tray holds the berries just fine.

Patching Things Up Cocktail

EQUIPMENT

- Vegetable peeler
- Plastic bag or covered small glass mixing bowl to make the oleo saccharum
- Saucepot for making the oleo saccharum and blueberry syrup
- Wooden spoon or potato masher
- Fine mesh strainer
- A small tray for the freezer for the garnish berries
- Bar tools: cocktail shaker, strainer, jigger, channel knife
- 2 small ramekins for making the sugared berries
- Collins glasses
- Garnish skewer or pick

INGREDIENTS

- 1 to 2 limes
- Crushed ice
- 2 ounces oleo saccharum
- 3 ounces raspberry gin
- Blueberry syrup for drizzling
- Sugared berries for garnish

INSTRUCTIONS

1. A day before, make the oleo saccharum, blueberry syrup, and sugared berries found in chapter 13.

2. Using the channel knife, carve some lime pigtails with one of the limes; set aside.

3. Use a veggie peeler to get a couple of lime peels to express over the drink; set aside.

4. Add crushed ice to the cocktail shaker.

5. Add 1 ounce oleo saccharum and 1½ ounces raspberry gin per serving.

6. Whip, shake, and roll the cocktail shaker, then strain into a tall glass with ice.

7. Drizzle the blueberry syrup on top and express one lime peel.

8. Take frozen berries and lime pigtail and wrap them around a garnish pick.

9. Serve with the following toast:

May our love be protected

May our happiness be centered

May we be grounded in now

Stronger together and how!

NONALCOHOLIC VARIATION

Replace the raspberry gin by muddling some raspberries, adding a little soda or tonic water, and then straining the berries.

Feed the garnishes to your happy hour date if you want to up the romance.

Persephone Rising

Often spring can be a season of frustration. As the sun is higher and closer to us, and as we start to peel the layers of woolies off, winter's cold blows back in and reminds us that the season is far from over. This recipe puts the rose back in the cheeks and the fire in the belly and maybe even activates that heart center—or, if chakra yoga is a part of individual practice, anahata.

This recipe is not quick. The strawberry-basil-infused tequila and rose salt take time to ready. This magic takes a small amount of planning ahead. This is one of the recipes where you'll use the mortar and pestle. A food processor works, too. Alternatively, substitute a small coffee grinder for a mortar and pestle.

If dried rose petals aren't in the cupboard, find an herbalist or Hedge Witch to help. Sometimes the bulk food section of the local food co-op has them. The recipe calls for preparing this in a punch bowl, but you can choose to make individual drinks, too. The punch bowl serves ten, so divide the measurements by ten to make individual cocktails.

Cheers!

ROSÉ MARGARITA
P U N C H

Equipment

- Mortar and pestle, food processor, or coffee grinder
- Punch bowl and ladle
- Sterilized quart-size mason jar with plastic lid or other such container
- Large fine mesh strainer
- Large bowl or measuring cup with pour spout
- Rocks or punch glasses
- Small plate for salting rim
- Garnish skewers or cocktail picks

Ingredients

- 10 ounces strawberry-basil-infused blanco tequila (instructions in step 1 below)
- 5 ounces lime juice, freshly squeezed
- 4 ounces agave syrup
- One bottle (750 ml) sparkling rosé
- Ice cubes
- 1½ cup strawberries, sliced; 1 cup for the tequila, ½ cup for garnish
- ½ to 1 cup fresh basil leaves
- One bottle (750 mil) blanco tequila
- Lime wheels, garnish
- 4 tablespoons fine sea salt
- 1 tablespoon dried rose petals

Instructions

1. First, make the strawberry-basil-infused blanco tequila. Combine 1 cup sliced strawberries and ½ cup fresh basil leaves in a glass mason jar. Pour the bottle of tequila over it. Seal the jar tightly and let it sit out of direct sunlight, unrefrigerated, for three to five days.

2. Shake daily while imagining that you are shaking off the winter sloth and heating up the home with love.

3. After the allotted time, strain out the solids and compost them, then rebottle the infused tequila. The infused tequila is traditionally kept in the fridge, but it's unnecessary. While straining and bottling this concoction, ruminate on the color, warmth, and vigor it conjures.

4. Make the rose salt. Add sea salt and dried rose petals to a mortar and pestle and gently grind. While grinding, focus on the breath. Bring the belly into the ribs, stack the spine, and breathe as you grind. Put relaxation energy into the salt. Put half of the mixture on a plate for glass rimming. Store the remaining rose salt in a 4-ounce mason jar with a plastic lid as salt and metal don't mix.

5. To make the drink, combine tequila, lime juice, and agave syrup in the punch bowl.

6. Add ice cubes and stir with a ladle to mix.

7. Top with the sparkling rosé.

8. Rim punch or rocks glasses with rose salt before serving. Arrange garnish of sliced strawberries on skewers or cocktail picks for guests to add to their glasses.

9. Enjoy, knowing warmth is inside and all around you, and it won't hurt to be outside soon. If feeling particularly energetic, raise this toast:

> *Cheers to the Wheel of the Year as it cycles and shifts*
> *With the promise of spring, Nature's warm gifts.*
> *A time of planting, a time of rebirth*
> *When new life arises inside us from Mother Earth.*
> *We have a new dawning, an eager fresh start*
> *A chance, once again, to follow our heart.*
> *Rejoice in the promise that the equinox brings*
> *And may we find balance and peace with all things.*

NONALCOHOLIC VARIATION

Replace the tequila with either agave juice (not syrup) or coconut water. Another option is to take strawberry juice and infuse it with basil.

Balancing Masculine Energy

Returning sippable spellcraft into the hands of the people must pay special attention to women and their bonds as a way of healing past and future. When women work together to rebalance the energies in our world away from its patriarchal leanings, they take care of business in a way only women can. We stand today to continue the work of those who came before us. That includes the fight against patriarchy, which we still endure as our ancestors did. It may be different in many aspects, but it's absolutely the same in oppressive systems, and some say we're headed backward. The importance of what has been defined as feminine energy has often been downplayed. In the mixology workings within this chapter, you'll begin to heal that, sip by sip. We'll connect to the feminine within ourselves, our relationships, and our spiritual practice.

Connection to the sacred feminine—the yin, if you prefer—is a core part of many a Witch's practice. Instinctually, we know that this is both resistance and inclusion. We understand that it is necessary. Regardless of gender, this next drink spell helps find that feminine power, connect with the matriarchal ancestors, or identify your circle. Or, if desired, connect with a feminine deity, often noted as the Primal Mother that flames inside all of us, regardless of Craft path. When we connect with this sacred feminine energy, we're not just balancing the scales of energy here on earth but also conjuring harmony within and without. We also balance the scales for all those alewives, brewsters, and wise women victimized in innumerable ways under oppressive cultural values.

The ingredients needed for this next magical mix are like a summertime hug from a favorite auntie—hence its name. Inspired by matriarchal ancestors, finding harmony within that bilateral spectrum of male and female energies continues in their name today. Basil brings peace. Lavender layers on protection. Lemon focuses on happiness. Gin's magical properties are health and energy. Last but not least is sugar and its forever love properties.

Find fresh lavender and basil at the local food co-op or farmers market. Super busy Witches may find flavored simple syrups readily available and already brewed, especially at markets featuring extensive selections of liquors.

Sitting with the Aunties

EQUIPMENT

Cocktail shaker

Cocktail strainer

Cutting board and knife

Glass (Witch's choice)

SERVES
1

INGREDIENTS

1½ ounces gin

1 ounce fresh lemon juice

¾ ounce basil-lavender syrup

Ice cubes

½ ounce tonic or club soda or sparkling water

Fresh basil, lavender, and lemon half moon for garnish (optional)

INSTRUCTIONS

1. To an empty cocktail shaker, add gin, juice, and syrup.

2. Add ice to fill the shaker almost to the top. Shake vigorously for about 30 seconds or until cold to the touch. See the temp change via condensation on the shaker.

3. Strain into a glass with fresh ice and top with a choice of tonic, soda, or sparkling water. Garnish with a lemon-basil-lavender spear, using the lavender as the skewer.

4. Serve immediately.

NONALCOHOLIC VARIATION

Zero-proof gin is available everywhere. It brings the botanicals of gin without the alcoholic effect. Pick something more herbal instead of fruity. There are a variety of flavors available. Alternatively, simply skip the gin and increase the level of tonic, club soda, or sparkling water.

Smart Ancestral Work

This next drink's energy focuses on boosting strength and energetic protection and clearing the way for connection when working with the ancestors. It is essential to send out the right energy in order to receive and welcome appropriate connections and messages from them.

Brew this up to use when we naturally seem to migrate thoughts of our ancestors—during Samhain or Yule or if personal tradition focuses on ancestor work at Imbolc or Beltane. However, this is available whenever individual practice calls for it.

This working uses hawthorn berries (*Crataegus monogyna*). Hawthorn has a long magical history in Britain, where it was planted to mark sacred wells (Cunningham 1985, 132). In places like Serbia and Croatia, it was used as a ward for any creature associated with the underworld (University of Washington, n.d.). Hawthorn holds Mars energy and is considered to be connected to the Goddess of Witches, Hekate. Wreaths and branches of hawthorn were used to protect livestock from evildoers. And, as many may know, hawthorn is sacred to those who practice Druidry. This drink holds the energy of protection. You may source these dried berries anywhere that typically sells bulk tea.

This brew also features cinnamon, which deepens our intuition and brings abundance. The vanilla bean holds the energy of passion. Don't spend much money on the red wine here. Don't get something awful; decent wines for less than ten dollars are perfectly acceptable for this working. I would advise you to avoid anything that says fruit wine (e.g., strawberry wine). Although pleasant to drink in some circumstances, in this working it'll be too sickly sweet, potentially attracting all the ancestors that would love-bomb their way into the connection and block things from those whose connection you need.

Like the living, there is a spectrum of energies emitted from the realm of spirit, or what some Witches call "the veil" (Auryn 2017). Because of that, we bring cardamom into the brew. It is often used in sex magic, but for our purposes here, it is for the energetic properties of courage. Meanwhile, allspice's magical property is to help the Witch go between the living and the dead, moving from one side to the other of that "veil" with ease.

Behind the Veil also uses blackcurrant syrup, but blackberry syrup is a good alternative and likely easier for most readers to find at any given market or in gardens and wild fields. Both syrups' energies are all about truth and are swallowed most sweetly. This helps set an aura of kindness around the connections and is like a neon sign that says, "Be kind or leave."

This is another slow drink that takes a moon cycle. Consider starting this on a full moon and then working the ancestor connection magic near the dark moon. It's easier to see into something if you're in the dark and they are in the spotlight. Consider charging the wine under a moon such as a Scorpio full moon or on astrological Beltane, even if you don't use the wine until closer to Samhain.

It will keep for a couple of months. If refrigerated, it will last up to six months. After refrigeration, allow it to come to room temperature before drinking, for taste's sake. However, if you prefer it chilled, that is not a problem.

BEHIND THE VEIL
C O C K T A I L

EQUIPMENT

- Measuring cups and spoons
- Sterilized quart mason jar with leakproof lid
- A cleansing smoke bundle
- Matches or lighter
- Crystal to help connect with ancestor, such as lepidolite, fluorite, or amethyst (optional)
- An offering cup or bowl
- Ancestor altar or personal altar
- Rocks glass
- Fine mesh strainer
- Pitcher or mason jar for storage

SERVES
2

INGREDIENTS

- ½ cup fresh or dried hawthorn berries
- 2 cinnamon sticks
- 1 vanilla bean, sliced lengthwise
- 1 teaspoon whole cardamom berries
- ½ teaspoon whole allspice berries
- 2 tablespoons blackcurrant or blackberry syrup
- 2 cups full-moon-charged red table wine

INSTRUCTIONS

1. Immediately following a full moon, gather jar and cleansing bundle. If using the optional crystal for this potion, be sure it's charged, too.
2. Light cleansing smoke bundle and move the smoke inside and around the jar, saying, "Air, fire, water, earth; cleanse; dismiss, dispel." Visualize any negativity departing the jar.
3. Add all dry ingredients to the jar.
4. Pour the syrup and wine over the dry ingredients. Put on the no-spill lid.

5. Shake the jar to combine everything thoroughly while saying this prayer:

> *I call upon those who have lived on this earth, whose energy flows through my energy, my ancestors; my kindred. I call on those who dreamed the best for future generations and upon whose lives my own was built. It is with gratitude and deep appreciation I call upon them to teach me. Show me the way.*

6. Keep the jar in a cool, dark place. Optionally, place a crystal that helps amplify ancestral connection near the jar. Infuse until the dark moon, shaking the brew daily and saying the prayer daily while shaking the jar.

7. At the dark moon, decant and strain this cocktail-infused wine. Put the strainer over a storage jar/pitcher and strain the liquid from the brewing jar into the pitcher. Discard the spices in the compost; return the crystal to an altar where it can be cleansed.

8. Keep somewhere cool and out of direct sunlight until use.

NONALCOHOLIC VARIATION

Zero-proof red wine is available. However, perhaps choose the more economical cranberry or pomegranate juice. Some no-alcohol red wines can be as costly as their alcoholic counterparts.

Firming Up Finances

Many modern Witches have spent time doing spells to survive in our capitalistic society. Many Witches who read for the public often have clients asking about career, jobs, employment, or finances. Additionally, I often see trends in spring and post-Yule with dream interpretation clients that money is a big focus of their dreams' symbolisms, signs, and messages.

The focus on the wallet is not bad, but a better start is directing our energies toward good health, without which it is difficult to achieve good wealth. Good health is the prime focus of the following drink. Plus, it looks pretty and is super tasty. Sometimes we need something special to boost us, so why not help boost the health and wealth coming to us?

Before making this drink, a small quantity of meditation happens. It doesn't have to be ritual in nature, either. Do this with a partner or housemate, even kids—they will relish this goodness here. Visualize what being healthy looks like for yourself. Be open to abundance. Know in heart and mind you are prosperous. Don't wish. Know. Allow.

This drink features pineapple juice, which has the energy of abundance. Its energy helps us gain abundant healing, money, protection, and love. It is paired with sparkling pear cider, which holds the energies of longevity and money. The pomegranate arils and juice give us fertility, creativity, and money energies. Honey syrup is used for purification, health, love, sex, happiness, spirituality, and wisdom. Whipped cream provides not only fun but more wealth and money, à la prosperity!

This working does have some follow-up homework. When receiving a boost in health and wealth, please give back. As Witches we understand that sacred exchange of energy. It's a spiral that is never-ending. Volunteer with an organization doing work you support or provide a monetary donation to the same or both. The spell is not complete until this is done.

Straws are called for in this bit of mystical bartending, but they're optional. Reusable glass and metal straws are an eco-friendly move. Find some dishwasher safe ones and invest in a straw brush for extra scrubbing when the party runs late and the dishes sit too long before washing. Many reusable straw sets are sold with their own cleaning brushes.

SHOW ME THE MONEY
MOCKTAIL

EQUIPMENT

- Collins glass
- Bartender's spoon
- Reusable drinking straw (optional)

INGREDIENTS

- 3 ounces pineapple juice, chilled
- ½ ounce honey simple syrup (options: Capricorn moon, Libra solar)
- 1 ounce pomegranate juice, chilled
- 2 ounces sparkling pear cider, chilled
- Whipped cream for garnish
- Pomegranate arils for garnish

SERVES 1

INSTRUCTIONS

1. Into the glass, pour in the pineapple juice; as you do, say, "I welcome abundance."

2. Next, pour in the honey syrup; say, "I easily find my way to good health."

3. Add the pomegranate juice; say, "I deserve extra income."

4. Pour the pear cider over the other ingredients, making sure you leave room for the whipped cream; say, "I am flourishing."

5. Take the bartender's spoon and gently move it sunwise nine times, saying, "Health and wealth to mine and me, by fruit and cream and honey bee; so it is."

6. Add the whipped cream and pomegranate arils, visualizing what health and wealth look like to you. There are no words right now. Put that image in the mind alongside the addition of cream and garnish.

7. The last part of the spell is to allow each person drinking these mocktails to say aloud the abundance they want most, such as "I am choosing healthier paths daily" or "I share because I am able" or even "Bring me the money, honey!" Sip to health and wealth.

8. After a moon cycle, give back based on the abundance that has come to you. The spell is not complete until this energy is exchanged. Once complete, expect the cycle to continue: health, wealth, sharing, caring, rinse, and repeat.

Make it into a cocktail by substituting the sparkling pear cider with a hard pear cider. The energy is the same, but how it's received may differ slightly. Another option is cherry brandy.

Braving Battles

Thinking back to the grandmothers and grandfathers that came before us—heck, even our parents' generation—there are straightforward ways in which our lives in the twenty-first century have improved. I often think about how many generations survived so much with so little so that the stars aligned for me to arrive here. It's easy to imagine them looking at us getting ice cream delivered to our doors as if we're royalty. Bravery was a requisite in their lives, and it is still required now to survive (despite ice cream). Whatever the battles in life, we need to do hard things. Sometimes we need a little boost to have the courage to be brave and face what is ahead.

Fortune Favors Boldness is for when we need to channel their bravery and fortify our mettle. Take a moment and reflect while working with the energies of the drink; find some awareness. This then breeds more boldness in our steps. Be sure to do so with a friend or family member who also feels less than robust. It's like having a battle buddy in the war to create peace and harmony in our lives.

This working will be what we call a top shelf drink. As a Witch, we constantly strive to improve, do better, and live better. Much like aligning the chakras in a yoga practice, we can use this potion to get the different parts of ourselves back in equilibrium—to tune into our fortune and boldly go, even in the face of doubt. This can be a heady drink, which is one of the reasons it's only an occasional, maybe a once-a-season drink. Therefore, it requires the best ingredients.

This drink recipe is an oldie but goodie. I learned to make it early on in my bartending career. However, I might have found it in an entirely different format, as many drinks have similar names. For this version, it is a rather stout drink, and the leading spirit is vodka. Magically, vodka, like most white spirits, elevates the ingredients with which it's made. The good stuff will be located behind the tender or in a pretty but locked display case. Some vodka on the top shelf of the easy-access aisle works for this. Vodka is naturally a neutral flavor, so spending extra is not necessary. But if vodka is the preferred spirit, and it may be given its magical properties, have them unlock that case. Maybe set an intention to only use that bottle for special magic like Fortune Favors Boldness. Although vodka can be distilled from just about anything, traditionally, it's made with potatoes. Potatoes hold the correspondence to earth, and their properties are all about compassion and protection. Then, you will work with compassion for yourself and rely on protective energy to keep you from more distress. Considering how vodka pairs with the other ingredients, you'll want to avoid the flavored vodkas.

In my humble witchy opinion, this drink also features some of the best sweet vermouths. It is a sweet vermouth called Carpano Antica Formula. The recipe for this brew goes back to 1786 and was developed by Antonio Benedetto Carpano. He was an herbalist and alchemist—okay, distiller. He likely did things other than brew booze, but that was what he was famous for—creating the aperitif of "vermouth," which he derived from the German word *wemuth*, meaning wormwood. Every time I pour a small quantity of this, I think about this pioneering Italian herbalist growing, harvesting, and fermenting wormwood and other herbs with the red wine. When drinking it, Antonio and all his descendants share their personal magic. That's pretty powerful. A small bottle will run about twenty dollars, but only small amounts are used in most drinks; therefore, in my experience, it lasts awhile.

You'll need a fortified wine, too: sherry, aka Fino sherry or Manzanilla sherry, which is fino sherry produced and matured around Sanlúcar de Barrameda. Either way, they are both dry white wine, aged for at least two years under a layer of flor yeast. A decent Manzanilla sherry will run about twenty dollars; consider it since the sherry is the vehicle for the vodka and vermouth. You'll find many producers who qualify for the Manzanilla label, but they all work with the palomino grape. You taste more of the wine and less of the harder alcohol. Magically, it's like wine and raises energy to celebration levels. Because it's sherry, the magical properties are a bit leveled up because it's been fortified and aged. Try a connection exercise with the sherry, and don't be surprised if you taste the salt spray of the Atlantic Ocean.

Cointreau is an orange liquor that is like drinking sunshine. This element in the working brings the "clear the decks and start fresh" energy. It is also lovely as a small aperitif before dinner. Its orange goodness will remind you to view everything from the perspective of love.

Edible flowers are featured here and are available from early spring through late autumn. There is the option to choose one or a combination; you decide. You might choose from the following:

* **Pansies** for love
* **Violas** for healing
* **Marigolds** for protection
* **Borage** for courage
* **Squash blossoms** for psychic connection
* **Roses** for love
* **Lavender** for peace
* **Nasturtium** for harmony
* **Brassica flowers** for protection
* **Herb blossoms** for health

Another option is to simply choose a small amount of all of them. Many farmers markets and food co-ops will stock edible flowers. Explore and find which you prefer or pick one based on its magical correspondences, or properties. It is included in this working to remind us to sometimes look for things we would not typically do to achieve balance (i.e., eating flowers). Once again, this ingredient is optional.

Fortune Favors Boldness

EQUIPMENT

Cocktail shaker and strainer

Bar jigger

Rocks glass

Divination tools (optional)

INGREDIENTS

SERVES
2

Ice (options: Gemini moon, Virgo sun, equinox)

1 ounce vodka (feel free to replace with gin or white rum)

½ ounce Carpano Antica Formula sweet vermouth

2 ounces Manzanilla or fino sherry

½ ounce Cointreau orange liqueur

Seasonal edible flowers for garnish (optional)

INSTRUCTIONS

1. Fill cocktail shaker with ice halfway. Add the vodka, vermouth, sherry, and Cointreau. Shake until condensation appears on the shaker.

2. Strain into a rocks glass.

3. Garnish with edible flowers.

4. You can double the recipe to share with a business partner or friend, then share the spell below. If you're a solopreneur, say both parts of the toast.

5. Toast to regain balance, peace, ultimate harmony, and establish a good equilibrium. Feel free to share verse with all present.

   WITCH #1: To balance: may we find that delicate status between work and leisure, ambition and contentment, the yin and yang of life.

   WITCH #2: To peace: let us cultivate the tranquility that dwells within our hearts and extend it outward to touch the lives of those around us.

WITCH #1: To harmonize our lives, may we listen to the symphony of existence, where every note, every voice, and every living thing plays a part.

WITCH #2: Here's to the journey we undertake, individually and collectively, toward a life imbued with the energies that unite us in strength, diversity, and abundance.

BOTH TOGETHER: Let us raise our glasses high with hope: to balance, to peace, to harmony. All of this or better. So it is!

Enjoy a drink together and have a conversation where each participant gets an opportunity to vent, ask for counsel, or even give one another some divination (runes, tarot, or other). Sip slowly; this is a potent cocktail. Serve this with a water back (a fancy bartender way to say a glass of plain water alongside).

Nonalcoholic Variation

Use a zero-proof replacement for the vodka, sweet vermouth, and sherry. Many of these nonalcoholic beverages are infused with botanicals, so there is some extra magical plant energy there. As for the Cointreau, substitute some simple orange syrup or oleo saccharum. Edible flowers are a must in the mocktail version.

Rally 'Round the Kindred

Whether it's a birthday, anniversary, graduation, promotion, or other important milestone, it's important to celebrate—even the tiny things. Creating a drink to signify that recognition of success, especially while kindred and community rally around one particular individual, creates a circle of goodness that permeates the celebration and beyond. Not that a reason is needed to create this Celebration Cider Punch, but it's meant to be shared with a large group. If supplying the ale for the coven's cakes and ale, this is a surefire win.

The magic here is all about elevation. It's also fun to elevate the good stuff; it can't all be realignments, cleansings, clearings, or manifesting. Relishing the moment, the accomplishment, or the benchmark is needful magic. Whatever the celebration, bring out this punch. Watch the good vibes permeate everyone.

The whiskey is a blessing of additional abundance. This spirit is made of barley, ruled by Venus, and corresponds to the earth. Witches use whiskey's energy toward money, fertility, and sex. Here, it's to make these good times fertile and create more opportunities for celebrations and punch-making.

Apples, also a Venusian ingredient, bring love, health, and peace to the punch. Cut them into stars, and you're connecting the stardust in all of us to the brew. Its partner, lemon juice, brings in watery moon energy and happiness. Plus, it keeps the apple stars exceptionally bright and fresh in the punch bowl. Apples and ginger beer are an excellent pairing. The ginger beer is bubbling with love and abundance energies. Although it's called beer, it's not alcoholic.

The ice is another way to layer on even more magic. It also looks fantastic when taking the time to create ice molds for gatherings and celebrations. Depending on what the celebration is, the mold choice may echo it. There are so many cool ones from which to choose. An ice-ring mold with star-cut apples or other festive things like edible flowers looks festive for a punch bowl. Regardless of the choice, those shapes have their energies and symbols. Know what is in hand before proceeding.

CELEBRATION CIDER
P U N C H

EQUIPMENT

- Punch bowl set or party decanter
- Ice mold(s) of moon water or fruit puree (optional)
- Medium mixing bowl
- Cutting board and paring knife
- Wooden spoon

SERVES
7

INGREDIENTS

- Ice (molded; optional)
- Full moon water for washing punch bowl/party decanter
- 1 apple, sliced into stars (optional)
- 2 tablespoons lemon juice (if using the apple stars)
- 4 cups apple cider
- 1 cup whiskey
- 1 bottle ginger beer (1½ cups)
- ½ cup simple cane syrup
- 2 to 3 whole cinnamon sticks

INSTRUCTIONS

1. Make sure you've planned and have the ice molds ready. If not, have some ice to fill the punch bowl or drink decanter.

2. Wash the bowl/decanter with full moon water. While drying bowl/decanter, imagine the celebration going smoothly and everyone's spirits being jolly. Once dry, set aside.

3. If using the apple stars to garnish the punch, slice them now.

4. Put the apple stars in the mixing bowl and sprinkle them with some lemon juice. Lightly coat the apples in the lemon juice; don't soak them. Set aside.

5. Inside the bowl/decanter, combine the apple cider, whiskey, ginger beer, and syrup. Add love energies and positive intentions while stirring the wooden spoon thirty-three times sunwise. For example:

*Let's celebrate the big and small milestones that
mark the journeys that define us, our kindred,
and our community. At the benchmarks that we
gather in joy, may we also find ourselves deep in
gratitude and savoring the moments of the simple
pleasures in life. May our hearts warm, connect, and
cherish one another. All of this or better; so it is.*

6. Rub the cinnamon sticks against each other above the punch, saying, "Cinnamon, cinnamon, strong and true; lend your magic to this brew." Put those sticks and one more into the bowl/ decanter and stir thirteen times sunwise.

7. Add ice and garnishes if using. Serve in health, happiness, and longevity.

NONALCOHOLIC VARIATION

Replace the whiskey with some cranberry juice or a zero-proof version with a splash of sparkling lemon water. Or add a shot of apple cider vinegar with a teaspoon of vanilla extract.

Magical Electrician

One of the hardest things I've had to learn in life is changing my default setting to glom onto the worst possible outcome. While studying psychology, I learned the term "stinking thinking" and dove into working on that during personal therapy (Kirschman 2020). It was hard to break the stinking thinking pattern in a mindset. When pummeled with multiple traumatic events and then left to pick up the pieces, it is easy to see how our human computer might get stuck in a lousy algorithm. However, it doesn't serve us.

Stinking thinking can be a significant problem in being our most authentic selves and living our best lives. Negative thought patterns are often the brain trying to protect itself. Thank you, monkey mind. Creating a ritual focusing on changing that bad habit of always assuming the worst is a natural path for many practitioners. To stop the future-tripping, as I call it, or carrying shizzle that isn't yours to carry, the Witch works the energy of a whole lot of sage, among other magical things.

This ritual suggests summer solstice or Gemini moon water. Summer is an excellent time to work on yourself, especially if there is a struggle with the stinking thinking. Although introspection or self-work always seems more traditional during deep winter, the sun's power is helpful and healing here. Also, Gemini energy is all about adaptability and pursuits of the mind. You want that energy here. In a pinch, some Mabon water—charged under the fall equinox sun—will work here, too.

A good muddler or mortar and pestle is needed for this drink. When mashing these herbs together, we are tuning into higher consciousness and taking a controlled action toward empowerment, as sage and rosemary lend themselves to this energetically.

You'll need dandelion simple syrup. The dandelion helps us get to a place where we can understand our emotions.

Cherry juice is a big part of this drink. Cherry and herbs may not sound like a delectable combo, but it is. Cherry provides some creativity, which a practitioner may find themselves in need of challenging their stinking thinking and learning to be kind to themselves and focus on the things in life that make them happy—all the things, from the dog's wagging tail to their kiddo getting engaged. This is something to do from full moon to dark moon.

Brandy is distilled wine that's been aged, typically in oak barrels. Like wine, brandy is used in workings to amplify the energies of the other elements in the spell. The flavors of brandy and cherry together are sublime, rich, and wonderful. And wonderfulness to ourselves is part of this working. Remember: the Witch is the magic; the drink is the spell's vehicle.

The borage flowers are optional, but they also bring the courage to face that stinking thinking, change our patterns, and smell the flowers along the way.

The Witch is the magic; the drink is the spell's vehicle!

Nah-Nah Stinking Thinking

EQUIPMENT

Mixing glass/tumbler

Muddler or mortar/pestle

Bar mixing spoon

Bar strainer

Rocks glass, chilled

NONALCOHOLIC VARIATION

Eliminate the brandy and increase the cherry juice to six ounces. Use a chilled draft glass instead of rocks glass. Beginning on the full moon and going through the dark moon, drink each night.

INGREDIENTS

2 to 3 sage leaves

1 sprig rosemary

½ ounce dandelion syrup

3 ounces cherry juice

1½ ounces brandy

Ice (options: Virgo or Capricorn)

5 to 6 borage flowers (edible, for garnish; optional)

SERVES
1

INSTRUCTIONS

1. Pick a full moon, waning moon, or even a dark moon for this working.

2. Muddle the fresh herbs (sage, rosemary) to release their flavors in a mixing glass or tumbler. As you muddle, activate those meditative brainwaves. Think about releasing the power of your higher consciousness. As you press and smash, recognize the potential of elevating your awareness and tapping into the wisdom of your expanded mind. The goal is to access the deeper levels of understanding and your intuition.

3. Add the dandelion syrup to the mixing glass/tumbler. Stir to combine well. Next, add the cherry juice and stir well again.

4. If making a cocktail, add brandy. Stir again.

5. Fill the glass with ice cubes and strain the mixture into it.

6. Garnish with borage flowers.

7. Drink this on the full moon and again on the dark moon.

Deadline Drinking

The next working is one you will only want to do from time to time, as it's not a cure to the chronic stress that is late-stage capitalism. As magical mixologists, it's another tool in our our belt to create a better world. Choose this coffee cocktail when you're stuck at work and deadlines loom and there is no wiggle room. Look at it as a magical assistant. However, as Witches, embracing this for times of fun is pure resistance to the capitalistic machine. In other words, feel free to use Shake That Money Maker All Night Long for fun, too.

This brew includes cherry brandy, which helps you dig what you do. The espresso liqueur is all about enhancing physical energy. Honey supplements the wisdom infused in vanilla, and this adds an attractant to what is wanted. As discussed in previous spells, whipped cream brings in health and healing—which, depending on how long you work, those energies are welcomed. And espresso chocolate? The fire in the belly to keep working for that cheddar.

Part of the magic of this brew is the absolute luxuriousness of it. You're working harder. This drink reflects something nearing a reward. Including the whipped cream and shaved chocolate, it certainly feels like a mini vacation.

This magical mix includes vanilla honey. It can be found commercially. A substitute could be vanilla simple syrup, which is a simple syrup with a splash of vanilla extract, either homemade or store-bought.

SHAKE THAT MONEY MAKER
ALL NIGHT LONG

SERVES
1

Equipment

Good coffee mug

Bartender's spoon

Grater or microplane for
chocolate shavings (optional)

Ingredients

½ ounce vanilla honey

3 ounces freshly brewed coffee

2 ounces cherry brandy

1 ounce espresso liqueur

Whipped cream (optional)

Espresso dark chocolate shavings (optional)

Instructions

1. Add the vanilla honey to center of the bottom of the mug. Add in the coffee and stir until honey blends into liquid.

2. Add the brandy and espresso liqueur and stir three times sunwise, envisioning yourself working effortlessly and meeting the deadline.

3. Add the whipped cream and sprinkle the shaved chocolate.

4. Drink before it gets cold. Be sure to have a napkin; this might leave a whipped-cream mustache.

A DIFFERENT *type of* HERBAL DRINK

In the United States, twenty-three states (along with Washington, D.C. and Guam) have decriminalized or legalized medical and recreational cannabis, with eleven others likely to enact new such laws in the next year or so (Sandy et al. 2024). Our Canadian neighbors' federal government legalized it as of October 17, 2018 (Berke 2018). Mexico legalized it in 2021 (Oré 2023), although some key regulations remain stalled in the Senate. Worldwide, there are more than two dozen countries where cannabis usage is legal. As I'm penning this, the United States government is looking at reclassifying cannabis from a no-value substance to one that is accepted for medical use and has a low potential for psychological dependence (Shortt 2023).

Clearly, the journey to more acceptance has had many benchmarks. There's no doubt it's becoming more accessible and common. As a Witch, watching the wave of canna businesses move across the continent was particularly educational. Cannabis's use as an entheogen is known and portrayed in our media. Using it this way does not connect with the Divine— at least not mindfully—whereas Witches are continually, cyclically even, inducing a higher state of consciousness through various ways, including using sacred plants. When it comes to magic and cannabis, it's all about expansion and clarity. It removes energetic blockers and elevates our intuition and psychic connections.

As with alcohol, cannabis usage is a personal choice. For many cultures and practitioners, cannabis is a part of their Craft. I know many Witches who forgo alcohol and caffeine but use cannabis in their magical workings. Although smoking is a common way to consume the plant, it is not necessarily the healthiest way to partake of this very magical herb. Rather, consider using its goodness by drinking. Drinking cannabis? Why not? It certainly doesn't have the potential negative impact on the body that smoking can have.

Before we cover making cannabis-infused drink ingredients, please be aware that drinks will affect the imbiber similarly as it would when partaking of cannabis edibles. If you do not have any experience with cannabis, make sure you know the applicable laws, rules, and regulations for cannabis use in your area. Just as some states don't allow alcohol sales on Sundays, you may live somewhere where a cannabis dispensary is illegal. Explore, Witch, but do no harm, especially to yourself.

Getting to Know Cannabis

Cannabis has two distinct "flavors," if you will. They are called strains. They are indica and sativa. Legally purchased cannabis flowers may be labeled with either of those or "hybrid," which means the plant it was harvested from contains both strains. The flower's strain can influence the effect experienced when using cannabis. Sativa is often used to uplift energy levels and mood and boost creativity, whereas indicas, nicknamed by users as "in da couch," are often sought out as a sleep aid, anxiety reliever, and for general stress reduction and relaxation. It's easy to see, therefore, why a hybrid might be something cannabis users seek out. Getting some of what both strains offer can be a nice balance.

Before using cannabis in any adult beverage, knowledge of the strains and how they might influence workings needs considering. You'll need to decide if a sativa, indica, or hybrid portion will be used to make the drink. Consider any counterbalances for possible energies with the type of water used. Is it solar charged? Solstice charged? Full moon charged? That can have an impact. Regardless, the energy and intention are the most powerful, so don't get too wrapped around the axle on this. Be aware and work from there.

Everything to do with cannabis is measured with the metric system because the metric system is more exact for such small measurements. Flower purveyors sell their products in grams. A good budtender will help you stay within legal ranges. The following syrup recipe uses cannabis that is about 15 percent tetrahydrocannabinol (THC), the chemical in cannabis that gives you the "high." This means there will be about ten milligrams of THC per two tablespoons of syrup. Be aware that the cannabis you're using to create this syrup may have lower or higher THC, so the dosage will be different. Test each batch made. Chef's bonus! Feel free to use a strain that is grown to be more cannabidiol (CBD) heavy, as that can relax the body without the high of THC. That may be easier or harder to find, depending on where you live.

Remember, taking too much of anything is not good. However, ingesting cannabis is very different from smoking a joint. It has to go through the digestive system, which, on average, takes about an hour. However, that hour can be shorter or longer depending on a whole host of things, from diet to metabolism, hormonal influences, weight, and overall tolerance to cannabis. Understand that low and slow is how to approach cannabis. A little goes a long way.

The following recipe will make about twenty-four ounces of canna-bis syrup. Two tablespoons is a serving. But if you've never had a drink with cannabis syrup in it, test yourself and any guest you're hosting. Start with two teaspoons and wait four hours before assessing the reaction to its strength and effectiveness. As a Witch, remember to connect with the buds when creating the syrup; that will also give you more information.

For this recipe, you'll want a tobacco grinder as most folx don't want to use their spice or coffee grinders with cannabis. A hand-held tobacco grinder gives more control. You can also break the bud up manually, of course—make it a meditation if called. You will also need vegetable glyc-erin. Be sure it's food-grade and purchased from a reliable source. Most markets and some health food stores carry it.

Cannabis must be decarboxylated in order to infuse into tea, syrups, and other drinks. That means you're going to bake it. (I'll pause while you giggle.) Be sure to use the vent hood over the stove when making this, but also be aware that the neighbors will smell the baking cannabis. Hopefully they are 420 friendly—another reason to be sure you are on the right side of the law here.

Do not substitute honey in this working because you have to create a cannabis-honey tincture first and then it still doesn't infuse well, from my experience.

Sacred Cannabis Simple Syrup

SERVES
24

Equipment

- Rimmed baking sheet
- Tobacco grinder
- Medium saucepan with lid
- Cheesecloth
- Fine mesh strainer
- Canning funnel
- Heatproof large measuring cup with a spout or a quart-size mason jar
- Favorite spatula or wooden spoon

Ingredients

- 4 grams cannabis (15 percent THC), coarsely ground
- 3 cups water (options: Taurus, Virgo moon, or solar)
- 3 cups sugar or agave nectar
- 3 tablespoons food-grade vegetable glycerin

Instructions

1. Preheat oven to 250°F (121°C). While it preheats, take a moment and energetically connect with the cannabis buds. You may even want to talk to them like you would houseplants.
2. Put the cannabis on a baking sheet and bake for 45 minutes.
3. Combine the water and sweetener of choice in a medium saucepan. If you're bringing in energy with the intention here, stir sunwise; if you're releasing energy with intention here, stir widdershins. Bring to a low boil over medium heat.
4. Add the decarboxylated cannabis and cover the saucepan. Cook for twenty minutes.
5. Add the glycerin and reduce the heat. Simmer for about seven minutes. Stir occasionally as the mixture thickens. Remember the intention here. Share energy with the liquid.

6. Line the strainer with cheesecloth and place over a large heatproof measuring cup with a spout or a quart-size mason jar with a funnel.

7. Very carefully pour the mixture from the saucepan through the cheesecloth into a jar or cup. At this time, take a moment to set your intention aloud while straining the liquid from solids (e.g., "With this syrup, I cultivate peace.")

8. Take a spatula and squeeze the herb to extract as much liquid as possible. Do this longer than you think. Take a good bit of time. Continue energetic connection and be mindful of set intention.

9. Allow remains and syrup to cool to room temperature, then remove the cheesecloth, gather it into a ball, and squeeze any remaining liquid into the syrup. As the remaining liquid enters the syrup, visualize its use as healing, healthy, and revitalizing (or pick intention). Dispose of the remains mindfully. Composting is excellent.

10. Transfer to an airtight container or a mason jar with reusable top. Be sure to label and date. It will keep for up to three weeks.

Composting is excellent.

Winter Blazing Blues

Bhang tea is one of the oldest known methods of ingesting cannabis. It is served during the Hindu festival of Holi each year. Holi is a popular and significant spring festival. It celebrates the eternal and divine love of the gods Radha and Krishna. The day also signifies the triumph of good over evil. It's normally celebrated on the full moon of the Hindu month of Phalguna, which is in the February/March timeframe in the Western calendar.

A neighbor introduced me to this drink only a decade ago when I lived in a little Cascade foothill valley. Inspired by this ancient beverage and the positive energies surrounding it, as well as how tasty and satisfying it is, I created Weed Out the Weary Tea. My neighbor's brew was probably even more homemade, but I have found this recipe to be very similar to what they made and close to other similar recipes published.

In February and March, many folks are tired of winter. If you're living in Southern California, maybe you're struggling with a project at work that cannot seem to find The End. Whatever is causing the weariness, this tea will refresh and ready you to handle the business at hand—whatever is on the Witch's planner.

I prefer sativa or sativa hybrid strain for this working, and I try to keep it close to 15 percent THC, although in today's dispensaries that can be hard to find. Again, a good budtender will assist with this requirement. As in the simple syrup, adjust the dosage accordingly.

Be prepared to bathe or shower with this working. This energetically washes some of the weariness away and revitalizes the Witch for the next steps in this work.

Have your intention in mind—you're deciding between releasing or receiving. Be specific. Be actionable. Be positive. "May Freyja protect me." "I release worry and doubt about my work."

WEED OUT THE WEARY

T E A

SERVES
2

EQUIPMENT

Rimmed baking sheet

Tobacco grinder

Medium saucepan with lid

Cheesecloth

Fine mesh strainer

Favorite wooden spoon or spatula

Sterilized quart mason jar or heatproof
   sizeable measuring cup with spout

Bar spoon

Offering cup for kitchen or main altar (optional)

Your favorite teacups for serving

INGREDIENTS

4 grams cannabis, coarsely ground

1 cup water (options: Aries sun; Sagittarius moon)

½ tablespoon unsalted butter

2 cups whole milk

1 tablespoon almond flour

⅛ teaspoon garam masala

1 teaspoon loose chai tea

¼ cup honey

Half-and-half or cream, to taste (optional)

INSTRUCTIONS

1. Preheat the oven to 250°F (121°C). While it preheats, take a
   moment and energetically connect with the cannabis buds. You
   may even want to talk to it like you would any houseplant.

2. Place the coarsely ground cannabis on a rimmed baking sheet
   and bake in the oven for 45 minutes. Take a bath or a shower
   while the flower bakes. Once done, remove from oven.

3. Bring the water, butter, and milk to boil in a medium saucepan. Observe. Don't let it scorch. It is a choice again whether to stir sunwise to bring in goodness or widdershins if using this to help with protective work.

4. Reduce the heat to low. Add the decarboxylated cannabis, almond flour, and garam masala. Cover and simmer for at least 30 minutes but not longer than 45 minutes. Consider cleansing the kitchen altar and freshening it up during this time. Light a candle and incense, and prepare an offering cup for guides, ancestors, or preferred deities.

5. Remove from the heat and add the chai tea to the saucepan. Steep for seven minutes. During this steeping time, put in the intention for this brew (e.g., "I will finish" or "I easily find myself reaching new levels of energy for my life").

6. Line a fine mesh strainer with cheesecloth and place over a sanitized quart mason jar or heatproof measuring cup with a spout. Mindfully pour the warm liquid through the cheesecloth. Press to extract any remaining liquid through the cheesecloth. Dispose of the remains mindfully.

7. Add the honey to the jar and stir with a bar spoon until dissolved.

8. Pour the offering first, then the other servings. Say a small prayer of gratitude for the brew: "With this tea, from weary we are free; our hearts and cups are full."

9. Add any desired creamer. Sipping, visualize yourself moving past weariness.

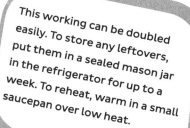

This working can be doubled easily. To store any leftovers, put them in a sealed mason jar in the refrigerator for up to a week. To reheat, warm in a small saucepan over low heat.

A Kushtail

As many a Witch is unable to use alcohol in their Craft but will use canna-bis, a different type of adult beverage might be an option. Cannabis sim-ple syrup can be used to create that different type of cocktail—a kushtail. You'll mix it up using the canna syrup instead of any alcohol. Again, in the mix, you'll be layering the magic of the cannabis herb and whatever other ingredients are preferred. Remember, the canna syrup can taste slightly herbal, so use that as a guide when you're making mix choices.

Following is a favorite nonalcoholic kushtail. This drink plays on the iconic American cocktail, the screwdriver, which is simply vodka and orange juice. I like blood orange juice for this, which often means hand-squeezing the juice. However, pomegranate, pineapple, or plain orange can be used—there are many choices. Can't decide? Use energy connection skills, listen to intuition, and let imagination and magic play.

Consider creating a cannabis simple syrup from some flower that is higher in CDB to elevate what is called a "body high" as opposed to the euphoric high of a more THC-heavy variety. Depending on the strain and percentage of THC in the flower used to make the syrup, it does not mean you won't get a little lit. Proceed in knowledge.

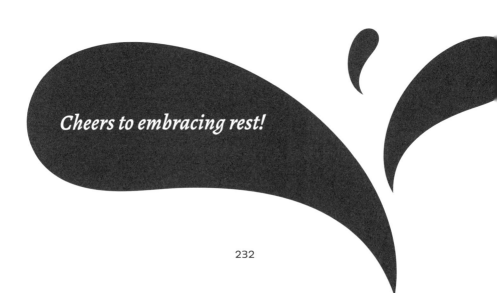

Cheers to embracing rest!

Kush Driver

EQUIPMENT

Bartender's mixing glass or pint measuring cup with a spout

Bartender's spoon

Rocks glass

Jigger

INGREDIENTS

3 to 4 ounces blood orange juice per serving

2 tablespoons cannabis syrup made with intention

Ice (options: Witch's choice)

Nonalcoholic cocktail cherry or blood orange wheel garnish (optional)

INSTRUCTIONS

1. Into the mixing glass, add juice and canna syrup. Stir thirteen times sunwise, putting in the intention that is desired (e.g., "Rest is doing; I will embrace rest").

2. Add ice to rocks glass and pour the juice mixture over the ice.

3. Garnish with cherry or orange wheel or both.

4. Drink to a healthy balance between activity and rest.

Dark Chocolate and Mary Jane

One of the most unexpected pleasures is dark chocolate and cannabis. Pull this working out when creating a loving environment, especially when sitting around or in front of a fire. There is a deep undercurrent of laughter in the properties of this potion because our dopamine receptors are spreading happy neurons all over the brain and body thanks to the drinking chocolate in this brew.

Dark chocolate has a place in anyone's cup because physically it is known to increase heart health, reduce stress, balance the immune system, improve brain function and mood, combat diabetes, and even boost athletic performance. Magically, it brings prosperity, wealth, and health. Mix it with cannabis, and it clears the way for all this stuff and strengthens intentions and intuition. And again, it's a boost in the humor of any event.

This is different from hot cocoa and is a drinking chocolate. Well-known in regions of Italy and France, drinking chocolate is a special treat. It is luxurious and suitable for those "giggle with your besties" occasions. The recipe below is for one drink. Multiply amounts as necessary. Tell funniest puns around the fire with your boo or bestie while enjoying this. Laugh until you cry. Alternatively, take in a thermos and go deep into the forest and laugh with the spirits of the trees.

CACKLING
AROUND THE FIRE

EQUIPMENT

- Cutting board and knife
- Small saucepan
- Favorite spatula
- Whisk
- Sturdy mug or thermos

INGREDIENTS

- 4 ounces good quality bittersweet chocolate, chopped
- ¾ cup whole milk
- 1 tablespoon unsalted butter
- 1 teaspoon light brown sugar, lightly packed
- ¼ teaspoon pure vanilla extract
- ⅛ teaspoon instant espresso powder
- 1 small pinch of salt
- 2 tablespoons cannabis simple syrup
- Whipped cream (optional)
- Chocolate shavings or sprinkles (optional)

INSTRUCTIONS

1. When chopping chocolate into small chunks to melt faster, put in the intention for fun, humor, and general feel-good vibes.
2. Heat the milk in a small saucepan over medium heat until steaming.
3. Whisk in the chocolate until smooth and creamy, and then the butter, brown sugar, vanilla, espresso powder, salt, and cannabis simple syrup. Make sure everything is combined well.
4. Heat until steaming, then remove from the heat.
5. Serve immediately. Top with whipped cream and some sprinkles if desired.
6. Get ready for the warmth and good feelings to arrive shortly.

Super Magical Lemons

In the United States, National Lemonade Day is celebrated on August 20. Lemons from our country's more temperate regions are plentiful then. It's also within Leo season. Leo is ruled by the sun, and little lemon slices look like perky little suns on the edge of a glass. It may be muggy with the summer heat, and a lot of porch, balcony, or patio—heck, even fire-escape sitting is required. That sitting needs a cool drink. There is nothing better in that environment than lemonade. Perching in a favorite sitting spot goes well with an ice-cold, fresh-squeezed lemonade. This drink can be a bridge between all the preferences—nonalcoholic, alcoholic, or cannabis-infused. Drink it lusciously plain or add a little gin or insert some cannabis simple syrup. It's recommended not to do cannabis syrup and gin at the same time.

With the exception of October, California lemons are available year-round. Look for lemons that feel heavier than their size. They need to smell like lemons. No wrinkling on the skin. The lemon gives slightly when lightly pressed. Not too soft. And no mold, please and thank you.

Lemonade historically came to be in Paris in the mid-1600s. They make theirs with sparkling water. However, I love the simplicity of noncarbonated water to create this drink. If you want to get fancy or have ample sparkling water, feel free to exchange or experiment (maybe half and half). This traditional summer drink is super easy to pack up and enjoy while splashing by the river, lake, ocean, or pool. That lemonade of ol' Paris featured honey, not sugar. You already mastered that syrup back in chapter 13.

The magic element within this working is the simple stirs of a favorite wooden spoon and decided intention. It's hot. Workings need to be low energy yet impactful.

LEO SEASON LUSCIOUS
L E M O N A D E

EQUIPMENT

Hand juicer

Pitcher (preferably a chilled glass one)

Long wooden spoon

Quart mason jars, chilled (for serving)

SERVES 6

INGREDIENTS

4 cups cold water

1½ cups lemon juice (approximately 9–12 lemons, hand-squeezed)

1 cup honey syrup or rich syrup

1 ounce gin or 2 teaspoons cannabis syrup per glass (optional)

Ice (options: Leo, solar, or moon)

Lemon wheel for garnish (optional)

INSTRUCTIONS

1. Pour water, lemon juice, and syrup into a chilled pitcher. With a long wooden spoon, stir three times sunwise to bring positivity and three times widdershins to banish negativity.

2. If choosing to add gin or cannabis syrup, add it into a mason jar.

3. Fill mason jar with ice. Pour the lemon juice mixture over the ice. Stir again, reinforcing your intention.

4. Add garnish and sip.

Sip to the sun and lean into lusciousness!

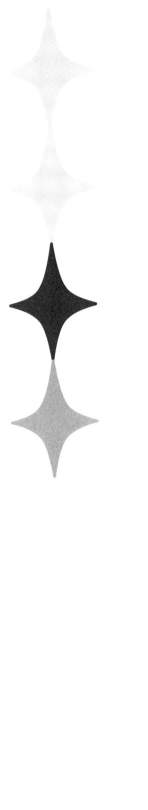

Many modern Witches follow a seasonal calendar based on a conglomeration of northwestern European cultural views and languages, but many around the globe, while marking these solar points, have a different name, title, or even marking point. Within this text I've added some seasonal names for those of us from more Germanic and Nordic backgrounds. All of these have secular names for them, too. Each drink and its observance will be labeled as such with a short explanation. Depending on the practice, there may be another name for it. Regardless of the label, the energies are where we're focusing. Refer to the following image for a visual explanation.

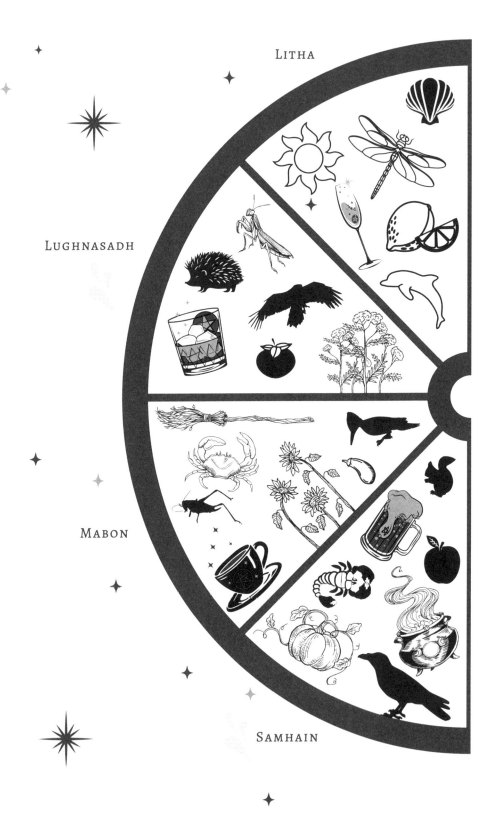

LITHA

LUGHNASADH

MABON

SAMHAIN

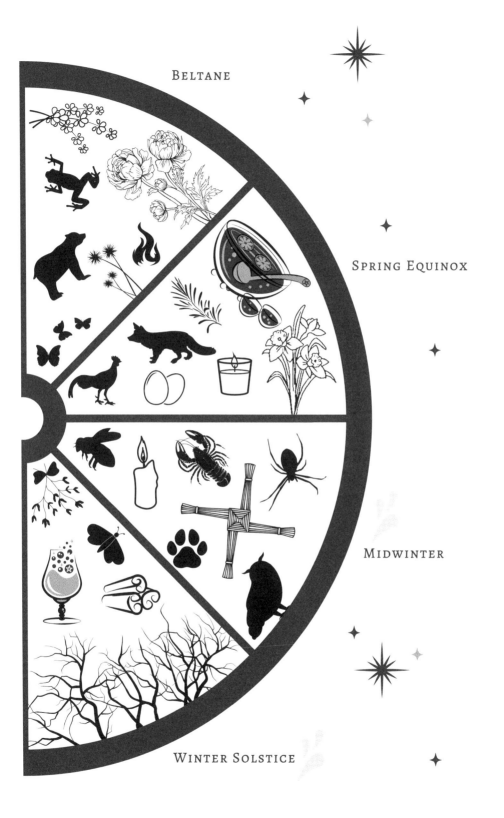

BELTANE

SPRING EQUINOX

MIDWINTER

WINTER SOLSTICE

Marking our time with the seasons and marking the magical points on that rotating compass are the sabbats, points along the solar year where its influence of energy creates festivals and feasts. Additionally, this chapter gives drinks for larger gatherings, observances, and rituals to include during these times. We'll start with the Witch's New Year, Samhain, aka Halloween, and then we'll end with the Witch's Thanksgiving, happening on or near the autumn equinox.

Samhain (Winter Nights or Witch's New Year)

DATES: GENERALLY RECOGNIZED FROM SUNSET
OCTOBER 30 TO SUNSET NOVEMBER 1

It's said we're the product of thousands. Take a look in the mirror. Your face is the creation of more than four thousand ancestors. Take a minute and think about all the drinks your ancestors consumed. How hard might it have been to get clean, drinkable water? Remember, brewing up drinks was because often water wasn't safe to drink. Those who stand behind you are marveling at how amazing this life is. Samhain is a good time to connect with all the energies and ancestral inheritance—not necessarily wealth—for which you enjoy. Gather 'round the fire, sip this drink, and watch the flames for messages.

This drink gets its name because of everything our ancestors have gone through. This drink has the effect of being smoked simply because it's made over an open fire. You'd have to get some fancy cocktail smoker to get the same taste, which would likely be half the fun. The ambiance of autumn lends itself to the telling of stories—with perhaps a ghost story thrown in for good measure and fun. Then get ready to tell a story about what you know from the ancestors or even memories of those you did know or from those who have passed on. This is a great way to get the elders in the family or community to talk about their past and the memories they have, so be sure to try to do this with them. That way, these important stories get shared. Now get ready for the fire to warm the Witch like it did the ancestors, have a warm drink from a bubbling cauldron, and peer into the lives of those who came before you.

The atmosphere of autumn seems to lead us to a willing attitude to focus on the connection with the spirits of the land, ancestors, and guides. Samhain may also provide a much-needed time out to focus on that connection. The next working is all about finding that connection—and comfort—while drinking this mouthwatering concoction. Magically, this brew brings in the energy of all the ingredients contained in the spirits—corn, wheat, rye, apples, cranberries, lime, and honey. Therefore, the energy of protection, health, love, strength, and wisdom are mixed into this warm toddy.

If you are fortunate to possess one of those tripod-hanging cauldrons, then you probably have attempted something like this already. Many fire pits are equipped with a grate, so you don't necessarily have to have a pot that features a tripod, but the pot needs to be flame-proof and hover above the fire. The pot you choose will always be the pot for the campfire because it will get sooty.

I use a cast-iron 3½-quart Dutch oven with three legs that rest sturdily on the grate. It features a lid, but you don't need one for this. In fact, you want some of the campfire smoke to permeate the drink, so don't use the lid until it's brewed.

Through the Fire & the Flame Toddy

EQUIPMENT

  Fire pit/circle

  A large cauldron that can be put over the fire

  Large ladle to serve the drinks

  Fireside mugs plus one for the ancestors

  Oven mitts/gloves for handling hot cauldron

  Musical instruments (optional)

  Bowls or other vessels to hold salt and sage

  Favorite wooden spoon

  Small offering table to hold the ancestor mug

  Liquid thermometer (optional)

SERVES 10+

INGREDIENTS

  Salt for sprinkling around the fire circle

  1 cup Canadian-style whiskey

  1 cup apple schnapps

  2 quarts cranberry juice

  ⅔ cup honey-lime syrup (found in chapter 13)

  Fresh sage leaves (culinary, not white), at least one per participant, plus one extra for the host/chef

INSTRUCTIONS

1. Sprinkle salt around the fire circle where you'll gather. It simply needs to be sprinkled from the hand; don't pour out a lot. Invoke the salt's protection energy. If it's in your practice, call in the directions and the elements. Visualize an energetic bubble over the ritual area. "For Kindred Only" is the energetic "sign" and connection to put out there. This step also keeps nosey neighbors uninterested. Make sure there's a space where the mug presented for the ancestors is placed, like a small table. Nothing fancy is necessary.

2. Get the fire going. Take a moment to think about how many ancestors have started fires to gather around. Put these thoughts into the fire as you tend to its energy. Be ready for this energy to spread to all participants around the fire. Do not put the cauldron on until the fire is going well and there are some strong coals forming before moving to the next step.

3. Take one of the sage leaves, light a small tip of it, and let it begin to smoke. Use that smoke and energetically cleanse the cauldron. Pass the smoking sage leaf in and around the cauldron while chanting, "Air, fire, water, earth; cleanse, dismiss, dispel!" When complete, toss the sage leaf in the fire.

4. Add the liquids into the cauldron. Stir well. Once the liquid stills and before it begins to simmer, take a look inside the cauldron. Think about who you'd like to connect with or ruminate on everything it took for you to get to this point. What do you see? What thoughts come to mind? Allow your focus to go there.

5. It shouldn't take too long for the cauldron to simmer and warm to a drinkable temperature (170°F or 77°C). We want to heat it and not boil it. During the time it takes to warm, make sure all the participants have a sage leaf.

6. Ladle warm beverages carefully into mugs, making sure to begin with one for the ancestors.

7. Ask some questions to begin getting the connections to memory or ancestors brewing from those present around the fire: e.g., What's your favorite summer memory? What do you remember of them? Talk about your first kiss. What's your favorite jack o-lantern carving memory?

8. If there is a good connection, psychically call on ancestors for whom questions need to be asked. Have a little chat. This may be a more silent working, but feel free to speak aloud: e.g., Papa Felix, who was your father? Why does our line stop with you? And why does my nose get cold every time I think of you?

9. Once everyone has a mug of the brew, raise the mugs and toast, "To the kindred!" If you've lost someone since the last Samhain, you may call out a cheer to them.

10. Next, start with the oldest participant (age has its privileges) and allow them to burn their sage leaf. This smoking leaf is a signal "for kindred only" to arrive. Ask the participants to think about what has brought them to this point and the people who helped them get there, then allow them to speak while the sage leaf smokes. When they are finished, have them toss

their sage into the fire. The remainder of the circle responds with a toast of gratitude: "Thanks for the story, Grandpa!" or whatever suits the circumstance.

11. Move to the next oldest participant and repeat until everyone has gone. Refill mugs as necessary between speakers.

12. Once everyone has had an opportunity to speak, be sure to refill mugs for those who want; say, "To all those who paved the path we walk today, we raise our mugs with gratitude and love!"

13. Next, invite everyone to mingle and enjoy the warmth of the fire. Pass out treats if that's in your practice. Play music together, dance, or sing. Eat, drink, and be merry, for you and yours are who those kindred ancestors once hoped for. Be ready for messages that come in from the ancestors. Pay attention to the intuitive downloads you get of signs that are sent in the next three days following this working.

NONALCOHOLIC VARIATION

Eliminate the whiskey. Substitute the apple schnapps for one part apple juice and one part fine applesauce. Place the applesauce in the cauldron first. The sauce cooks down and provides a substantial creaminess and mouthfeel.

Winter Solstice (Álfablót or Yule)

GENERALLY OBSERVED BETWEEN SUNRISE
DECEMBER 21 AND SUNSET JANUARY 6

The winter solstice, December 21 in the northern hemisphere, is the longest night of the year. The amount of daylight you've been receiving between the autumn equinox and now is a noticeably small amount. But the winter solstice marks the moment on that solar wheel where the scale of darkness begins to tip back toward an even balance. However, even with the return of light, temperatures dip. Winter is only getting started. We watch the wildlife begin to spend more and more time resting and sleeping. This is nature's time to rest. As Witches, we embrace a slower cycle and opportunity to enjoy our kindred, and, for those who work close to the land, the harvest from autumn. Historically it is a time for laying low and staying warm. For our ancestors, it was very much about making sure their communities survived the winter. For those with northern European and particularly Scandinavian lineage, this was when the beer from the last harvest was ready to share, and animals were fat and ready for dispatch. This is *Álfablót*, translated to "elven sacrifice," and it was conducted in sacred privacy. Therefore, if you're not part of a covenstead, your presence and energy is not required. This was not for greed but for energetic protection, especially from Odin or the beings from the realm of Alfheim, one of the nine realms in Norse mythology. There are not many reasons found for this, but as someone who lives close to the land, I understand the privacy part. Butchering animals is not an act for show. In the back of the book, I've listed some recommended texts regarding such traditions and where to read about them if you're curious. But for our purposes here, you're safe to share this working.

In the modern world, getting through winter is still hard. Within the Western overculture, this time is observed with celebration, too. Myths of the energy of the season of winter hover all about and through all of our preferred celebrations. As Witches, our focus continues on the land, its energies, and its continuing flow with the seasons. We also mark the winter solstice with celebrations, feasting, and rituals, and it's not just an eve and a day; it's weeks because part of getting through winter includes bringing light energetically and physically. Many of the rituals focus on things like lighting the Yule log, putting lights on an evergreen tree, and giving offerings—cookies and cake—to one another and our ancestors or deities.

For light-bringing efforts during this time post–winter solstice, we traditionally bring some ingredients together with the intention of creating peace and harmony. Often the holidays can be fraught with unmet expectations and drama. With Good Forward Nog, we're leading with love to create peace and harmony. You'll use locally made fresh eggnog. It brings the energy of renewal; the light has returned. Also, if you think about the shell of an egg, it's very protective. This energy is contained within the eggnog, too.

Rum is made from sugar cane juice and is often aged to create different flavors. As you've learned, where there's sugar, magically, energetically, there is love. You've already gotten to know the energies of brandy from chapter 14, and orange, that powerhouse of love and cleansing, is heaping on the abundance in this drink. If you think about our ancestors in the middle of winter, especially in the northern climes, an orange would be completely exotic. Therefore, sometimes the intention is that this orange reminds us of more tropical locales and the interconnectedness of our planet. The cream is that hug from nature and physically adds a little protein (along with the eggnog), making this very rich. The combination of spices not only reminds many of this time of year but also feeds our intuition, luck, comfort, and strength. All together, we head into the season with good intentions and goodwill toward kindred.

The recipe gives amounts for single-mug servings. Multiply as needed to make enough for a crowd.

GOOD FORWARD
N O G

Equipment

Measuring spoons

Small bowl

Microwave-safe pourable measuring cup or saucepan with spout

Bartender's spoon

Jigger

Favored mug

Ingredients

2 tablespoons powdered sugar

½ teaspoon ground nutmeg

¼ teaspoon allspice

¼ teaspoon ground cloves

1 teaspoon cinnamon

¾ cup eggnog

1 ounce aged rum (ron añejo)

1 ounce cognac or aged brandy

Orange peel for expressing

Whipped cream

SERVES
1

Instructions

1. Add the powdered sugar and all the spices to a small bowl. Mix it up, imagining safety and warmth and cozy feels. Set aside.

2. Heat the eggnog either on the stove over low-medium heat, making sure not to scorch it, or in the microwave in thirty-second bursts, stirring in between times. While stirring, remember that this cooks away any dysfunction and only takes the good forward.

3. Into the holiday mug, add the rum and brandy.

4. Add the eggnog. Pour it into the mug as you think of pouring in health.

5. Stir, and think or say aloud:

> *Mix in a little extra labor, an extra dash of healing;*
>
> *Stir in more love for neighbor; patience for dealing;*
>
> *A sprinkle of humor; take the good of the begettted,*
>
> *Even those who knew no better;*
>
> *Take a step forward and sip the reward.*

6. Express the orange peel, knowing you're putting in prosperity and harmony.

7. Top with whipped cream and sprinkle with the sugar-spice mixture.

8. Serve and enjoy. Toast to a blessed winter.

Serve a whole crowd by using a slow cooker to keep this warm. Heat on low for one to two hours, and then set the crock to warm.

A Calendar New Year

I often joke that going out on New Year's Eve is for amateurs. Maybe you're fortunate enough to watch the ball drop in Times Square or the fireworks over the Space Needle in Seattle or the calendar New Year's celebration in Sydney Harbor; such events may be a lasting memory. The powerful energy of such a large collective in one place is good for a Witchling to experience. I did mine in Frankfurt, Germany, and that was a culture shock and a big education. Every New Year now, for some thirty years, I pause and think about that particular New Year's Eve. The dose of the power of that collective energy rises up again when I do that, too. Now I take it with me to do more quiet, smaller observances, celebrations, and rituals at home.

Simple at-home rituals when we go from one calendar year to the next can be super strong energy, which is a great time to work magic. Unlike Samhain, we're focused on the past calendar year and specifically our own lives. The beverage that accompanies this time of year has a long history. Of course, we're talking about wassail. We sip it while reviewing our Good Things Jar—a year-long ritual of recording, you guessed it, good things. Then burn that goodness in gratitude up to the universe. If there is a local orchardist who makes cider, I highly encourage you to support those folx. But cider may be hard to come by this time of year, so substitute apple juice. What you can't substitute is the mulling spices! Especially the clove-spiked orange, which is my favorite. That said, make these individually; you can easily mull the cider in the microwave.

I always have a crock of it going from winter solstice through the Yuletide, including New Year's Eve—apple cider, amaretto, some bourbon and a little orange juice along with pierced oranges with a cinnamon stick and cloves, floating some star anise and keeping the crock on warm and serving in holiday mugs. Everyone gets festive and calms down very quickly, especially if you serve them with holiday cookies. Wassail and those cookies are an immediate balm to holiday frazzles. However, my recipe here is to help you do so a mug at a time. It even uses that modern marvel: the microwave. If you're not a microwave fan, heat this slowly on the stovetop in a saucepan or slow cooker, as mentioned above.

Apple cider holds the energy of peace; amaretto is for healing; orange juice is for love and purification. All those holiday spices are little tiny bombs of patience, abundance, and awareness. Make sure holiday guests have a comfortable seat, a drink, and a sweet, and even the staunchest scrooges and grinches can smile for an hour or so.

The magic of this is how smooth and juicy it is, peppered with the winter spices we all know and love. Be careful; this can go down quickly. Try to drink it before it gets too cool because then it may be guzzled too fast. Remember it's a spirited cocktail.

Mug by Mug Wassail

EQUIPMENT

- Serving mugs
- Mulling bag or cheesecloth
- 4-cup microwave-worthy pourable measuring cup
- 2-cup microwave-worthy pourable measuring cup
- Kettle
- Bartender's spoon

INGREDIENTS

- Hot water for prewarming mugs
- Two cinnamon sticks
- Two whole star anise
- One orange, peeled; peels reserved
- 1 tablespoon whole cloves
- 1 tablespoon whole allspice
- ¾ cup apple cider per mug
- 1 ounce orange juice per mug
- 1 ounce amaretto per mug
- 1 ounce bourbon per mug
- Three drops orange bitters per mug (optional)

SERVES
1

INSTRUCTIONS

1. Prep your mugs first by putting some hot water in them and allowing them to warm while you prep the rest.

2. Take the cinnamon sticks, star anise, orange and peels, cloves, and allspice and put them into a mulling bag or tie them into a little bouquet garni and put in a large measuring cup. While creating this bouquet, imagine everyone staying healthy, feeling calm, and having a good time.

3. Pour apple cider over it and put it in the microwave for about two minutes until nice and warm. Depending on the microwave, it could take up to three minutes to warm to 180°F (82°C). Leave the bouquet of spices in the juice and let it steep.

4. Pour a small quantity of orange juice into the smaller pourable cup and heat in the microwave. You won't need but one ounce per serving, so it won't take as long as the apple cider to heat.

5. Discard the water from the mug and pour in the amaretto and bourbon. Add the orange juice and the three drops of orange bitters.

6. Fill the rest of the mug with the warmed, spiced apple cider.

7. Stir sunwise with the intention, again, of health, calm, and ease. Serve.

8. Toast to everyone's health and calm nerves.

Midwinter (Disting or Imbolc)

Generally Celebrated from Sunrise February 1 to Sunset February 2

By the time February rolls around, many of us are so ready for some sunlight and daylight that a bit of cabin fever has set in, and we can begin feeling stir-crazy. This point in the solar wheel of the year marks the beginning of the end of winter. We are at the midpoint between the winter solstice and the spring equinox. This is a time of reflection traditionally. We've made it halfway through winter. There is much to celebrate. Even with the modern versions of shelter and warmth, winter is still tough. We're still in winter mode, but we're starting to wake up, like the flowers and trees.

In many Imbolc rituals, milk and tea are traditional. This is because they likely still had stores of herbs, tea, and the first milk of the season after the drought of winter started to flow in most of the livestock. Spring goddesses are often venerated and provided offerings of those now seasonally abundant herbs and milk. Traditionally milk is used as an offering. The same is true for the *Disting*, sometimes referred to as the *Disablot*, meaning sacrifice to the divine feminine and honor of female ancestors. *Ting* is a term for a great assembly. When I lived in Germany, the Disting is when everyone begins to come out of winter hiding, and new markets and gatherings begin.

The following tea is made with some of the "dew" or snow that is available outside on the morning you're observing this midwinter point on the solar wheel. I often put out a bowl with some water, cover it with a tea towel, and let it infuse with the moon overnight; whatever dew gets into it, gets into it. Then use that water. Alternatively, use some solar or moon water. White tea is delicate, so it's very important not to overheat the water. This tea is harvested in the spring and is called white because of the pearly white hairs on the buds of the tea plant, Yin Zhen Bai Hao (aka Silver Needles) or the Bai Mudan (aka White Peony). Whatever white tea being used, steeping is important here. If there are more leaves than buds, five minutes will do; if there are buds in the tea, it will take eight minutes. Let it only steep for four minutes if you're using bagged white tea.

255

The magical qualities of this tea lean more toward the courage part, as opposed to raising consciousness. The Imbolc dew water you're using to boil is all about rebirth and transformation. What are you going to blossom into come summer? The time to plan for that is now. With this little midwinter tea ceremony, as with other workings in this book, the milk here brings in love and spirituality. Especially at this time of year, milk is associated with life. An offering of milk to a preferred deity is appropriate here.

This working relies on intuition because you're going to be doing a little drink divination. We're going to be looking at the messages the milk sends when it hits the tea, as well as the steam on the mirror, and putting the messages together.

REFLECTION
T E A

EQUIPMENT

Kettle

Teapot, strainer, or infuser

Creamer pot with spout

A small handheld mirror

Favorite teacup

Sketchpad or journal with favored writing instrument (optional)

SERVES
1

INGREDIENTS

2 cups dew/snow water (or Witch's choice moon/solar)

1 tablespoon white tea

Whole milk (half and half will work, too), to taste

Wild violet syrup, to taste (optional; found in chapter 13)

INSTRUCTIONS

1. Heat the water to 170°F (77°C). Do not let it get warmer than 180°F. This is a delicate tea we want to brew gently.

2. Add the white tea to your choice of tea brewing device. Pour heated water over. Steep for five to eight minutes. While it steeps, connect with the tea. Feel its delicate cheerleading. It might even whisper, "You got this, Witch."

3. Pour the tea. Sit down with the tea and the milk or half and half in the creamer pot. Put the mirror over the tea and ask a question for deities/the universe/the ancestors; e.g., How can I become more independent? What can I do to prepare for the changes I desire?

4. After you've asked the question, take the mirror off and quickly lay flat on the table. Look at the condensation on the mirror from the steam. What do you see? What does that make you think about? Note it.

5. Take the creamer and pour desired amount in. Watch the shapes it makes. Do not stir the milk in until it stills. What do you see as the milk hits the tea? What are the shapes, scenes, and symbols? What do you see? Make a note of it.

6. Now add the violet syrup. What personal message is there for you between the cup and the mirror? Note it.

7. Drink tea as you ponder these things. You may want to write down whatever comes to mind. If it's in your practice, sketch what you see or what other images it brings to mind.

8. When finished, thank the tea, the mirror, and any gods, ancestors, or spirits you worked with during this.

9. Clean up all the tea supplies.

Spring Equinox

As we transition from the dark of winter into the brightness of summer, there's a lot of back and forth between winter's grasp and spring's arrival, paving the way for summer. The best part is between March and July, when pineapple is in season and readily available. I lived in Hawai'i for nearly five years and can be on the beach there, lickety-split, with Aloha Pineapple Water. And who doesn't dream of being on a beach come the spring equinox? Although much of the pineapple production in the places I used to live there left completely around 2008, pineapple still reminds me of the wonderful welcome that the land of Hawai'i and its people gave me as I tried to figure out who I was at that time in my life (early twenties). Today, when I drink pineapple water, I can smell the air of the magical place that is Hawai'i, soaked rich in the scent of pikake and plumeria, the latter of which, like the pineapple, is not native there. This fact is something that made me understand how full of aloha the Hawaiian people are. My haole fanny, the pineapple, and the plumeria were not native, but the land and its people, as well as the ocean, had a whole host of lessons to teach. And they did so with grace, kindness, and a whole lot of laughter.

This drink's presence in my life has developed into a ritual of welcoming in the change of seasons both within and without. Every time I taste the acidity of passionfruit (*lilikoi*)—another immigrant to that Pacific archipelago—I recall a lesson regarding the importance of *pule* (prayer) in one's life. Pule is, in my opinion, the core of Hawaiian magic. It is so absolutely powerful and authentic when you see it. For example, a protection pule over a household would be recited at sunrise and sunset for an entire *kēlā pule* (week), which also shows how important these prayers and requests to the *Akua* (divine) were; it helped define the word *week* in their language. The Native Hawaiians have a core value of *mālama 'āina*, which means "to take care of the land." I credit their influence on the earth-healing focus of my practice.

The pineapple's magical correspondence is healing and protection as well as abundance and love. Who doesn't need a bit of extra love? You can use frozen pineapple that's been thawed. I have not found that canned pineapple works for this, as it tends to be too sweet.

Here's how to pick a ripe pineapple in the store. Pick one that has a balance of yellow to green in its color. Smell the bottom of the fruit. You should be able to detect that pineapple smell. The leaves should be green, and the fruit should have a small amount of flex when you gently squeeze it. It should feel heavy in your hand; just like lemons, it should feel heavier than its size. Lastly, give a pull to one of the fronds (leaves). It should pull out easily to indicate freshness and ripeness. If it's difficult to tug a frond out at the top of the pineapple, it may not be ripe.

Passionfruit is not something easily accessible for most. You have to find yourself some passionfruit syrup. As the passionfruit is very delicate, shipping it from Brazil, Australia, or Hawaii can be difficult. The passionfruit syrup taste is distinctive and quite possibly so tasty you'll want another.

If you cannot find passionfruit syrup, make a simple cane syrup as a substitution. The taste will be different but still refreshing, welcoming, and full of the possibilities that are spring.

This recipe calls for Valencia oranges because, again, they are easy to find in Hawaii. But any variety of oranges will help bring even more pure love into the beverage.

E ola iā 'oe! To your life!

Aloha Pineapple Water

EQUIPMENT

Blender

Large fine mesh strainer

Large 8-cup pourable measuring cup

Spatula

Hand juicer

Pitcher

Garnish skewers

Collins glass

SERVES 4

INGREDIENTS

4 cups fresh pineapple chunks

1⅓ cups cold water (Libra moon water is good here)

Juice of 2 Valencia oranges, freshly squeezed (about ½ to ⅔ cup)

¼ cup passionfruit syrup

Ice (options: Cancer or Pisces)

Valencia orange wheel for garnish (optional)

Pineapple wedge for garnish (optional)

INSTRUCTIONS

1. Place pineapple chunks and water into a blender. As you do, think about the healing and protection you'd like to take with you and your kindred into spring. Blend until smooth—between one to two minutes.

2. Strain the mixture into your large pourable measuring cup (you can skip this step if you prefer keeping the pulp). As you strain, imagine more aloha (love) pouring into the mixture. Love for self. Love for others. Love for the community. Love for our planet. See yourself, your kindred, and others at peace and protected.

3. Strain a second time into pitcher, then add orange juice and syrup. Stir. Connect that loving energy within yourself to the ingredients before continuing.

4. Pour over a collins glass filled with ice. As you pour, say: "Enter, spring; let us grow within and without." Repeat with each glass you fill.

5. Garnish as desired with orange and pineapple. Give to your ʻohana (kindred) and spread some aloha (love).

May Eve Day (Walpurgisnacht or Beltane)

GENERALLY OBSERVED FROM SUNSET
APRIL 30 TO SUNRISE MAY 2

Beltane is the traditional solar holiday, marking the awakening of the earth and the renewal of life. It marks the midpoint between the spring equinox and the summer solstice. The days are markedly getting longer. This is when Witches feel this huge pull to connect with the natural world and express, much like the autumn equinox, the harmonious balance—light and dark, masculine and feminine, the passivity of winter to the action of summer, and the ebb and flow of the natural world here on earth. For Witches, Walpurgisnacht may hold more pull to Beltane as the name means "Witch's night."

Germanic in origin and adopted by a good portion of northern Europe, the celebration is a very Halloween-like festival, with bonfires, games, costumed parades, and lots of food and drink, especially mead-featured punches. Often the bonfires would be started with a wooden "Witch" figure that very much looks modernistically crooked-nosed and wart-faced. Spiders are symbolic here, too, and are often worn on the cloaks of those who embody the Witch's spirit in costume and attitude.

These practices are particularly strong in the towns around the Harz Mountains, especially near its highest peak of Brocken (Pottamkulam 2023). There you'll see this mountain jutting out of thick evergreen forest. Strange rock formations shoot out from the mountain's side. Most notably, this area has an odd weather phenomenon that creates auras around its summit, giving it quite the mystic feel. It's easy to see how this region suffered from some of the worst Witch hunts in history. Stories to explain the weird colors and clouds around the mountaintop were blamed as evil spirits doing Witches' biddings and all manner of tales of uppity women plotting to take over good churchgoing folk. There, Walpurgisnacht is known as Hexenbrunnen, the burning of the Witches. Since then, the area has remained one that attracts those much like Salem, Massachusetts, does in the United States. Modern heathens and Witches crawl all over that area, especially the towns of Goslar and Thale, during this time of year.

After a long winter, especially in mountain range elevations, April 30 feels balmy, and the world looks welcoming again. Our ancestors celebrated that energy at Beltane. The Catholic Church came in and took one Saint Walpurga and made her feast date align with Beltane. Today, while there are Pagans drumming on Walpurgisnacht, the Feast of Saint Walpurga has many devotees making a pilgrimage to her tomb in Eichstätt to seek her intercession and blessings or collect a vial of her healing oil. Saint Walpurga was an English nun who traveled to Germany, where she founded several monasteries. She was said to have the power to heal the sick and cast out demons. Sounds very witchy, yes? She was a healer who helped people integrate their shadow selves in healthy ways. Yeah, sounds pretty witchy to me.

Mead is associated with this midway point between spring and summer, and its sweetness aligns with early strawberries, which have a more tart flavor and acidity than their closer-to-summer counterparts. Because mead is made with honey, it holds the same properties. Its energies include purification, health, love, sex, happiness, spirituality, and wisdom.

If unable to find mead, substitute a German Rhine wine, Riesling, or Moselle. Hearty beer steins are traditional, but a draft glass works well, too. But holding onto a beer mug is a whole lot easier as you're socializing around the fire. No harm, no foul if you choose to use some more outdoor-friendly tumblers.

Prepare this at least a day before serving it. Leftovers can be refrigerated for about three days. It's said that lovers who drink this punch on Witch's Night end up following each other through the eons. On May Day eve, invite your best Witches' circle to sit around the fire or plant flowers—a favorite activity for this mini festival of Witches. Eat some waffles or pancakes and drink some Party Hearty Punch.

Prost!

PARTY HEARTY

P U N C H

EQUIPMENT

A ½ gallon mason jar
with reusable lid

Fine mesh strainer

A punch bowl or other
drink dispenser

Garnish skewers

Beer steins

INGREDIENTS

One bottle (750 ml) of mead

1 sprig fresh tarragon

Ice cubes made from Aquarius moon water (fun shapes optional)

1 cup strawberries, hulled and sliced

16 ounces German schnapps

Whole strawberries, hulled, 1 per serving mug (optional)

Candied tarragon spears, 1 per serving mug (optional)

Favorite spring edible flower such as Johnny Jump Ups (optional)

INSTRUCTIONS

1. Pour mead into the mason jar. Put one sprig of tarragon into
   the mason jar with the mead. Let it sit in the mason jar for at
   least thirty minutes, but preferably overnight.

2. Before serving, take remaining tarragon and create candied
   sprigs. This is optional but gives it that really festive feel as
   well as balancing the sometimes strong flavor of the tarragon.
   Another simple option is to spear the whole strawberries with
   an unsugared tarragon sprig.

3. To serve, add ice to the punch bowl or drink decanter.
   Strain the mead into the serving vessel. Add in the prepared
   strawberries and the German schnapps, if using. Stir well.

4. Dispense or ladle into beer steins. Garnish with edible flowers and candied tarragon–strawberry spears.

5. Toast to the "Witches" that they burned and the ones who survived so the present Witches can dance around the fire.

NONALCOHOLIC VARIATION

Use some sparkling pear cider to substitute for the mead and add a little honey syrup. Use a nonalcoholic substitute of choice for the schnapps; anything plum or cherry would give similar tastes.

Summer Solstice (Midsommar or Litha)

GENERALLY OBSERVED FROM SUNRISE TO SUNSET
ABOUT 48 HOURS BETWEEN JUNE 19 AND JUNE 26

Inside my heart is a soft spot for those artists that dance with fire. I find it completely amazing and utterly terrifying all in one. Seeing fire performers on or near the summer solstice is a tradition for a lot of practitioners, although it's thrilling any time of year. They are a great way to mark the shedding of winter routines and get our summer fired up.

A flaming cocktail brings in that ooh and ahh that a fire performer would. You might consider doing this only for small, intimate parties, as too many people and flaming drinks are asking for trouble. Sparkle up the solstice with some flaming aquavit shooters. Inspired by the land of fire and ice, this work embraces the sun-drunk energy of this time of year, especially in the northern climes. Get the fire goddess involved (however that looks for you), dance around the bonfire, run off and star gaze, or soak in a hot tub to ring in Midsommar.

In Iceland as well as Denmark, Sweden, and Germany, aquavit is an important part of the culture. As you may have surmised, its name is a derivative of the Latin *aqua vitae*, meaning "water of life." As with many spirits, the brew depends on the region. Generally speaking, the herbs and spices used in brewing aquavit are dill, coriander, and caraway. However, individual recipes may vary. It is a clear spirit typically enjoyed chilled. It's rarely used as a mix, save the kaffeepunch you might find in Copenhagen during winter.

The first time I had aquavit was in Denmark in the mid-90s. I went to a pub in a little village north of Hamburg, Haderslev. They automatically brought out the aquavit when they learned our party was American. It showed me its magic that day, and I was grateful to find it produced in the United States, too. Magically, this brings in all the properties and correspondences found with aquavit and cinnamon and sugar: abundance, connection, and love. The lemon, that ubiquitous symbol of the sun and the summer solstice, is used in this drink much like you would after a tequila shot.

Flaming shots must be approached with caution. Make sure to use high-proof alcohol responsibly and be aware of the fire risk. Always be in control, and never drink a flaming shot that is still on fire. Have a fire extinguisher on hand. Snuff it out with a large enough coffee mug. Please ensure this is done in a well-ventilated area.

Solstice Flaming Shot

Equipment

A shot glass for each serving, chilled

A large coffee mug that covers the shot glass

A long fireplace lighter

Mixing glass or large measuring cup with spout

Bartender's spoon

SERVES 1

Ingredients

1 ounce aquavit

½ ounce cinnamon schnapps

A dash of 151-proof rum

Lemon wedge for garnish

Instructions

1. Make sure glass has chilled no less than fifteen minutes.

2. In a mixing glass, combine the aquavit and cinnamon schnapps. Pour into shot glass.

3. Using the back of a spoon, gently layer a dash of the rum on top of the aquavit and cinnamon schnapps mixture. The rum floats on the surface. This is fuel for flaming.

4. Ignite one shot at a time for safety's sake. The rum will catch fire and produce a small blue flame.

5. Once the shot is flaming, only let it burn until smelling the aroma of caramel. Snuff flame with a coffee mug. Make sure the flame is extinguished before moving on.

6. Serve shot immediately while it's still warm but not flaming. Garnish it with a lemon wedge.

7. Toast to summer, good harvests, good health, and all the toothsome fire energy (e.g., "Health and growth to flora, fauna, and kindred. Skål!")

8. Squeeze a little lemon juice into mouth after taking the shot. The contrasts of flavors are an ignition in energy and tastes.

First Harvest (Lughnahesh or Freysblöt)

About the first part of August, some of the early cordials I brew each year start to be ready. We won't actually partake of these potions until Witch's Thanksgiving, or the autumn equinox, but the infusions make some of the best sangria—an iced punch typically made of wine, fruit, and sparkling water. Gatherings around this time, whether termed Lughnahesh, Freysblöt, or the more modern Freyfest, feature our First Harvest Sangria. I take the cherries that were in the brandy, the raspberries that were in the rum, the blackcurrants that were in the gin, and whatever else I'm infusing (herbs, even) and put them in a giant drink decanter with some decent rosé wine, a bit of fresh juice, and ice, and we literally are drinking the fruits of our labor. It makes a nice offer (*blót*) to the spirits of the lands or other energetic connections.

You don't have to brew up cordials like I do, but have this festive punch to feed a whole work party while working together to bring in the beans, tomatoes, peppers, and mid-season fruits—plums start coming in right about now. Bread baking is a large part of this season since the first harvest is often grains (or hay); serving this alongside some bruschetta, with the bread and garden veggies turned into a nice roasted spread, is summer heaven on earth.

The magic during this turn of the solar wheel is about community, especially when sharing abundance, energy, and other resources. If you want to get fancy, make sure there are drinking horns available for everyone, or tell folx to bring their own. Consider any rustic pottery available as appropriate. A lot of the mood during this holiday is about rest. This tends to be a more casual ritual for many.

The fruit and wine mixture is set aside and allowed to meld for at least one hour. Make this up a bit before you'll be serving during the high summer festivities.

FIRST HARVEST
S A N G R I A

EQUIPMENT

A large punch bowl or gallon pitcher

Drinking horns or other rustic drinking mugs

Cutting board and knife

Favorite wooden spoon or spatula or bartender's spoon

Gallon pitcher for mixing

Cherry pitter (optional)

INGREDIENTS

SERVES
8

1 bottle (750 ml) rosé wine, chilled

½ cup white rum

½ cup orange or pineapple juice, chilled

½ cup pitted cherries

½ cup blackberries

1 orange

1 plum or peach

1 lemon or lime

4 cups lemon-lime sparkling water or soda

Ice (Cancer moon/solar or Aquarius moon/solar) in fancy shaped molds (optional)

INSTRUCTIONS

1. In a gallon pitcher, combine the wine, rum, and juice. Refrigerate.

2. While the wine mixture is chilling, prepare fruits. Slice into wheels or other thin, elegant shapes. Pit cherries. Leave blackberries whole. While slicing, imagine ancestors having to process the first harvests of wheat, corn, rye, and the like.

3. Add the fruit to the wine mixture. Refrigerate for at least one hour.

4. Before serving, add enough lemon-lime sparkling water or soda to fill the dispenser or punch bowl to the top. Stop and bless it for strength to know when to rest and when to work. Put away all the tools before toasting with this seasonal sangria.

5. Fill the drinking horns or other glassware with ice, then ladle or pour sangria over it. Toast to deities, the universe, ancestors, and kindred:

> *We give our sweat to the earth; she gives us water.*
> *We give our bones to the earth; she gives us food.*
> *We give our hearts to the earth; she gives us shelter.*
> *She honors us with her energy,*
> *so we give her ours in exchange.*
> *To the first harvest! To the earth!*
> *Connected in energy, heart, and body!*
> *Blessed be!*

Autumn Equinox (Mabon or Haustmánuður)

The autumn equinox is the prelude to the season of the Witch. You'll notice many practitioners giggly for the change of the season and all the psychic energy that invades come October. Pumpkin spice and sweater weather jokes aside, it begins a very powerful quarter in our ever-turning planet and lives. It's all done from a foundation of gratitude for all the abundance in our lives and to firm up plans to maintain, share, and care for said blessings. Forget November and all that negative energy; this is the time of Thanksgiving—the Witches' Thanksgiving.

You'll want the punch bowl set for its festive energy and garnishes like sliced apples and cinnamon sticks. Consider having two bowls, one alcoholic and one nonalcoholic, for your Welcome Autumn Punch. Next, we look at our table settings. Perhaps make sure the tablecloth and napkins are ready to go. Optionally, spritz or launder linens with some lemongrass or mint hydrosols for some intentional aromatherapy. Both hold mood-boosting and calming properties. As guests dab their mouths, they will be given a little spiritual hygiene. It's a simple little spell, but it works wonders.

Also, turn the dining table into an altar of sorts. Candles in the center for the element of fire are accessorized with crystals that represent the air we breathe, such as clear or smoky quartz, sodalite, and gold jasper. The crystals reflect the candlelight and create a warm glow for all around the table. If youngsters are at the table, consider opting for LED candles so you don't have to worry about any accidents with lit candles.

Salt and pepper and butter dish are placed intentionally to the north of the center candles to symbolize the element of earth and how much our wondrous planet gives to us.

A pitcher of water that was moon water from a past new moon may be placed to the west of the candles and blessed with these words:

Drink in thanks, drink in peace.
All are loved beyond this joyful feast.
So It Is.

Then there is the autumn punch recipe that will be blessed with these words:

Sip, love, and smile
Join together tonight.
We gratefully pause awhile
Loving with all our might.
May the wine remind
The blood that ties
Our ancestors from behind
To strengthen us love wise.
So It Is.

Welcome Autumn Punch

EQUIPMENT

Large punch bowl or beverage dispenser

Small party mugs or punch bowl mugs

Cutting board and knife

Jigger

Ladle

SERVES
26

INGREDIENTS

6 cups ice

1 gallon hard apple cider

1 bottle sparkling wine, champagne, or prosecco

2 (12-ounce) bottles ginger beer

1 cup spiced rum

2 to 3 sliced apples for garnish (optional)

2 to 3 cinnamon sticks for garnish (optional)

INSTRUCTIONS

1. In a large punch bowl or beverage dispenser, add all the ingredients. Stir to combine. Use the blessings noted above. Say it or chant it. You decide.

2. Add garnish, if using. Drink up and enjoy!

NONALCOHOLIC VARIATION

Use mulled cider or juice and flavored sparkling water (maybe pick something autumnal).

CHAPTER
17

We all have a story about a spell where things don't work out as planned. Perhaps a cord-cutting spell didn't remove the connection completely, and now you're feeling a magical hangover. Or that candle pouring failed to set correctly, making your brain drained because you can't figure out what went wrong. Or maybe those aftereffects occurred because you've not been hydrating properly, and you didn't even drink, smoke, or do magic. Whatever the reason you're feeling down or punked by wayward workings, always take a breath, brew a drink, have a think, and deepen the magic for a quick way of feeling better.

TENDING THE *worked-over* WITCH

Overdoing it with magic or drink may happen to the best Witches. I certainly have had my fair share of magical and physical hangovers. When—not if—it happens to you, don't beat yourself up over it. Instead, focus on returning to a state of being centered and grounded. To do no harm. To do good.

You've likely heard of "hair of the dog" tactics when it comes to curing a drinking hangover. That is the last thing the poor liver needs. It's the same with being magically and energetically hungover or drained. You don't go conducting a rune-casting reading party when the energetic cup is empty. Drinking alcohol to cure a party hangover doesn't make sense either. Both types of hangovers suck. You may not be surprised that both can be attended to similarly. It's understood that everything is connected when you're tapping into the magical realm.

Nourish and Refill

With this next working, we'll be resetting, nourishing, and refilling all the places that make us feel low and sick. It provides everything you need for any hangover—dream, divination, or a ding-dong drunk one. Riffing off the infamous Bloody Mary, this one is sans any vodka to be kind to the liver as well as provide hydration, electrolytes, a bit of fuel, and even some anti-inflammatory properties. It's also sans tomato because the acid is too much when we're in this state. Carrot juice brings in clarity and is kind to our throat, belly, and gut. It gives almost a lust for taking better care of ourselves and seemingly lightning insight into new directions to be the best Witch you can be, even after you were a bloody foolish Witch.

When we consider the energy and the deep forgiveness you'll need for making a misstep, this drink hosts the papaya. Papaya is all about love. You need love to forgive. Frozen papaya here is actually preferred because nobody wants to prepare a papaya when feeling nauseous. If you're not that woozy and want something fresh, go for it. If you don't have access to papaya, mango is usually more available; feel free to use that. It's still bringing love. Cranberry energy is no stranger to you at this point in the book. You're going to need to protect the energy for a bit while you heal up and recharge. Cranberries will also help heal the body by assisting the kidneys and liver in cleansing the overdo out of the system.

Much of the world knows about coconut water. It's in this drink to hydrate, which it sometimes does even better than plain water because it provides essential electrolytes such as potassium, sodium, and magnesium—all great for recovery. Together with the banana, which magically strengthens our connection to spirit, the coconut water makes you start feeling more yourself. When that happens, magic is more powerful. Fenugreek brings luck and money so that while you rest, you're open to energetic windfalls (and maybe a surprise check). That smack of mint served as garnish helps soothe an upset belly. It's also a nice little tactile movement to push a little anger out. Slapping the mint is a part of this potion. Doing so releases a gentle aroma that probably smells better than hangover breath. It's also there to nibble on for some tummy settling. Mint brings abundance because you may need a few ideas to overcome any problems created from overdoing it. It's normal to be a little disappointed in ourselves when we overindulge. Focus on the sweetness of the drink's honey, which not only calms the belly but also feels good against the throat and gives you a little energetic cleanse.

This recipe calls for using a blender. This may not be ideal when you're irritable from excess and may be fighting a headache, but it's brief. Plus, the relief it brings is amazing, and it does most of the work. The most effort is peeling a banana and sticking everything in the blender.

BLOODY FOOLISH
W I T C H

EQUIPMENT

Blender

Quart mason jar

Peeler

Measuring cups and spoons

Cutting board and knife

SERVES
1

INGREDIENTS

¼ cup carrot juice

½ cup cranberry juice

¼ cup coconut water

One ripe banana, peeled

½ cup papaya or mango, chunked, frozen or fresh

½ teaspoon fenugreek powder

Honey, to taste

Mint stems or leaf for garnish (optional)

Ice cubes, optional (options: Aries, Cancer, or Sagittarius)

INSTRUCTIONS

1. Gather ingredients. Connect to each one as if you were waving to a neighbor you passed on the road. A sweet hello. Nothing deep. You are reserving energy while still connecting.

2. Put all the ingredients except mint into the blender.

3. Blend (high pulse) for a good thirty seconds. Cover ears with hands if you need the relief.

4. Taste and blend additional honey, if desired. Start with a half tablespoon until you achieve the desired level of sweetness.

5. If you'd like a daiquiri-like consistency with this drink, add some ice cubes into the blender and use the high-pulse setting until smooth.

6. Pour into a quart mason jar.

7. If using the mint, slap the entire stem with leaves or a single leaf alone, depending on preference. Do so by putting it in one palm and then clapping the other palm into it, deftly and quickly slapping the mint between palms. Garnish.

8. Enjoy! Drink it all, you bloody foolish Witch. This is as far as the magic goes. You're on spell rest. No divination. Nope, no holding tarot cards. If you want to connect with the drink and say thank you, that's allowable, but nothing else until drinking is complete.

Don't be surprised if you feel like going for a walk after drinking; make it a gentle stroll. Then spend the rest of the day resting as much as possible. Journaling and daydreaming are encouraged.

Pre-Func Mitigation

Another way to make sure you don't overdo it with magic or beverage is by planning ahead. Don't overschedule your Witch work. Understand your own energy management and keep strong boundaries. Chunk out time to prioritize self-care. If you've got an evening out planned or a romantic dinner with wine, any of the hydrating or healing drinks from earlier chapters may be applied here. Drink those things ahead of time to make sure your body is nourished and hydrated. Again, making sure you're not celebrating with an empty stomach goes a long way. There's always the Witch-ade or Positivity Tea or perhaps Chill Witch Juice. Do stay away from whatever it was that made you overdo it.

CONCLUSION

Don't Stop Pouring

You've now gone through an introductory exploration along the path of sippable spellcraft, a collection that in itself is one long working. The study does not have to stop here. There is so much more to investigate. Now that you've moved through the recommendations, spells, rituals, and other magical workings here, I encourage you to seek out your own path within sippable spellcraft and deepen your knowledge of all the ingredients we use in our cocktails, teas, juices, coffee, etc. Use ingredients that are accessible, sustainable, and appear in your life most frequently. Continue that connection energetically and physically, and create new and even more expansive magic through drink.

At any time, if you find you need practice, go back to chapter 6 and do that water connection exercise, then build those skills up again with the other workings. Check out the reading suggestions that follow and deepen your understanding and knowledge of the magical properties and energies of everything you consume. Remember, the Craft is a practice. You are always going to be learning. Embrace it, draw it in, and record it. Hopefully, you feel the strong energy I am sending out through this book, which is fueled by a strong undercurrent of excitement for other Witches to take this journey through drink. Consider performing this liquid-based magic for a moon cycle, a season, a year, or any chosen time frame.

Regardless, what an adventure awaits you, Witch! Go now and find the magic in your cup. Drink up!

ACKNOWLEDGMENTS

Writing this book was a journey I was not expecting to take, but it very much has been an adventure into the roots of my own Craft practice and my personal Witch identity. Such a journey, though mostly solitary, is supported by kindred, without whom I may not have brewed the big giant spell that became this book. It is with great gratitude that I recognize them here.

To Gregor, my favorite pub and life partner: your support helped birth this book. Our partnership has weaved together such a life where growth, creativity, and magic are foundational. As we joke often, we are two halves of a whole nerd. Thank you endlessly for all you do to help build and maintain a life that allows book-writing, growing food, and magic to happen.

To my family, especially the newest member of it, my dear Grand Witchling, thank you for making my life so full and wonderful. Thanks for sending me notes like "I think this is your year, Mom," or "You really helped me with my practice" or the favorite: "Home safe." Working to create a family that is strong, united, and bolstered by deep love and support under extraordinarily hard circumstances is the miracle before us. Your resilience is amazing and inspiring. This book is a testament to our continued hope. It's also another way I endeavor to teach you good things. Everything in moderation, kiddo, even moderation.

To the Tarot Lady's Hierophant Writers: Thank you for showing up week after week, month after month. I have learned so much from each and every one of you. I see you. Thank you for seeing me. Keep writing, friends. Keep Witching and writing hard.

Theresa Reed: Thank you for your solid wisdom, your honesty, and your generosity. I appreciate your belief in my work and the support you showed by writing the foreword here. Thank you for pushing me to do better and not give up. May you forever have daymakers around you.

To my "Greenies," "Easties," Cali-Witches—my dear friends: Thank you for making sure I checked myself before I wrecked myself. Your feedback, counsel, and support were so very important to the completion of this work. More importantly, however, I appreciate your friendship and ability to geek out over dreamwork, growing food, making booze, astrology, and all manner of Witchcraft. May my gratitude blossom goodness in your lives.

To my patrons, thank you so much for your support. You've been with me on this journey the entire way. I'm so thankful and recognize your impactful role within the little covenstead. It has allowed me to lean in even harder into the Craft and create a space where others can learn their own path. Thank you. Let's continue to brew up magic together. No telling where it'll lead us, but I'm excited to do so and see all our lives blessed by it.

To my editor, Heather Greene, thank you for keeping me off the side quests and bringing me into the sixteenth edition of formatting and generally tightening up my magical mixology and writing. Your patience is a blessing. And a big appreciation to all the good folx at Llewellyn who have labored for many decades to create a space where books on magic, Witchcraft, and all that goodness are accessible and growing.

To all the bartenders, baristas, and other alchemists who have inspired, taught, and led by example on how to get magic in any cup: you are all magical creatures, and sharing that magic makes you demigods among humans. May your tips be threefold your expectations regularly.

Runa Troy
Unceded Coast Salish Territory

RECOMMENDED READING

Beyond the bibliography, listed below are some books that may help you further create magic in your cup. Please consider the following as you dive deeper into magical mixology and Witchcraft. Additionally, there are listed resources for pieces and parts of the workings.

Astrology

The Book of Houses: An Astrological Guide to the Harvest Cycle in Human Life by Robert Cole and Paul Williams

Practical Astrology for Witches and Pagans: Using the Planets and the Stars for Effective Spellwork, Rituals, and Magickal Work by Ivo Dominguez, Jr.

Astrology for Real Life: A Workbook for Beginners by Theresa Reed

Cannabis

Weed Witch: The Essential Guide to Cannabis for Magic and Wellness by Sophie Saint Thomas

Witchcraft Foundations

Anatomy of a Witch: A Map to the Magical Body by Laura Tempest Zakroff

By Rust of Nail and Prick of Thorn: The Theory and Practice of Effective Home Warding by Althaea Sebastiani

Drawing Down the Moon: Witches, Druids, Goddess-Worshippers, and Other Pagans in America Today by Margot Adler

Dreaming the Dark: Magic, Sex, and Politics by Starhawk

The Green Witch by Arin Murphy-Hiscock

The Holy Wild Grimoire: A Heathen Handbook of Magick, Spells, and Verses by Danielle Dulsky

Inspiring Creativity Through Magick: How to Ritualize Your Art and Attract the Creative Spirit by Astrea Taylor

Truth or Dare: Encounters with Power, Authority, and Mystery by Starhawk

DREAMS AND DREAMWORK

The Curious Dreamer's Practical Guide to Dream Interpretation by Nancy Wagaman

Jungian Dream Interpretation: A Handbook of Theory and Practice by James A. Hall

When Brains Dream: Exploring the Science and Mystery of Sleep by Antonio Zadra and Robert Stickgold

Women Who Run with the Wolves by Clarissa Pinkola Estés

ENERGETIC CONNECTIONS

Chakras and the Vagus Nerve: Tap Into The Healing Combination of Subtle Energy and Your Nervous System by C. J. Llewelyn

The Hidden Messages in Water by Masaru Emoto

Talking to Spirits: A Modern Medium's Practical Advice for Spirit Communication by Sterling Moon

GROWING INGREDIENTS

Gaia's Garden: A Guide to Home-Scale Permaculture by Toby Hemenway

The Herbal Alchemist's Handbook: A Complete Guide to Magickal Herbs and How to Use Them by Karen Harrison

The Magic Harvest: Food, Folklore and Society by Piero Camporesi

Thirsty Days of Rewilding: Find Your Place in Nature and Watch Your Family Bloom by Lucy Aitken

NORSE/GERMANIC PAGAN RESOURCES

Nordic Runes: Understanding, Casting, and Interpreting the Ancient Viking Oracle by Paul Rhys Mountfort

The Way of Fire and Ice: The Living Tradition of Norse Paganism by Ryan Smith

Wild Soul Runes: Reawakening the Ancestral Feminine by Lara Veleda Vesta

WOMEN AND DRINK

The Bartender's Manifesto: How to Think, Drink, and Create Cocktails Like a Pro by Toby Maloney

Blotto Botany: A Lesson In Healing Cordials and Plant Magic by Spencer L. R. McGowan

Drink like a Woman: Shake, Stir, Conquer, Repeat by Jeanette Hurt

Edible Cocktails: From Garden to Glass—Seasonal Cocktails with a Fresh Twist by Natalie Bovis

Tea Magic by Jenay Marontate

A Woman's Place Is in the Brewhouse: A Forgotten History of Alewives, Brewsters, Witches, and CEOs by Tara Nurin

YOGA

Yoga for Witches by Sarah Robinson

BIBLIOGRAPHY

Althea Press. 2014. *The Practical Herbal Medicine Handbook*. Althea Press.

Auryn, Mat. 2019. *Psychic Witch*. Llewellyn.

———. 2017. "The Veil Between the Worlds." *Patheos*, October 11, 2017. https://www.patheos.com/blogs/matauryn/2017/10/11/the-veil-between-the-worlds/.

Ballard, H. Byron. 2023. *Small Magics: Practical Secrets from an Appalachian Village Witch*. Llewellyn.

Bauer-Petrovska, Biljana. 2012. "Historical Review of Medicinal Plants Usage." *Journal of Medical Plants Research*. https://www.ncbi.nlm.nih.gov/pmc/articles/PMC3358962/.

Bendix, Aria. 2020. "Cities with the Worst Tap Water in the US." *Business Insider*, March 17, 2020. https://www.businessinsider.com/cities-worst-tap-water-us-2019-3#charleston-west-virginia-is-still-recovering-from-a-massive-chemical-spill-10.

Berke, Jeremy. 2018. "Canada Legalizes Marijuana, Becomes First G7 Country to Do So." *Business Insider.* June 20, 2018. https://www.businessinsider.com/canada-legalizes-marijuana-first-g7-country-to-do-so-2018-6.

Blue, Naomi. 2022. "Benefits of Blackcurrant Tea." *Simple Loose Leaf* (blog), November 23, 2022. https://simplelooseleaf.com/blog/black-tea/black-currant-tea-benefits/.

Bro-Jørgensen, Maiken Hemme, et al. 2018. "Ancient DNA Analysis of Scandinavian Medieval Drinking Horns and the Horn of the Last Aurochs Bull." *Journal of Archaeological Science* 99 (November 2018): 47–54.

Burns, Eric. 2004. *The Spirits of America: A Social History of Alcohol.* Temple University Press.

Byer, Rebecca. 2022. *Wild Witchcraft.* Simon Element.

Calabrese, Salvatore. 2019. *The Complete Home Bartender's Guide.* Sterling. Kindle.

Campanelli, Pauline. 1993. *Wheel of the Year: Living the Magical Life.* Llewellyn.

Campbell, Joseph. 1991. *A Joseph Campbell Companion: Reflections on the Art of Living.* Edited by Robert Walter. Joseph Campbell Foundation.

Cardoza, Riley. 2017. "The 11 Worst Ingredients in Soda That Aren't Carbonated Water." *Eat This, Not That!* June 23, 2017. https://www .eatthis.com/chemicals-in-soda/.

Cheung, Lilian, et al. 2020. "Coffee." The Nutrition Source, Harvard T. H. Chan School of Public Health. July 2020. https://www.hsph.harvard .edu/nutritionsource/food-features/coffee/.

Crawford, Jackson, trans. and ed. 2015. *The Poetic Edda: Stories of the Norse Gods and Heroes.* Hackett Publishing.

Cunningham, Scott. 1989. *The Complete Book of Incense, Oils, and Brews.* Llewellyn.

———. 1985. *Cunningham's Encyclopedia of Magical Herbs.* Llewellyn.

———. 1990. *Wicca: A Guide for the Solitary Practitioner.* Llewellyn.

Daab, Margaret. 2022. "America's Blackcurrant Ban." *In Custodia Legis: Law Librarians of Congress.* October 2022. https://blogs.loc.gov /law/2022/10/americas-blackcurrant-ban/.

Davies, Sioned. 2012. "Transforming the Mabinogion." Cardiff University Research Impact and Innovation. https://www.cardiff.ac.uk /research/impact-and-innovation/research-impact/past-case -studies/transforming-the-mabinogion.

Dominguez, Jr., Ivo. 2012. *Casting Sacred Space: The Core of All Magickal Work.* Weiser. Kindle.

Dugan, Ellen. 2012. *Witch's Tarot* (kit book). Llewellyn.

Elagizi, Andrew, Evan L. O'Keefe, and James H. O'Keefe. July 2021. "Here's to Your Health: Why a Drink with Dinner Might Improve Longevity." *Mayo Clinic Proceedings* 96(7):1706–1709. https://www .mayoclinicproceedings.org/article/S0025-6196(21)00421-3/pdf.

Fairtrade America. 2024. "Fairtrade Coffee Products." https://www
.fairtradeamerica.org/shop-fairtrade/fairtrade-products/coffee/.

Greenleaf, Cerridwen. 2016. *The Book of Kitchen Witchery: Spells, Recipes,
and Rituals for Magical Meals, an Enchanted Garden, and a Happy Home*.
CICO Books.

Haight, Colleen. 2021. "The Problem with Fair Trade Coffee." Stanford
Social Innovation Review. June 2021. https://ssir.org/articles/entry
/the_problem_with_fair_trade_coffee.

Hall, Judy. 2004. *The Crystal Bible: A Definitive Guide to Crystals*. Walking
Stick Press.

Harvard T.H. Chan School of Public Health. 2018. "Study says no amount
of alcohol is safe, but expert not convinced." https://www.hsph.harvard
.edu/news/hsph-in-the-news/alcohol-risks-benefits-health/

Higgins, Diane. 2018. "The Discovery of Merlin's Spirit within the Trinity
of Robert de Boron's *Le Roman de L'estorie dou Graal*." DePaul University.
August 2018. https://via.library.depaul.edu/cgi/viewcontent
.cgi?article=1263&context=etd.

Kenney, Erica L., et al. 2015. "Prevalence of Inadequate Hydration among
US Children and Disparities by Gender and Race/Ethnicity: National
Health and Nutrition Examination Survey, 2009–2012." American
Journal of Public Health (online). June 11, 2015. doi:10.2105
/AJPH.2015.302572.

Kirschman, Ellen, PhD. 2020. "Stinking Thinking: How Our Thoughts
Determine How We Feel." *Psychology Today*. October 17, 2020.
https://www.psychologytoday.com/us/blog/cop-doc/202010/stinking
-thinking-how-our-thoughts-determine-how-we-feel.

Klesiaris, C. F., et al. 2014. "Health Care Practices in Ancient Greece:
The Hippocratic Ideal." *Journal of Medical Ethics and History of Medicine*.
March 15, 2014. https://www.ncbi.nlm.nih.gov/pmc
/articles/PMC4263393/.

Kruyswijk, Anna. 2018. "Let Food Be Thy Medicine." July 17, 2018. https://
www.drgoodfood.org/en/news/let-food-be-thy-medicine-hippocrates.

Kurlansik, Stuart L., and Annamarie D. Ibay. 2012. "Seasonal Affective
Disorder." American Family Physician. December 1, 2012. https://www
.aafp.org/pubs/afp/issues/2012/1201/p1037.html.

Kynes, Sandra. 2017. *Llewellyn's Complete Book of Correspondences*. Llewellyn.

LaBerge, S., L. Levitan, and W. C. Dement. 1986. "Lucid Dreaming: Physiological Correlates of Consciousness During REM Sleep." *Journal of Mind and Behavior* 7: 251–58.

Lermen, Gustavo. 2018. "How the Commodification of Water for Profit Fuels a Global Crisis." *The Inertia*. April 19, 2018. https://www.theinertia.com/environment/how-the-commodification-of-water-for-profit-fuels-a-global-crisis/.

Lewis, Kiara. 2021. "What Does 'There's No Ethical Consumption Under Capitalism' Truly Mean?" *Sunstroke Magazine*. April 4, 2021. https://www.sunstrokemagazine.com/archive/2021/4/22/what-does-theres-no-ethical-consumption-under-capitalism-truly-mean.

Lewis, Marsha. 2023. "Greens Gone Bad: The Dark Side of Drinking Your Veggies." News4Jax. March 20, 2023. https://www.news4jax.com/health/2023/03/20/greens-gone-bad-the-dark-side-of-drinking-your-veggies/.

Mankey, Jason, and Laura Tempest Zakroff. 2018. *The Witch's Altar: The Craft, Lore & Magick of Sacred Space*. Llewellyn.

Mascitelli, Luca, Francesca Pezzetta, and Jerome L. Sullivan. 2007. "Inhibition of Iron Absorption by Coffee and the Reduced Risk of Type 2 Diabetes Mellitus." *Archives of Internal Medicine* 2007; 167 (2): 204–205. doi:10.1001/archinte.167.2.204-b.

Mayo Clinic Staff. 2022. "Alcohol Use Disorder." May 18, 2022. https://www.mayoclinic.org/diseases-conditions/alcohol-use-disorder/symptoms-causes/syc-20369243.

Minkowski, William L. 1992. "Public Health Then and Now: Women Healers of the Middle Ages: Selected Aspects of Their History." *American Journal of Public Health* 82, no. 2 (February 1992): 288–295.

Morris, Rebecca. 2017. "6 Health Benefits of Black Currant." *Healthline*. September 14, 2017. https://www.healthline.com/health/health-benefits-black-currant#easy-on-the-eyes.

Nunez, Kirsten. 2023. "Benefits of Drinking Water in the Morning." *Real Simple*. June 12, 2023. https://www.realsimple.com/health/preventative-health/benefits-of-drinking-water-in-morning.

Oré, Diego. 2023. "Mexico's Legal Cannabis Business Takes Next Step with CBD-Focused Firm." Reuters. https://www.reuters.com/world /americas/mexicos-legal-cannabis-business-takes-next-step-with -cbd-focused-firm-2023-03-09/.

O'Meara, Mallory. 2021. *Girly Drinks*. Hanover Square Press.

Pacheco, Danielle. 2023. "Drinking Water Before Bed: How It Affects Your Sleep." Sleep Foundation. December 7, 2023. https://www .sleepfoundation.org/nutrition/drinking-water-before-bed.

Parker, Julia, and Derek Parker. 2020. *Parker's Astrology: The Definitive Guide to Using Astrology in Every Aspect of Your Life*. Penguin Random House.

Patsiaouras, Georgios. n.d. "All Articles: A Bottle of Water." *Social Worlds*. University of Leicester. https://le.ac.uk/social-worlds/all-articles /bottle-of-water.

Petrovska, Biljana Bauer. 2012. "Historical Review of Medicinal Plants' Usage." *Pharmacognosy Reviews* 6, no. 11 (2012): 1–5. doi:10.4103/0973 -7847.95849.

Porterfield, Andrew. 2019. "Study Finds a Lack of Adequate Hydration Among the Elderly." *UCLA Newsroom*. March 5, 2019. https://newsroom. ucla.edu/releases/study-finds-a-lack-of-adequate-hydration-among -the-elderly.

Pottamkulam, Naina. 2023. "Walpurgisnacht: The German Night of the Witches Explained." IamExpat in Germany. April 30, 2023. https:// www.iamexpat.de/lifestyle/lifestyle-news/walpurgisnacht-german -night-witches-explained.

Pruthi, Sandhya, et al. 2022. "Water: How Much Should You Drink Every Day?" *Mayo Clinic Proceedings*. October 12, 2022. https://www .mayoclinic.org/healthy-lifestyle/nutrition-and-healthy-eating /in-depth/water/art-20044256.

Radin, D., G. Hayssen, Emoto, M., and T. Kizu. 2006. "Double-Blind Test of the Effects of Distant Intention on Water Crystal Formation." *Explore* (NY) 2, no. 5 (2006): 408–411. doi 10.1016/j.explore.2006.06.004. PMID: 16979104.

Regan, Gary. 2003. *The Joy of Mixology*. Clarkson Potter.

Robb, Alice. 2018. *Why We Dream: The Transformative Power of Our Nightly Journey*. Mariner Books.

Sandy, Eric, Melissa Schiller, and Tony Lange. 2024. "States That May Legalize Cannabis in 2024." *Cannabis Business Times.* January 22, 2024. https://www.cannabisbusinesstimes.com/news/states-that-may-legalize-cannabis-in-2024/.

Seladi-Schulman, Jill. 2023. "The Endocrine System: Functions, Diseases, and How to Support It." *Healthline.* December 21, 2023. https://www.healthline.com/health/the-endocrine-system#function.

Shoemaker, SaVanna, et al. 2024. "What Is BPA and Why Is It Bad for You?" *Healthline.* January 29, 2024. https://www.healthline.com/nutrition/what-is-bpa#where-its-found.

Shortt, Daniel. 2023. "From Schedule I to Schedule III: Potential Shift in Marijuana's Legal Status." *McGlinchey.* August 30, 2023. https://www.mcglinchey.com/insights/from-schedule-i-to-schedule-iii-potential-shift-in-marijuanas-legal-status/.

Shyu, Jeffrey Y., and Aaron D. Sodickson. "Communicating Radiation Risk to Patients and Referring Physicians in the Emergency Department Setting." *The British Journal of Radiology* 89, 1061 (2016): 20150868. doi:10.1259/bjr.20150868.

Spearing, Sinead. 2019. *A History of Women in Medicine: Cunning Women, Physicians, Witches.* Pen and Sword History. Kindle.

Spector, Dina. 2016. "The Surprising Reason You Can't Buy the Best British Candy in America." *Business Insider.* October 14, 2016. https://www.businessinsider.com/blackcurrant-america-vs-europe-2016-10.

Spence, Charles, and George Van Doorn. 2017. "Does the Shape of the Drinking Receptacle Influence Taste/Flavour Perception? A Review." *Beverages* 3, no. 3: 33. https://doi.org/10.3390/beverages3030033.

Spiller, Jan. 2008. *New Moon Astrology.* Bantam Dell.

Starin, Dawn. 2013. "Kola Nut: So Much More Than Just a Nut." PLoS Biology. December 2013. https://www.ncbi.nlm.nih.gov/pmc/articles/PMC3842857/.

Stewart, Amy. 2013. *The Drunken Botanist: The Plants that Create the World's Great Drinks.* Algonquin Books.

Stilwell, Blake. 2021. "The Art of the Coffee Pause: How Beethoven Took His Coffee." *Coffee or Die Magazine.* February 11, 2021. https://coffeeordie.com/beethoven-coffee.

Storl, Wolf D. 2012. *The Herbal Lore of Wise Women and Wortcunners: The Healing Power of Medicinal Plants*. North Atlantic Books.

Telesco, Patricia. 2005. *Kitchen Witch's Guide to Brew and Potions*. Red Wheel.

University of Washington. n.d. "Hawthorn (*Crataegus* spp.)." https://depts.washington.edu/treetour/61_hawthorn.html.

Virginia Commonwealth University. 2005. "Stinking Thinking." TBI Today. https://tbi.vcu.edu/media/tbi/nrc-articles/Vol3_3StinkingThinking.pdf.

Wagner, Stephanie, et al. 2007. "Herbal Teas for Soothing Common Ailments." University of Wisconsin School of Medicine and Public Health. Department of Family Medicine and Community Health. September 28, 2007. https://www.fammed.wisc.edu/files/webfm -uploads/documents/outreach/im/ss_herbal_teas.pdf.

Wasim, Shehnaz, et al. 2020. "Neuroprotective and Neurodegenerative Aspects of Coffee and Its Active Ingredients." *Cureus*. August 12, 2020. https://www.ncbi.nlm.nih.gov/pmc/articles/PMC7478584/.

West, Kate. 2009. *The Real Witches Kitchen: Spells, Recipes, Oils, Lotions, and Potions from the Witches' Hearth*. Llewellyn.

Wigington, Patti. 2019. "Dandelion Magic and Folklore." *Learn Religions*. March 11, 2019. https://www.learnreligions.com/dandelion-magic-and -folklore-4588986.

Wittbrodt, Matthew T., and Melinda Millard-Stafford. 2018. "Dehydration Impairs Cognitive Performance: A Meta-analysis." *Medicine & Science in Sports & Exercise* 50, no. 11: 2360–2368. https://pubmed.ncbi.nlm.nih .gov/29933347/. https://doi.org/10.1249/MSS.0000000000001682.

Wolf, Laurie, and Mary Wolf. 2016. *The Medical Marijuana Dispensary: Understanding, Medicating, and Cooking with Cannabis*. Althea Press.

Woodward, Laurel. 2019. *Kitchen Witchery: Unlocking the Magick in Everyday*. Red Wheel/Weiser.

Wu, Shana. 2022. "Time for a Fresh Brew: Oldest Tea in World Discovered." *The Art Newspaper*. January 10, 2022. https://www .theartnewspaper.com/2022/01/10/time-for-a-fresh-brew-oldest -tea-in-world-discovered.

Xiang, Yi, et al. 2023. "Tea Consumption and Attenuation of Biological Aging: A Longitudinal Analysis from Two Cohort Studies." *The Lancet* 42, article 100955. November 21, 2023. https://www.thelancet.com/journals/lanwpc/article/PIIS2666-6065%2823%2900273-0/fulltext#secsectitle0165.

Zakhari, Samir. 2006. "Overview: How Is Alcohol Metabolized by the Body?" *Alcohol Research & Health* 29, no. 4: 245–254. https://www.ncbi.nlm.nih.gov/pmc/articles/PMC6527027/

Zakroff, Laura Tempest. 2019. *Weave the Liminal: Practical Magic for a Vibrant Life*. Llewellyn.

———. 2017. *The Witch's Cauldron: The Craft, Lore & Magick of Ritual Vessels*. Llewellyn.

Zhao, Jinhui, et al. 2023. "Association Between Daily Alcohol Intake and Risk of All-Cause Mortality: A Systematic Review and Meta-analyses." *JAMA Network Open* 6, no. 3: e236185. https://jamanetwork.com/journals/jamanetworkopen/fullarticle/2802963.

To Write to the Author

If you wish to contact the author or would like more information about this book, please write to the author in care of Llewellyn Worldwide and we will forward your request. Both the author and the publisher appreciate hearing from you and learning of your enjoyment of this book and how it has helped you. Llewellyn Worldwide cannot guarantee that every letter written to the author can be answered, but all will be forwarded. Please write to:

Runa Troy

℅ Llewellyn Worldwide

2143 Wooddale Drive

Woodbury, MN 55125-2989

Please enclose a self-addressed stamped envelope
for reply or $1.00 to cover costs. If outside the USA,
enclose an international postal reply coupon.

• • • • •

Many of Llewellyn's authors have websites with additional information and resources. For more information, please visit our website:

WWW.LLEWELLYN.COM